Plato's Logic

Plato's Logic

Tommi Juhani Hanhijärvi

HAMILTON BOOKS
an imprint of
Rowman & Littlefield
Lanham • Boulder • New York • London

Published by Hamilton Books
An imprint of The Rowman & Littlefield Publishing Group, Inc.
4501 Forbes Boulevard, Suite 200, Lanham, Maryland 20706
www.rowman.com

6 Tinworth Street, London SE11 5AL, United Kingdom

Copyright © 2019 by The Rowman & Littlefield Publishing Group, Inc.

All rights reserved. No part of this book may be reproduced in any form or by any electronic or mechanical means, including information storage and retrieval systems, without written permission from the publisher, except by a reviewer who may quote passages in a review.

British Library Cataloguing in Publication Information Available

Library of Congress Control Number: 2019931068
ISBN 978-0-7618-7089-0 (pbk. : alk. paper)
ISBN 978-0-7618-7090-6 (electronic)

∞™ The paper used in this publication meets the minimum requirements of American National Standard for Information Sciences—Permanence of Paper for Printed Library Materials, ANSI/NISO Z39.48-1992.

Printed in the United States of America

To Laala (1923–2016)

Was ein Philosoph ist, das ist deshalb schlecht zu lernen, weil es nicht zu lehren ist: man muss es 'wissen,' aus Erfahrung, [. . .] die Wenigsten kennen sie, dürfen sie kennen, und alle populären Meinungen über sie sind falsch. So ist zum Beispiel jenes ächt philosophische Beieinander einer kühnen ausgelassenen Geistigkeit, welche presto läuft, und einer dialektischen Strenge und Nothwendigkeit, die keinen Fehltritt thut, den meisten Denkern und Gelehrten von ihrer Erfahrung her unbekannt und darum, falls Jemand davon vor ihnen reden wollte, unglaubwürdig. Sie stellen sich jede Nothwendigkeit als Noth, als peinliches Folgenmüssen und Gezwungen-werden vor; und das Denken selbst gilt ihnen als etwas Langsames, Zögerndes, beinahe als eine Mühsal [. . .]—aber ganz und gar nicht als etwas Leichtes, Göttliches und dem Tanze, dem Übermuthe Nächst-Verwandtes! "Denken" und eine Sache "ernst nehmen," "schwer nehmen"—das gehört bei ihnen zu einander: so allein haben sie es "erlebt." Die Künstler mögen hier schon eine feinere Witterung haben: sie, die nur zu gut wissen, dass gerade dann, wo sie Nichts mehr "willkürlich" und Alles nothwendig machen, ihr Gefühl von Freiheit, Feinheit, Vollmacht, von schöpferischem Setzen, Verfügen, Gestalten auf seine Höhe kommt,—kurz, dass Nothwendigkeit und "Freiheit des Willens" dann bei ihnen Eins sind.[1]

—Nietzsche

---

1. My translation: What a philosopher is, that is difficult to learn because it cannot be taught: one must 'know' it, from experience [. . .] only few know it, are allowed to know it, and all popular opinions about it are false. For instance the real philosophical combination of a bold and frisky spirituality which runs presto with a dialectical rigor and necessity and which takes no false steps is unknown to most thinkers and scholars from their own experience and therefore also something implausible, if anyone should present it to them. They imagine necessity as hardship, as the awkward duty to follow and to be forced, and thought itself is for them something slow, hesitant, almost plight [. . .]—but not at all something easy, divine, dance-like, and arrogant! "Thinking" and taking something "seriously"—these for them belong together: only so have they "experienced" it. Artists may have the finer scent regarding this: they know all too well that, if nothing is "arbitrary" any longer and everything is made necessary, their feeling of freedom, fineness, authority, of creative positioning, ordering, and shaping reaches its peak—in brief, that necessity and "freedom of the will" are for them one and the same thing.

Contents

Preface		xi
1	Introduction	1
	1.1 Thesis	3
	1.2 Versus Vlastos Etc.	9
	1.3 Versus Fine, Irwin, and Nehamas	14
	1.4 Versus Owen, Gallop, Castañeda, Etc.	23
	1.5 Plato, Anti-Plato, and Totalitarianism	28
2	The Hippias Major	37
	2.1 Definitions (287B–289D, 291D, 292C–E, 293C–294D, 299D–300B)	38
	2.2 Complexes (300E–303C)	44
	2.3 Self-Causation (297A–D, 303E–304A)	45
	2.4 Irony (281A, 286C–E, 287B–C, 288A–B, 292C–E, 298C, 304C–E)	48
	2.5 Dialogue About Dialogue (282E, 287E, 291D, 296B, 297D, 304D–E)	50
	2.6 Versus Woodruff (Definitions)	52
	2.7 Summary	55
3	The Phaedo	57
	3.1 Pleasures (60B–69C)	57
	3.2 Virtues (68D–69B)	58

	3.3	Forms (73D–75A)	60
	3.4	Psyches (73C–76A)	61
	3.5	Mathematics (75C–D)	63
	3.6	Method (63C–64A, 85C–D, 89D–91C)	64
	3.7	Reincarnation (79E–84B)	67
	3.8	Harmony (85E–88B, 92A–93D)	68
	3.9	Opposites (70C–72E, 102A–E, 104B–107D)	69
	3.10	Simplicity (78B–84D)	72
	3.11	Causality (94A–95A, 96A–99D, 100B–102D, 105B–D)	75
	3.12	Versus Bostock I (Forms)	78
	3.13	Versus Bostock II (Virtues)	80
	3.14	Summary	82
4	The Symposium		85
	4.1	Love (199C–212A)	86
	4.2	Creation (206B–207E, 208B–209E, 210C–D, 211C, 212A)	90
	4.3	Evolution (208E–209B, 210A–E, 211C–D)	91
	4.4	Lack (200C–204D, 206A, 207C–D, 212A)	94
	4.5	Opposites (199D–200A, 202C–D, 203E–204A, 206C–D, 207A–C)	97
	4.6	Beauty (210E–211C, 211D–E, 212A)	99
	4.7	Speeches upon Speeches (Entire Work)	104
	4.8	Versus Nussbaum (Risk)	104
	4.9	Summary	107
5	The Republic		109
	5.1	Simonides (331C–332C)	110
	5.2	Internal and External (357A–368C)	115
	5.3	Justice (370A–B, 374A–D, 397E, 430E–431B, 441C–442E, 443B–444B)	116
	5.4	Er (614B–621D)	120
	5.5	God (377E–392C)	122
	5.6	Relativity (472B–E, 475E–D, 476A–480A, 510B–511E, 522C–526A, 583B–588A)	125
	5.7	Dialectic (510B–511C, 532A–537C)	133

		Contents	ix

	5.8	Sun, Line, Cave (507B–509C, 509D–511E, 514A–520A)	137
	5.9	Versus Reeve (Good)	141
	5.10	Summary	143
6	The Laws		145
	6.1	Self-Superiority (625E–628E)	146
	6.2	Virtue (631B–D, 689D–E)	150
	6.3	Pleasure (653A–654D, 659D–660A)	150
	6.4	Gymnastics (653A–654A, Book 7)	151
	6.5	Music (653E–656C, 667E–671A, 700A–701C)	152
	6.6	Theater (657E–663D, 700A–701C)	153
	6.7	Education (643A–645C, 653A–673D, 788A–822D)	154
	6.8	Discourse (720A–724A, 880D–E, 885B–899D)	156
	6.9	Crime (859D–864B)	158
	6.10	Labor (704D–705B, 806D–E, 918C–919E)	160
	6.11	Ancestor Worship (656D–657C, 715D–718D)	162
	6.12	The Deluge (677A–682E)	163
	6.13	God (893B–899E)	164
	6.14	God's Thoughts (895E–897B)	169
	6.15	Versus Bobonich (Non-Philosophers)	171
	6.16	Summary	173
7	The Lysis?		175
8	The Gorgias?		177
9	The Meno?		181
10	The Protagoras?		185
11	The Phaedrus?		189
12	The Timaeus?		193
13	The Theaetetus?		197

Bibliography	201

Preface

Initially it can sound outlandish to hear that Plato is the great liberator of human thought, for this is not ordinarily said. But consider first that the "Socrates" of the *Apology* lives the examined life, seeking self-knowledge. True, the Greek word for freedom (*eleutheria*) does not appear in the text of the *Apology* but the point in it is clearly to criticize endlessly and to seek perfection as an individual. (Thus we do not need the word.) As Plato's career evolves this view only becomes more radical and more positive. The Forms (Ideas) and Gods are presented as models of perfected freedom, and after his transitional period around the time of the death of the historical Socrates Plato's works tend to circle around these ideals. In Plato, philosophical ideals and Gods are always instruments to human liberation because they are always objects of emulation. In many of the world religions one needs to submit to God and to obey Him and to not inquire boldly about the roots of His authority, His origins, His purposes, His constituents, et cetera, but in Plato the situation is the reverse. In Plato one needs to study God intrinsically in order to become Godlike, and the more one manages this, the better. God is perfectly autonomous. Similarly, a Form is wholly self-sufficient, indebted to nothing outside itself. Gods and Forms stand above us not in order to suppress us but to lift us upwards. All possible questions need to be asked, and nothing is simply trusted. Philosophizing frees the mind.

Of course, this is not the first time in history that someone preaches the need to return to Plato for the sake of human dignity or open research. The German tradition of *Bildung* was about that and so was the *Humanitas* of Renaissance Italy. Even the Greek *paideia* itself seemed to depend heavily on Plato. Hence, like so many before me I am saying that Plato has merely been forgotten once again, like the Forms in the *Phaedo*. It is time to rewind:

time for *anamnesis*. But *Plato's Logic* does also break with those great traditions—for it is not as historicist or philological. I can illustrate this difference best by means of an analogy. What Plato teaches us is, in a way, what medieval Arabs teach us when they teach algebra. We learn from the Arabs to count in particular ways, and to solve an associated spectrum of problems. But we do not thereby find reason to cling to the original symbols, such as "al-jabr." We do not need to speak Arabic. For the lesson is abstract. We are to internalize patterns of argument and to put them to our own uses, in our own symbols. That is how we *do* algebra. We solve problems; we do not parrot anybody *verbatim*. Similarly, free thinkers are not obliged to keep parroting things about "Plato" or "Greece," for that would go against the highly abstract and timelessly valid argument that Platonism itself is. It is not the point to learn to say "*logos*," e.g., for what is in the word, any word? It is the operations with their structures that count. The Romantic and Renaissance scholars did not adequately distinguish between valid formalities and the contingent histories, and this shortcoming still holds back scholarship.

Now I have made grand assertions. Are they true? This book consists largely of debates about whether they really are. There will be allegations that he makes category mistakes in logic or grammar, that he is a totalitarian and the very opposite of a libertarian, that his rationalistic perfectionism is insensitive to the experiences and contingencies of individuals, and that his position cannot be represented schematically and timelessly because it is a part of a specifically ancient and Greek environment.

This has been a first sketch of this book's argument. Finally for this preface let me make a more personal note and a dedication.

In my own small life Plato's overall framework has provided some much needed stability, because through the years and decades I have lived in numerous countries and countless neighborhoods without having much of an overarching identity or plan other than that of an idealistic teacher and author. My dependence specifically on Plato has been heavy because as I see it he is the archetypal (Western) idealist, even if this is partly for some rather contingent reasons (such as that texts from so many other authors have been lost). I like to imagine that I, too, play some small part in a long tradition, like a minor current in a long and wide, winding river. In my dream I have future readers, however few, who consciously supersede me. They will say things that are better than I can now even imagine, but I will have been one of the scholars who prepared the ground for them. This is wishful thinking, but the hope is honestly motivating when you write. Still, such future prospects are not the main dish on the idealist's menu. The main event is to only *look* at some well pondered symbols, with the greatest attention. It is the dignity in this, the precise respect, that has no *Ersatz*. Nothing has the focus of a Form or a God. Yet also *humility* is required. For look at what for instance Plato tried to do! If there were some fallacies in his result, they are insignificant compared to the nobility of the effort. I have seen some Mediterranean gardens in which ancients used to speculate and read their poems, and I am not always sure that anything was supposed to happen after them.

This book is dedicated to my own dear grandfather, who always treated me with such warmth and interest. Whenever we met he had patient and penetrating questions for me about philosophy and the unstable life I was leading. Between us it was only the hours and days that ended, never the questions. Officially he was very far from being a philosopher, and this is probably a reason why his questions were never merely academic. He was a businessman, a devout Christian, and a war veteran. At seventeen he was made to run in the snowy forests to fight the Russians. The Finnish army was so poor that the only piece of equipment many soldiers received for the front was a belt or a hat, but the Soviet troops came with tanks. Laala always quietly refused to talk about the Winter War. May he now have peace.

TJH, Rome October 2018

Chapter One

Introduction

Plato philosophizes about a heaven of Forms and Gods. It is our true home, he writes, because we are animals or sensual beings only superficially. We can never quite identify with the material world. If we learn to philosophize then we begin our ascent, and if we philosophize well enough then we will ultimately think according to the perfect patterns of the Forms and Gods. In that way we would reach a kind of purity and immortality.

However the reaction to Plato's idealistic message has not been overwhelmingly positive. Already in his own time we encounter some main kinds of negative response. Aristotle identifies numerous supposed fallacies in Plato's idealistic argument, and Aristophanes ridicules both Socrates the public buffoon and the birds' utopia of Cloudcuckooland.

What if anything can be done in behalf of Plato's idealism? Where is the cause of its failure? Apparently Plato has seemed quixotic primarily because his crucial expressions about the Forms and Gods are too often merely poetic or ambiguous. For this has made it seem too many that the archetypal idealist engages in mere dreamwork. He is carried away by fictions. He is not realistic about this world of sweat and dirt.

But then how can the idealistic idioms be improved? Or can they not be? Is improvement impossible given that Plato's language is only rhetorical or poetic in the crucial places? (Should one lie about how he writes to make his idealism seem firmer than it really is?) The strategy of this book is to argue that Plato's texts are flowery only superficially. Deeper down they instance a solid logic. In consequence of this, the idealism is not really a laughing matter. Rather, if anything it is a pity that so many humans through the generations have lived so brutishly, neglecting their better sides.

One obstacle to this can already be formulated. Can such a "deep" level of a text ever be truly discussed? For does a text not *consist* only of a surface? What evidence is there in any piece of writing beyond the surface level of letters, words, sentences, and so on? Consider a few analogies to see this. In speaking her native language, a speaker uses verbs without thereby necessarily singling the verbs out explicitly as "verbs." Similarly, logical operations are performed not by saying "logic" or "operator" but by using certain rules. One does not even need to define, prove, or at all to describe the rules to *use* them. But this is just how things are in Plato. He *uses* a logic. So this is how there is a "deep" level to his texts.

All of this book is a defence of Plato's logic. This introductory chapter (1) begins with a direct statement of that logic, in 1.1. In reading 1.1 the reader should come to understand the *meaning* of this book's thesis as easily as possible. It is important to note that the *truth* of the thesis should not be obvious yet at this point, however. The truth can be shown only by studying Plato's individual works and passages in Chapters 2–13. I am aware that this book's thesis will not strike many readers as obviously true. It is not supposed to.

After 1.1 I will attempt immediately to show why this logic works against Plato's different enemies, because this shows how the logic is a useful for his idealism. Thus in 1.2–1.4 I use the logic to solve the main problems raised by Plato's hostile readers. Hostile readings come in rather different versions, and I here distinguish between three of them (in 1.2–1.4 respectively). For each I have nominated certain current or recent spokespersons.

In 1.2 the first group of anti-Platonists is represented by Vlastos. They say that Plato's talk of Forms and Gods is paradoxical or nonsensical, or in general faulty in point of logic. The error in this is to project the fallacious vocabulary to Plato, I argue. It is not Plato's own, and he can be read with much more charity.

In 1.3, several currently esteemed scholars claim to defend Plato but they do this in a way that is not really idealistic at all. Thus Fine, Irwin, and Nehamas take Plato to say things that are only quite ordinary. Hence, they accept him, yes, but in order to do that they must first belittle him. They say that all Plato wants is explanatory properties, universals, or essences. They ignore that he is a moral revolutionary. Socrates *dies* for his beliefs. Something is amiss.

Section 1.4 comes to more technically oriented, relational scholars like Owen and Castañeda who read Plato with great philological and logical care but with an exclusive focus on small details. They inspect the small variations with such devotion that they ignore the larger hills and mountains.

Finally, 1.5 ponders why the *Zeitgeist* has been so anti-Platonic. What explains all this hostility to idealism in the current world? Why is it so difficult for people to respect it? I surmise that it is still often connected to totalitarianism. The talk of large revisions scares people away because in the past century we have already seen how that went.

1.1 THESIS

Plato's Forms and Gods do not emerge out of the blue. There is no sudden flash of light to change everyone miraculously into a believer. Rather, there are chains of causes (of all four of Aristotle's kinds; on them see his *Physics* II 3 and *Metaphysics* V 2). First, a is given. Then a is caused by b, b by c, and so on, until the whole series ends in z and z is a Form or a God.

If we formalize this a little, then the causal relation can be symbolized as $R, R', R'', \ldots$. In this way we already have the vocabulary of Plato's logic. There are

- relations: $R, R', R'', \ldots$ and
- relata: $a, b, c, \ldots$

We get series like these: $aRbRc\ldots$ and $aRbRcRdRe\ldots$.

Now how can Forms or Gods end these series? This book argues that they do this because of their structures, which are $\ldots zRR$ and $\ldots zRz$, respectively.

At this point I have already stated this book's thesis. It is that Plato always uses the structure $aRbRc\ldots zRz$ or $aRbcRc\ldots zRR$ to establish his idealistic claims. These structures are called $\mathbb{R}$. Thus $\mathbb{R}$ is Plato's logic. (If the symbol $\mathbb{R}$ has other uses outside this book then that does not matter here.)

As noted in the introduction to this Introduction (1), nothing said in this section (1.1) is supposed to show that this book's thesis is *true*. Establishing its truth will take time. I am informed that this book's view is quite unusual and that readers will often not be convinced of its truth very quickly. However the *meaning* of the thesis should become plain in this section (1.1). To that end, let me now make a series of notes that I think should be helpful.

First, how are the above symbols representations of what happens in *Plato*? Consider that

- the series $aRbRc\ldots$ are chains of causes, where R has a content such as IS MOVED BY, IS PROVED BY, HAS THE PARTS, or IS A MEANS TO.
- God, and therefore also the pattern zRz, is used mainly with the content IS MOVED BY (see Chapter 6 on the *Laws*).
- the Forms, and hence the pattern zRR, is instanced with a variety of contents from e.g. EQUALS (which equals itself in the *Phaedo*, see Chapter

3) to PROVING (which concerns proving itself in the abstract in the *Republic*, see Chapter 5).

Here we have relations (*R*) in capitals, and I will soon bring up many more (see 1.2). Note also that relations, and relational series, are in play also in the process of Platonic philosophizing. For the characteristic questioning of a "Socrates"[1] (or an "Athenian") is a search for a Form or a God along the same lines. For example, about an interlocutor's belief or value *a* he can ask *Why a?*, and if the answer is *b,* then Socrates will predictably ask *Why b?* To the further answer *c* he will react with *Why c?*, etc., until there is a conclusive answer in a Form or a God. The question may also be e.g. *What is ...?*, *What moves ...?*, *What proves ...?*, etc. But the structure of this process is once again $\mathbb{R}$ (see endnote[2] for why), so dialogical patterns do not require any separate or autonomous interpretive method (contrary to e.g. Gadamer[3]).

Second, and as already noted, *Plato's Logic* does not say that Plato *himself* describes, defines, or even names $\mathbb{R}$. He only *uses* it. Symbols like "$\mathbb{R}$," "*aRb*," etc. need not be found in Plato any more than the word "logic" must be used to do logic. (By that standard even Aristotle would not do logic.) It would also not be important to find that these symbols *translate* Plato's own idioms. Rather the explanandum and the explanans need to differ. There is no use repeating Plato if he requires explanation.[4] The explanation must be more orderly than the original. (See 1.4, where I oppose "positivists" like Owen and Castañeda.)

Third, what is so *special* about this view of Plato? How is this different from other versions of Platonism in the past or present? From Neoplatonism to contemporary scholarship (see 1.2–1.4), interpreters have tended to think that Plato's Forms and Gods are something especially *general*. In contrast, $\mathbb{R}$ makes them *extreme*. To illustrate this with the color white, as a generalist Plato would want to draw white*ness* apart from examples such as snow and clouds. But as an extremist he wants something whit*er*, or even whit*est*. This is the logical difference made by $\mathbb{R}$. (How does this bear on causal chains? For example, as a first mover God is the *über* mover, and by comparison every other link in the chain of movers is a mere puppet—not the puppeteer, see 6. Hence the first link in the chain is the superlative instance. Similarly, as the authority of authorities the Form of the Good is the only proper authority. The others are shams or copies compared to it. Again, the Form of Beauty is the end of ends, i.e. the ultimate satisfier—and so on. In general, $\mathbb{R}$ provides Plato with the superlatives that he needs to make the Forms and Gods superior to the ordinary run of things. This is what the generalist cannot do; see 1.2–1.4. This is a logical difference in one sense of "logical." Usually Plato scholars do not even consider the possibility of a logic in this book's sense

($\mathbb{R}$). Many focus on the elenchus, the method of hypothesis, the dialectic, and collection and division.[5])

Fourth, it is vital to note already at this point that zRR does not work with *all* of Plato's contents. No one moves motion, for example. That would be nonsense. For that content one needs zRz, as Plato clearly knows. Usually zRz is for Plato the pattern of self-moving Gods and psyches (as in *Socrates' psyche* MOVES *Socrates' psyche,* or *theos* MOVES *theos*; see 11 and 6.13-6.14 respectively; cf. Sedley 2000, Feibleman, and Solmsen). zRR makes sense for abstract patterns. There is an order for all orders, or an authority of authorities (see Chapters 2 and 5). The *Laws* outlines a law for all laws (see 6.1). The *Theaetetus* is a search for knowledge about knowledge (see 13). These are examples in which there is a relation R to R itself. They are not as in zRz but as in RR. At this point one may ask why $\mathbb{R}$ is made to cover both zRz and zRR if they are this different. Is this not contradictory? The first answer is that it merely so happens that Plato uses both of these structures. But another answer is that he has good reasons to do so, because only zRz works with some relations (see Chapters 3 and 6 especially) and zRR works with some others (see Chapters 2-5). Hence $\mathbb{R}$ is as precise as a unified generalization can get (α) about Plato in general or (β) about first causes in general. If one wants more precision then the price is a loss in generality. Then one can talk about *one* kind of first cause or *some* kinds of first causes, but not about all. Also, then one can be concerned with some works of Plato's, but not with very many.[6]

Fifth, $aRaRb$... is formally equivalent to ...$yRzRz$ just as *a* MOVES *a* MOVES *b* says the same thing as *y* IS MOVED BY *z* IS MOVED BY *z*. (The first relation is the "converse" of the second, and vice versa, see e.g. Russell 1903, Chapter IX.) Also the exact number of relata is indifferent, so $\mathbb{R}$ is instanced in $aRbRcRR$ as well as $aRbRcRdReRfRR$. (However there may be a minimum number of relata for communicating specific relations.[7]) Transitivity, which is often also brought up with relations, does not work with all relations below, for instance with the *Symposium's* LOVES: if I love you and you love *c*, it does not follow that I love *c*. In general, relations have their own, local characteristics, and only a limited number of generalizations is true of them all.

Sixth, my *symbols* are not entirely standard. This is as it should be because $\mathbb{R}$ is meant to make Plato seem unique. His thinking is not standard in our day or in any other (see the eleventh note below, still in 1.1). I capitalize relations in technical contexts (*Socrates* RECOLLECTS *the Equal*, for example) to draw attention to those relations. Relations are often written in the form Rab or $R(a,b)$ instead of my aRb, but my way of writing is more convenient for the formation of relational series like $aRbRcRd$ (see endnote[8] for the reason why). Another difference between the usual symbols and mine is that if several different relations are placed in the same expression they are usually distinguished by using different letters of the alphabet for them, as in *R, S, T* (see Tarski), but I tend to use many different relations inside any single expression so rarely that I distinguish the relations only as in *R, R', R''*, as above (5.6 on Good as the Idea of Ideas is the exception). The reader may ask whether I must use the exotic "*RR*." It is impossible to avoid because it is only in *RRaRbRc*... that we register how the *same* thing (*R*) figures as both the extreme case and the general standard. One cannot be explicit about this double role without writing *R* at the left hand extreme *and* repeatedly throughout the string.

Seventh, *quantifiers* can be used with relations both as in

- ($\exists x$) (*x* moves *x*), and as in
- ($\exists R$) (God *R* God),

where "moves" and "*R*" are relations (cf. e.g. Hylton 1990, p. 288). I do not use quantifiers in this book because they would often complicate expressions needlessly. However readers should now register that quantifiers can be used in more than one way. This implies that there is no easy or automatic way to police existential commitments based on the use of relational idioms (cf. Quine on quantifiers and existential commitments, and see especially his 1969, page 96[9]). To see this, consider that *God* MOVES *God* can be translated into ($\exists x$) (*x* moves *x*) *or* ($\exists R$) (God *R* God). Hence, perhaps it is motion and not God that is said to exist. I say this not merely as a point about the use of quantifiers or about existence but also about the philosophy of Plato, or about the Platonic philosophizing that other individuals may do. For if Plato says that a Form or a God exists while using the pattern ℝ then we can still tinker with his expressions to pin down what exactly he may see as the basic existent(s). One should therefore not be naive about this and say merely that of course it is the "theos," "demiurge," "idea," or "eidos" that he thinks is real. It is not that easy. For what are they? (By and large this book's emphasis is not on issues about ontology, however. Cf. Tarski on the use of quantifiers with relations. On some metaphysical and ontological versions of Platonism see Jubien 1997, Chapter 3.)

Eighth, one main reason to analyze Plato in relations has to do with their *flexibiliy*. For, as noted, ℝ consists of

- relations: *R, R', R''*, ..., and
- relata: *a, b, c*, ...

Examples of relations are MOVES and PROVES and examples of relata are an ape, a psyche, Socrates, God, a Form. However, and crucially for this book's argument, *overlap* between these two levels is allowed, so one can say for example that *RR'R''*, thereby placing the relations *R* and *R''* in a relation *R'* (cf. Tarski). This is important because it allows us in principle to insert relations for relata, thereby replacing God-talk or psyche-talk with motion-talk, for instance (see 6.1, 6.13, 6.14, and Chapters 11 and 12). What is even more pertinent to Plato's idealism is that a relation can coherently relate to itself, because this is what makes Plato's hyperbolical claims about the Forms intelligible. (1.2 will explain some basic aspects about how a relation can relate to itself, and many sections of this book are devoted primarily to this topic, see 2.1, 3.3, 4.6, 5.6, 6.1, 6.13, and 6.14. Also see Chapter 8 for illustrations. (Russell 1903, pp. 25–26 on "powers" of relations like *grandparent: parent: child* is one inspiration for this, though Russell does not use *zRR* or *zRz* exactly. I should note in passing that despite his youthful Platonism Russell is unprepared to read Plato in terms of powers or relations, see Russell 1945, pp. 128–129; cf. Scheibe for discussion.) On defining "relation" generically see endnote.[10])

Nineth, there is no *conjunction* symbol in series of the form $\mathbb{R}$. It is present tacitly, however, if e.g. *aRbRc* is read as "*aRb* and *bRc*." It is sometimes useful to distinguish portions in the series by using "and" (or Λ, which I use) in this way, as e.g. with beauty or harmony, see 1.2 and 4.6 below. Also parentheses may be used, sometimes in conjunction with conjuction symbols and sometimes in their stead, see endnote 14. (That Plato's thought often requires complex symbols should not be taken to mean that his unit of significance is as large as e.g. *aRbRcRd* or *aRb and bRc*. The reason is that the autonomy of the Forms, Gods, and philosophizing psyches requires that things of the form *zRR* and *zRz* can stand alone. In Chapter 5 we find that metaphysical and epistemological holists such as Reeve do not perceive this. The *Republic's* Sun Allegory communicates the main difference between these positions succintly. In that allegory the sun does not only illuminate other things, such as trees and rivers. It also illuminates itself. Moreover it illuminates itself *more* than it illuminates other things, because it is the brightest visible object (at least to technologically unaided observers on planet Earth). Thus the services of the sun are primarily services to the sun itself, and if it partakes in some greater whole, as with trees and rivers, then that is only of secondary importance. See 5.8 on this.)

Tenth, there is also no symbol for *negation* in $\mathbb{R}$, for in Plato's spirit $\mathbb{R}$ is a structure for generating hierarchies with *many* levels. In Plato one does not tend to find binary oppositions such as *no/yes, false/true, 0/1, white/black* so much as graded series with more numerous terms, like *a/b/c* or $a<b<c<d$ (here *{a, c}* and *{a, d}* respectively are pairs of *opposites*, not only negations of each other). This is to say that in Plato there are negations and affirmations

in different strengths. Heraclitus' content *ape: man: god* illustates the basic point of thinking in this way, because in this expression man is torn between his animal drives and his higher calling (on this see 2.1). Plato scholars call a phenomenon of this type the "compresence of opposites" (see 1.3 below; the key passages in Plato are *Hippias Major* 289A–C and 293B–E, *Phaedo* 100ff., *Symposium* 210E–211A, *Republic* 479A–B and 523A–525A); but they do not tend to notice that many levels must be stratified before the phenomenon is revealed. For in $a<b$ nothing is torn between two mutually exclusive pressures; b is in $a<b<c$. Plato scholars do often note that Plato uses hierarchies for various things, as for instance for beauties (see Chapter 4), truths (5), realities (3–6), but they cling to logical patterns that are too simplistic to make clear sense of Plato's reasoning about these matters. More precisely, they use dualistic schemes with negations (and conjunctions), universals, and particulars (or else one-place predicates and subjects), whereas Plato demands more levels, as in ℝ. (Cf. Fränkel 1994, and see 2.1; also see Vlastos 1981; Gosling 1960 and 1968 and Fine 1978 cling to hierarchies of truths in particular, and Robinson 1963 notes how parochial this is.)

Eleventh, *implication* is not central to ℝ because in Plato relations tend to be explored and not deduced from. His logic is one of discovery (*logica inventiva*). Somewhat as in Descartes' first two *Meditations*, one tries to silence the skeptic, that is, to find some ultimate answer to a persistent critic (like Plato's Socrates or Athenian; though of course Socrates and the Athenian are much more constructive than Descartes' radical skeptic; on the *Gorgias'* Callicles see Chapter 8). Plato's Forms and Gods are the conclusive, utopian answers to lines of inquiry, that is, something analogical in certain respects to Descartes' *cogito*. However it is not always *epistemic* ultimacy in particular that interests Plato, though that is Descartes' sole concern in his first two *Meditations*. In Plato that is only *one* tangent in a spectrum of inquiries; for as noted Plato studies *all* types of causes. Also, Plato is not about *private* foundations (or incorrigible one, contra Penner). What is more, and as Leibniz points out, Descartes is not really informative about any logic for his procedure. Leibniz's own logic of discovery bases on the principle of sufficient reason (besides a principle of non-contradiction, see e.g. *Monadology* §§ 31–32 and Craig Chapter 8, von Wright Chapter 2, and Sluga p. 11), and this is similar to ℝ. Also Kant's view of reason (*Vernunft*) is akin to ℝ. To be sure, "logic" is for Kant only a tool for the understanding (*Verstand*), roughly as in Aristotle: it uses already known generalizations in individual cases. But Kant's views of reason are self-consiously Platonic and not Aristotelian (*Critique of Pure Reason* A312–A320/B368–B377). Plato is not only the dogmatic voice of pure reason or the spokesperson for the theses in Kant's antinomies (A405–583/B432–611): he is also Kant's hero for the regulative ideals. Plato's archetypes or ideas form the utopian "horizon" to which the Kantian researcher must always aspire in interrogating reality (cf. Kim). (Major differences between these philosophies remain, however. The main one is that only Plato ever really seems to use zRR and zRz. More generally, plenty of philosophers have sought first causes, but the special logic of the Forms and Gods—zRR or zRz—which Plato attaches to the series $aRbRc$... seems to be his specialty. This is such a large induction that it is impossible to prove, but certain major comparisons are easily stated.[11])

Twelfth, *all relations* are not covered by $\mathbb{R}$ directly, because for instance IS LARGER THAN (in the *Republic*) or OVERTOPS (in the *Phaedo*) does not conform to aRa or RRa. However the *Republic* manages to cover them by introducing the Form of the Good as the Form of Forms. Then the Good instances RR and the other, lower Forms are only its relata. In this way Plato can be said to present a total doctrine of relations (see 5.6 and 5.7).

Thirteenth, it is morally significant that Platonic reasoning is never merely *mechanical*. It is not about blindly repeating *Why....?, Why...?, Why....?* no matter what happens. (Cf. Wos and Fitelson on mechanized relations.) Rather, one needs to track down each causal series to its end in a perceptive and fitting way. This is how things are in done in Plato's corpus. Mimicing others is the very opposite of this *ethos* (because questioning is so different from obeying), including the mimicing of Plato himself. One need not speak Greek. This liberates thought, as several Platonic commentators from different backgrounds have noted. (Cf. Irwin and Rowe as well as Jaeger, see e.g. 1944, vol. 2, pp. 77–86 and 354–357. Neokantians say that Plato teaches a "method" and not a result that is attained by using that method, see Natorp, and for discussion see Kim. Also certain existentialistic interpretations of Plato may be liberal in the present sense.[12])

1.2 VERSUS VLASTOS ETC.

Plato's wildest and most characteristic expressions are about Forms and Gods, but they do not make great sense in all vocabularies (this section, 1.2, is mostly about the Forms and ...zRR and only occasionally about the Gods or ...zRz). Surprisingly, the vocabulary that is popular among scholars is *not* sensible. Accordingly, Plato is being dismissed from the ranks of serious philosophers, and for whimsical reasons.

The popular vocabulary interprets Plato in terms of universals (or properties or concepts; 1.3 will find this fault in the major current scholars; cf. e.g. Owen 1987, Hamlyn 1955, pp. 301–302, Stenzel 1931, p. 96, Jaeger 1944, vol. 2 p. 263 (though also see p. 286), and Zeller 1980, pp. 129–134 on sources from the recent past). In its terms Plato may be thought to say such things as that justice is just or that the equal is equal (*Protagoras* 330C–D, *Phaedo* 74B–D), that is as if the property of justice had the property of justice and the property of equality instanced itself. That sounds like nonsense because it confuses the properties with their instances: length is not long, just as money is not rich.

A closely related vocabulary, which is also popular, consists of predicates. A predicate is used on itself if ... *is just* or ... *is equal* is predicated of itself. This is called "self-predication" in Vlastos' seminal article from 1954 (on the "third man" see also 5.6 on Dedekind). Then ... *is just* is just and ... *is equal* is equal, absurdly. (For of course ... *is just* is not just! Who would ever say such a thing outside *Alice in Wonderland*? True, ... *is a predicate* is a predicate, so there is at least one self-consistent content for this vocabulary, but it is or at least borders on a tautology. It is not of utopian interest. It will not convert anyone into an idealist. 1.3 will expand on predicates. A further alternative, which is not explored here, is to use particulars or paradigms instead of predicates. This possibility is mentioned at *Parmenides* 132C–133A.[13])

Observe what is happening here. Plato is made to play the fool. To illustrate this with an analogy, it would not be sound for an Egyptologist to study hieroglyphs and to report that they are nonsense. One would justly doubt that the Egyptologist in question has done her work well. It is better for the decoder to find intelligence in her source.

A healthier foundation for a logical discussion is obtained by not giving such a representative status to the passages which Vlastos selects (*Parmenides* 132A–B and 132C–133A; I do not have the space here to argue that much in Vlastos or the scholarship of his generation depends on this). Take instead the *Phaedo*'s Form of the Equal (see 3.3 for the details). Equality may seem like a property but its relational character comes out more plainly in EQUALS. Then *a* EQUALS *b,* and the self-related (not self-predicated, because we are now using relations and not predicates) pattern to represent Plato is EQUALS EQUALS *c*. But this is not nonsense any more than a topic like the meaning of meaning (compare Ogden and Rchards as well as Putnam). There is no nonsense in this because the higher order issues make good sense. We are not forced to discuss only meanings like *The cat is on the mat* or *I see red.* We can also discuss e.g. *love, structure,* or indeed MEANS. We are not tied to the most trivial cases in everyday life. We have the license to philosophize. *This* is how Platonism takes flight.

This leads again to numerous questions, which are best addressed outright.

First, if we say that *a* EQUALS *b* then must we not utter a *tautology?* No, because e.g. *water=H_2O* is no tautology. In general, identities are revealed everywhere in different areas of inquiry, not only in Chemistry, and few if any of them are plain and obvious to men in the street. Accordingly, there is no rational requirement to make our idioms seem grammatical in everyday speech. (A use of *RR* is often ungrammatical in everyday terms, and even if it is not, it is typically ambiguous on a grammatical plain. For example, in "MEANS MEANS *c*" the first token of "MEANS" is a noun and the second is a verb, but their meanings are the same. However this does not imply that we confuse verbs with nouns because our topic is meaning, which can figure in verb as well as noun constructions. Similarly, the meaning of *runs* or *running* does not change between *Li runs fast* and *That is running*, where "is" is the verb.) Truly everyday language should be seen as a kind of straitjacket. Populism does not hold back progress only in politics!

Second, does any of this conform to *Plato's own* vocabulary? He certainly uses *adjectives* (not relations) for what is good, beautiful, just, more or less fine, etc.—that is true, but he uses those terms *as well as* relational ones, and often for the *same* topics. For example, in the *Republic* the Form of the Good is not characterized *only* by means of the adjective "good" (or fine, *kalon*): it is also the final link in a chain of formal causes (see 5.6–5.7). We cannot worship any *word* in Plato, because his processes take place on several different levels. A philosophy is not summarized in a word (1.4 expands on this in opposing "positivist" scholars like Owen and Castañeda).

Third, does not *Russell's Paradox* refute this? Is it not inconsistent to not stratify between types such that each type concerns only the types *below* itself in the hierarchy? If yes, then *RR* becomes impossible because *R* is of the *same* type as *R*. It is not below itself. But Russell's Paradox is not this generally relevant, for the paradox arises for sets which consist of sets that are not members of themselves and $\mathbb{R}$ does not imply anything for the formation for such sets. To see this, consider a set that is not a member of itself, such as the set of animals. The set, call it *S*, consists of rabbits, tigers, etc. But *S* does not contain *S*. Why? Because *S* itself is not an animal. Now Russell's Paradox arises if one tries to form a set of all sets like *S*. But $\mathbb{R}$ is not about any set like *S* at all. Rather, $\mathbb{R}$ is only about such things which *do* cohere with themselves. E.g., if one advocates philosophizing by philosophizing then one is acting in a self-consistent way, and if fineness is measured by something that is itself also fine then there is a deep fit. (However see 5.6 on how Plato can include many more relations in a consistent way.)

Fourth, Plato holds that his Forms are *extremes,* not only generalities, as 1.1 already noted. How can EQUALS be an extreme? Picture this through MEANS. In a MEANS b, b is more meaningful than a, so there is progress with regard to meaning. MEANS itself is the most meaningful thing if it terminates the series, as in .... $xRyRzRR$. This would happen if we came by a semantic theory which is especially siginificant. That is not easy to do, certainly, but it is not fallacious. (And surely it is a philosopher's dream! Surely this type of an effort accords with the ambitions of a Plato.) Similarly with EQUALS. If we had a perfect theory of identity then the thing with the most defnite identity could be identity itself. Based on that we could pin down other things: a is b, c is d, etc. (And IS=R all the while. See 3.3 and 5.6–5.7 especially.)

Fifth (and lastly for 1.2), surely Plato is not only a *semanticist*. He writes about knowledge, God, virtue, utopia, education, and so on. Hence this thinking must be shown to work more widely in philosophy, that is not only in semantics but also in epistemology, theology, ethics, social or political philosophy, and so on. Are relations really adequate for philosophizing about all of these different topics? Some of Plato's range can be summarized now in three examples: order, justice, harmony.

Order. In Chapters 2 (on the *Hippias Major*) and 5 (on the *Republic;* on this matter see especially 5.6–5.7) order is presented as a first formal cause with the structure *RR* in the chain *RRaRbRc*.... It is then a structure that is both perfectly orderly in itself and a model for all of the more or less orderly other things that there are. This idea is understood quickly by thinking of a pyramid, if the pyramid's tip is drawn as a perfect miniature of the entire pyramid. For then the shape of the tip is not only the order or shape that is approximated by the entire pyramid. It is itself also the most orderly portion of the pyramid. *RR* is instanced in this way because a relation of ordering is now used primarily to that relation itself: R to R. This is the pyramid's tip. (Recall: it is the most orderly thing; it is not only a model for the pyramid as a whole.) Next, as we move to the right from *RR* in the series *RRaRbRc*... we simultaneously descend down the pyramid, and things get more and more complex and disorderly as we go. Then the same order (R) is instanced in less and less perfect versions in *aRb*, *bRc*, etc. In the *Republic*'s terms, the perfectly orderly thing is the Agathon, and the less orderly things are for instance numbers or colors and sounds. (Certain aspects of this view of order may be analytical of $\mathbb{R}$, but the pyramid structure is not, and Plato's structures can as well be e.g. trees, circles, etc.)

Justice. Justice is fundamental to Plato's major utopias, Kallipolis and Magnesia (see Chapters 5 and 6). It conforms to $\mathbb{R}$ if it is defined in a particular way. As I argue, Plato defines it roughly in the manner of several ancient sources, such as:

- Hammurabi's law that an eye should be taken for an eye,
- Pythagoras' possible view that for any x the just standard is x itself as in x times x, or x^2 (Sieroka p. 22), and
- the Biblical saying that one reaps what one sows (*Galatians* 6:7).

How does this echo $\mathbb{R}$? The simple answer is that relational actions are now paid back in kind. For example, if a IS EATEN BY b then justice is served if *b* IS EATEN BY *c*. For then the eater is eaten, as in *bRb*. However things get more nuanced because Plato requires a type of *consistency* of just relations. For, to use an example from the *Phaedo* (see 3.7), no one's proper fate is to be reborn as an ass unless she first acts *consistently* as an ass. The general thought is that one must first show one's true colors in a specialized way or one can not even *have* any distinct fate to deserve! This implies that there cannot be any justice unless people flourish first, and this leads me to argue that Platonic justice can apply only in utopia. Stated conversely, there cannot be justice (roughly: reaping what one sows) in pre-utopian life if too many agents fail to realize their true powers or interests (i.e. if they do not properly sow something in the first place). By comparison, Hammurabi, Pythagoras, and Jesus seem to be less worried that people are often *held back* from showing their true colors (e.g. by biased customs, diseases, or accidents). But Plato has this worry, and so he demands utopia first. There is no justice before utopia. (How is justice relational? There are easy ways to see this. Consider the metaphor of "scales" of justice first. If you put a weight n on one side of the scale, what do you put on another side? n, of course. That is how you weigh something on a scale: you match it. n for n, nRn. A second basis is less metaphorical: *reciprocation*. For justice is very often construed, traditionally, as payback. You incur a debt, you exchange money or goods, you take revenge, you are punished for your crime, or at any rate you should imagine how you would feel if others treated you like you would treat them (as in the Categorical Imperative and the Golden Rule). But each of these scenarios is about turning the tables, which is relational exactly as in *aRa*. Comparatively, any idea of a mere property to analyze the phenomenon is simply clumsy. Plato scholars have wasted their time using their irrelevant Aristotelian vocabulary.)

Harmony. Harmony is a relational pattern in Chapter 4 (see 4.6 on the Form of Beauty in the *Symposium*). Harmony exemplifies ℝ if there is

- some harmony within the different arts, as e.g. in music and poetry,
- more harmony between them, and
- most harmony with harmony itself.

This last item on the list is the Form of Beauty, I argue in 4.6. I admit that Plato does not quite come out and define beauty in this way, but he seems to express all of the needed premises. His musical examples derive mainly from the *Laws* (6) and partly also from the *Phaedo* (3). His views on verbal art and his own verbal artistry are instanced especially in the *Republic* (5), the *Phaedrus* (11), and the *Symposium* (4). The *Symposium* also contains the most direct statement of his overall aesthetic. As noted in 1.1, the topic of beauty or harmony seems to call for the explicit use of conjuction symbols; see endnote[14] for the reason why. (Perhaps I should note that the association of harmony with beauty is far from arbitrary. There is a long tradition of this type, perhaps most obviously in the area of music (see Rothstein). Moreover, harmony is certainly a relational structure. It is instanced between different musical intervals or rhythms, or else between verbal meters or rhymes or metaphorical analogies, visible colors or geometric ratios, etc. Conversely, it is quite obviously not well analyzed merely as a universal! That is once again a clumsy category for the expression and analysis of values. Nussbaum plays a role in the discussion of Chapter 4, but not because she calls this relational aesthetic into question. Rather, she raises moral objections to Platonic aesthetics. I argue that she confuse categories. The Form of Beauty is not supposed to be moral. Justice is. In general, the different uses of $\mathbb{R}$ take different directions. They are not all the same. Platonic reasoning is characterized by its mobility and variety, and it is striking how rarely scholars notice this. "Word worship" is one reason for it, see endnote 4 and Chapter 9.)

(Note that these are not the *only* consistent uses of $\mathbb{R}$. They illustrate *some* of the range of Platonic speculation, that is all. The totality of *all* extensions may in fact be impossible to lay out, see endnote.[15])

1.3 VERSUS FINE, IRWIN, AND NEHAMAS

The most renowned Plato scholars of our own day, such as Fine, Irwin, and Nehamas, do not say Plato is nonsense. They have a different way to belittle him, namely by pretending that he is no idealist at all. He is made to seem quite normal. All his student needs are explanatory properties, universals, or essences. Nothing as exotic as self-predication is necessary. They agree that the likes of Vlastos are wrong in discrediting Plato, but in a way they do even worse by ridding us of all of the wonders. (An analogy with Egyptian hieroglyphs may once again illuminate the situation. The Vlastosian Egyptologist would discredit the symbols about the dog-God Anubis: they are mere nonsense, not intelligible. The current scholars would say that the symbols are intelligible, yes, but they are only about a normal dog. They are not about any supposed God, as I think they are.)

This section (1.3) is best begun by introducing a small logical map before the introduction of the views of Fine, Irwin, and Nehamas.

In my view Plato does not exactly collect sets of things a, b, c such that each of them shares some property P. Rather, he collects sets of things a, b, c such that they are ranked, as in $a<b<c$ (or $a<b<c<d<e$, and so on, because

his hierarchies can have many more terms than three; cf. Fränkel 1994, and see 2.1; also see Robinson 1963, Vlastos 1981). Hence, he is not after a commonality but an extreme. Here is an example. For Plato the situation is never so simple that some *a* is (an instance of) education and some *b* is not (an instance of) education. Rather, his philosophizing requires more differentiation. Then some *a* is education, yes, but not properly. For in Plato the class does not consist of equal members. Some *b* is education in a way that is superior to *a*, but then there is some *c* which is even better. Then $a<b<c$, and *a-c* are all instances of education but they are a hierarchy. There is *über*-education and *unter*-education, as it were, and not only education *simpliciter*.

Now, this is a general and not an isolated point about Plato in this book. For it does not concern education alone: it is rather about Plato's manner of philosophizing—that is about *any* topic. He will seek the utopian optimum in every subject, from e.g. language (*Cratylus*) to justice (*Republic* and *Laws*, Chapters 5 and 6), knowledge (*Republic* and *Theatetetus*, 5 and 13), the psyche (*Phaedo* and *Phaedrus*, 3 and 11), love and friendship (*Symposium* and *Lysis*, 4 and 7), and so on. He never simply generalizes from cases, so *P* above is never the right vocablary for him.

One obvious objection to this view can now be refuted briefly. This is that surely *Plato* if anyone is an academic theorist and a generalist. After all, he is the creator of the millenial Academy, the first institution of higher learning in the West! What can be as academic? Moreover he is the designer of such deliberate utopias as the Kallipolis (see 5) and Magnesia (see 6). He is no intuitive child groping vaguely for the most fascinating examples. And is not *P* above therefore what Plato's thinking requires? He theorizes everything under the sun, does he not? To reply, Plato does also theorize, but that is for him not the only or the main affair. Moreover, $\mathbb{R}$ provides him with *both* hierarchy and generality whereas *P* gives us only generality, so $\mathbb{R}$ unlike *P* explains Plato's interest in theory *and* his perfectionism. $\mathbb{R}$ gives one generality in that $aRbRc$ covers all of *a, b, c* while also ranking them (if $R=<$). *P* does not give us hierarchy because properties are only had or not, so the situation is black and white though hierarchies require different shades of gray.

Now let us consider whether the above is not a straw man. Does anyone really maintain these universalistic views about Plato?

Yes. For some of the currently most respected scholars like Fine, Irwin, and Nehamas see Plato's Forms essentially only as universals. For example, the Equal of the *Phaedo* does not for them equal or equate with anything (see Fine 1993, p. 62; cf. Irwin 1995, Chapter 10, and especially pp. 154–157 in Fine 2000, vol. 1; also see Nehamas, and see Stahl and White 1987, p. 213n15 for discussion on Nehamas). Let us now interpret each of them based on their own terms, beginning with Fine.

Fine's position is most accessible in her "Introduction" (especially pp. 17–18; *On Ideas* (1993) is a longer and more complex discussion which compares Plato to Aristotle and Aristotle's criticisms of Plato; Fine herself says her views are the same in both sources in 2000, vol. 1, p. 18n51). With Owen (1957) she maintains that "self-predication" (see 1.2) is not intelligible and that Plato should be credited with a more rational position. For if the Form of the Equal is equal then it must be equal *to* something; but it cannot be equal to anything else without losing its independent character as a Form (against this see 3.3). In a different vein, the Form of the Large should be large—impossibly because largeness is an abstraction without size (see 3.11). How, then, does Fine propose to avoid self-predication? She views Forms as "explanatory properties" (p. 18). The Form of the Large, for instance, is "that in virtue of which large things are large" (ibid.). It is then not itself the largest thing (ibid.). Similarly with the Form of Justice, for example. Justice is predicated of people, actions, institutions, laws, and more (ibid.), and Fine seems to hold that all of these predications depend metaphysically and/or epistemologically (cf. p. 19) on the Form of the Just. In sum, a Platonic Form is for Fine an explanatory property and it is used in predication.

Irwin (1995, Chapter 10) assesses Plato's views of the Forms in diverse dialogues, among them the *Hippias Major*, the *Phaedo*, the *Symposium*, and the *Republic*. Clearly Irwin's view is that a single and systematic position can be revealed from Plato's works (see the first sentence in section 8 in Irwin's Chapter 10; however Irwin distinguishes the early dialogues' Socratic position from Plato's own, see sections 1–5 in Irwin's 1995, Chapter 10). Most of Irwin's questions about the Forms concern their non-empirical epistemological status. Why exactly are they not accessible to the senses?, he asks. One key problem in this area is the purported incoherence of what is accessed through the senses, and following others Irwin calls this problem "compresence of opposites." The Forms, as for instance of the Equal in the *Phaedo* or the Fine in the *Hippias Major,* should be free from that compresence, and empirically accessed entities seem to suffer from it. Irwin's terminology for unravelling this problem consists of distinctions between properties and instances or types and tokens (see section 8 in his 1995, Chapter 10 especially). What is Irwin's result? Its most direct statement is in the two last paragraphs of his 1995, Chapter 10. The Platonic Form is a "property," Irwin says there, and empirical phenomena do not instance the property in a way that is free of the compresence of opposites. Justice itself cannot ever be unjust, but whatever we meet with empirically will be just, at most, in some context and not in another.

This leaves *no question* as to whether Irwin identifies Plato's Forms with properties (universals). But this is to say that the issue which my book builds on, namely whether the Form of Justice is itself just or extremely just does not even arise in Irwin's text. (However Irwin refers to Bostock, whose discussion I find more informative; see 3.12–3.13 on it. Irwin's helpful discussion of the "craft analogy" in Plato's earlier works is built on in Chapter 9.)

Finally for this triplet let us look at Nehamas. In his "Plato on the Imperfection of the Sensible World" (1975) he, like Fine and Irwin, studies Plato's middle-period position as a single whole. Nehamas' concern is to refute the view of an older generation of British scholars. The key difference Nehamas finds between his own view and that of his opponents is that for them things other than the Platonic Forms are only *approximately* just, beautiful, or tall (somewhat as visible circles and squares are not precisely round or square), whereas for Nehamas non-Forms are only *accidentally* just, beautiful, or tall. Stated conversely, on Nehamas' view Plato's Forms are "essentially" just, beautiful, or tall, he says. The point is to depend on modalities at the expense of degrees.

What should be made of this? There is the possibility of disputing Nehamas' particular claims. His opposition to degrees of satisfaction seems naïve, considering that Plato so frequently establishes hieararchies between things (as I repeatedly argue, primarily in 2–6). For instance, it seems odd for anyone to deny that in the *Symposium* souls are *more* beautiful than bodies or that artworks like poems or political creations like laws are *still more* beautiful, without yet having the *extreme* beauty of the Form (see 4.6). Again, is there not more knowledge in philosophy than in the arts or sciences in the *Republic* (see 5.7)? *Plato's Logic* finds that hierarchies typify Plato's thinking.

But this is only to meet Nehamas' argument head on, and there is actually a deeper problem to prioritize. For how much sense can Nehamas actually make of Plato's position if he abolishes degrees?

In his section II Nehamas 1975 offers a logical explanation of the difference between Forms and empirical non-Forms as he sees it. Consider that predicates are either one-place or two-place. The former are single-termed, so they function atomically, or in isolation. Nehamas' examples are ... *is a man*, ... *is a finger*, and ... *is a stick*. In contrast, two-place predicates are relational, so that for instance ... *is tall* is true of a subject only in comparison to a shorter subject, but not in isolation and not in relation to an even taller subject. Hence its form is really ... *is taller than* ..., so it requires two subjects (because it demands a point of comparison for whoever it is who is to qualify as tall). Now, two-place predicates function only in certain conditions or comparisons or others, not atomically. To illustrate this, one and the same man can find that he is tall in China but short in Norway (and without shrinking). In contrast, he will be a man no matter where he travels, so the ulterior conditions or comparisons do not change his status as a man. But this is because of the difference between one- and two-place predicates. To this background, Nehamas says that there are Forms for the two-place predicates.

Now one would think that Nehamas would here see the opportunity to treat two-place predicates much as I have treated relations, so that the two-place predicate ... *is taller than* ... is a relational construction aRb where R=IS TALLER THAN. For this would take him rather naturally to gradations like $aRbRc$, where a IS TALLER THAN b IS TALLER THAN c. From this, again, it would be fitting for him, or for anyone, to draw that the extreme terms of the series are the tallest and shortest things there are. Those extremes would then be approximated more or less closely by the other (that is, the non-extreme) members of the same string, and this would make the "compresence of opposites" intelligible (more on this in 3.1, 3.9, 4.5, and 5.6). For then a and c would be polar opposites in $aRbRc$ and b would be torn between them (like Heraclitus' man in 1.1 and 2.1); so b would be positioned exactly in the way that b is both tall (compared to c) and not tall (compared to a). In contrast, if we have only a single token of a two-place predicate and no longer series, as in Irwin or Nehamas, then nothing is *between* anything (as b is between a and c). In "a is taller than b" or aRb no two opposites are compresent in anything. Compresence begins only once the series has at least three terms. It is illogical otherwise! But Nehamas will not have this, because he *objects* to gradations or approximations, as we saw.

Now we can turn around and challenge Nehamas on his own ground. How are "essences" to be understood as subjects of two-term predicates? This promises to be difficult to explain because two-term predicates are, recall, normally the predicates which do *not* function atomically or in isolation. For now they are supposed to work for the Forms, which *are* precisely atomic or isolated (or independent, immutable, simple, and so on, as everyone agrees; 3.3 discusses this supposed paradox at length, invoking a list of authors who have registered it in the recent past: Castañeda's problem of dyadicity, Geach 1956, Allen 1959, Tarrant 1957, p. 125, and Matthen 1982, pp. 97–98; also cf. Gallop 1975, pp. 122–123, Sedley 2006, Svavarsson 2009, and Silverman 2003). In other words, as subjects of two-place predicates the Forms appear as especially *de*pendent things, but their role is surely to be especially *in*dependent. But this is exactly backwards compared to what Plato needs. Hence, Nehamas' terminology of essences and one- and two-place predicates does not seem to accord well at all with Plato's Forms.

What is Nehamas' answer to this challenge? How does he make intrinsic sense of Plato's Forms based on his vocabulary of two-place predicates and essences? He has no such answer. He neglects even to consider the Forms' internal character. He is unprepared to explain how Plato's Forms or Gods could themselves play the foundational roles that Plato assigns to them. Like

Irwin, Nehamas is content to make *external* comparisons about the Forms. For both Irwin and Nehamas the main issue is the relationship between the Forms and empirical phenomena. Their question is never how the Forms (or Gods) can be the awe inspiring things that Plato says they are.

(This criticism would lose some of its force if Plato himself *wrote* of "properties" or "two place predicates" or "incomplete predicates," but he does not. Consequently these logical slots of the major current scholars have *neither* merit, (α) that of being literally true to the text, in effect only translating it, nor (β) that of making the ambitions of the text seem rational. Meanwhile, ℝ has advantage (β). I admit that it does not have (α), see 1.4 below.)

Before we move on it is worth noting in passing that earlier scholars have not always or usually been this superficial. An example is A.E. Taylor, who is among Nehamas' enemies in his article. Taylor holds that the *Christian God* is equivalent to Plato's Form of the Good (see Taylor 1926, pp. 288–289). While I do not agree with Taylor's conclusion, it is clearly in a different league from the predicates, properties, or types of Nehamas, Fine, and Irwin. How so? The difference is that Taylor interprets Plato's large thoughts in *large* ways. He does *not* make Anubis into a mere ordinary dog, to use the comparison made above. (By the way, Taylor's Christianity does not stop him from being astoundingly open-minded compared to the major scholars of today. See e.g. Taylor 1926, p. 293 on the relation of Plato's dialectic to the foundations of the sciences, Darwinism, logicism, and price theory.)

Observe that this is not a point about *philosophy*. It may be that Fine, Irwin, and Nehamas philosophize well, at least in some senses of "philosophize" (on this see endnote[16]). But *Plato* is not captured in their manner. *His* philosophy, and his way to philosophize, is a great deal larger in its scope and ambitions. It is about for instance the psyche's immortality, the validity of utopia, God's existence, and the perfection of the Forms. These are the kinds of things a charitable reader of Plato should try to save.

Let me now indicate how one might try to *prove* the validity of this demand in four separate ways: ethically, epistemologically, metaphysically, and pedagogically.

Ethical Version. The position of Fine, Irwin, and Nehamas deprives Plato of his great reason to live as a philosopher. For Plato believes there to be more equality, beauty, motion, goodness, and so on in the Forms and Gods. It is due to this that it makes sense by his lights to look upwards, that is to study the Forms and Gods as a philosopher. (Notice the performative aspect in this: *one comes to more equality, beauty, motion, goodness,* etc. in this way! For Plato philosophy is not a *plan* or an explanation of life but the highpoint of life itself!) For such an examined life will bring one to think in the Forms' and Gods' patterns. One will learn to adjust one's *psyche* or *eros* to these perfect role models. And this way one will find more, even much more, beauty, equality, and so on.

Now why exactly does Fine's, Irwin's, and Nehamas' position undermine this? Because if a Form is a universal (or a property or a predicated concept: these differences do not affect my argument) then it is not an instance of that universal (let alone an especially good one). If for instance a painting has beauty then beauty is a universal and the painting is a particular. Beauty then cannot *have* beauty without turning from a universal into a particular. This is just how the roles go on the Aristotelian, dualistic scheme. Everything is either/or, a universal or a particular, which is exactly why Plato's ideals cannot fit into the picture. They will appear as category errors (as if a universal were somehow a particular) or as banalities (as if Plato's Forms were mere universals: beauty is beauty; or in terms of predicates, ... *is beautiful* is indeed the same as ... *is beautiful*). On their reading the Form of Beauty is not extremely beautiful. It is not even moderately beautiful. Why not? It is not one of the beautiful *things* at all. Rather, as a universal it is something that the beautiful things *share.* It does not belong *among* them. Consequently it is also not the superior member in their set. And so on down the line, for not only beauty is interpreted like this, but all of the Forms. The generalization is that if Forms are universals then they are not of superlative value, and for that reason they will not be rewarding merely as such. But therefore it will not make sense to leave the concerns of the mundane *polis* with its materialism and busy-bodies behind and to steer upwards to the Forms and Gods for a more enlightened life and mind. Why not, exactly? Because the Forms and Gods are not anything more equal, more beautiful, more moving, and so on! All the impressive movers and aesthetic pleasures will be down in the city, not up in the sky. It will not make sense to convert to philosophy. I can illustrate this in terms of the *Republic's* allegory of the Sun (on this see Chapter 5). The sun of Fine, Irwin, and Nehamas shines only on all the things below, as on trees, valleys, cities, and so on, but the true Platonist's sun illuminates itself the most, because it is the brightest thing (for more specific uses of the logic involved in this see especially 2.1, 3.3, 5.3, 5.6–5.8, 6.1, 6.13, and 6.14). Hence if one seeks illuminated things then according to the true, idealistic Platonist one had better look up to the sun itself, because that is where light is at its most intense. *This* is how things need to be in a Platonic universe. For this is when the philosopher's examined life pays off. Fine, Irwin, and Nehamas write as if this played no part in Platonism. But if it does not then little of it is left. All the bold aspirations are forgotten.

It needs to be stressed that it is the *logic* of Fine's, Irwin's, and Nehamas' position which implies this conclusion, for they do not emphasize this. They do not at all advertize their anti-Platonic aspects (and I am not sure that they are aware of them). In contrast, especially Bostock and Nussbaum and sometimes Woodruff, Reeve, and Bobonich more consciously draw the relevant negative conclusions for Plato's idealistic view of life on similar premises, and this is why I focus on them in 2–6 below.

Epistemological Version. Epistemologically, invoking a universal merely as such will not silence a skeptic (like "Socrates"), because further questions can be asked about the universal. For instance, take it that a IS PROVED BY b, and b is a universal. Plato's Socrates then has the opportunity to ask what proves b. If the answer is c, he can ask his question again, and then this can happen with $d, e,$ *ad infinitum*. But then nothing is proved, so the skeptic wins the debate. The regress does not terminate; there is no foundation. But the positively thinking epistemologist will ask how this series of questions could possibly end. How could the skeptic be made to lose? By $\mathbb{R}$ the answer is: if some z proves itself (that is z, as in zRz) or/and if z is a proof about proof (as in zRR). Notice that the terminus here is not anything as ordinary as a universal (or a property, a predicate, a quality, etc.). A universal is not such as to silence the skeptic. Why not, exactly? Because it does not refer *to itself*. It begs a further question. This is different with self-proving things of the form zRz and zRR because they *themselves* answer the further questions. But the Forms and Gods in Plato are offered for this type of a role (e.g. the *Theaetetus* aims at knowledge about knowledge (see Chapter 13), the *Phaedo* equates the equating relation with itself (see 3.3)). In other words, they are taylor-made to function as endpoints in just the kinds of questioning series which Socrates always strives to make, so Plato creates both the demand *and* the supply—just as a proper dialectician should.

Here we may take a step back to make sure the situation is clear. Why exactly can a universal or a predicate not refer to itself? This is due to their logic. A universal is had by a particular, not by a universal; so the universal is logically incapable of referring back to itself. These logical categories exclude each other, and since the categories must none the less be used together, they cannot explain (or justify) themselves. The same is true of predicates, because they apply only to subjects. Dualism is built into these schemes. Therefore such schemes must always eventually depend on staring skeptics down. They cannot coherently justify or even thematize themselves so their advocates can only finally pretend that they are inevitable (which they are not). Put differently, the problem is that universals and predicates are simply *not like* the things they are about. That is why they cannot provide rational foundations for themselves (I lack the space to discuss Fine's or Irwin's coherentism at this juncture).

Metaphysical Version. How is the situation metaphysically? Formally it is just the same. This is because with $\mathbb{R}$ we always produce formally analogical scenarios. Thus, if *a* IS CAUSED BY *b* IS CAUSED BY *c,* then we have a causal chain, and in this setting the grand metaphysical issue (of Plato himself according to this book and also of Aristotle's theology, Aquinas' five ways, Kant's antinomies, Hegel's philosophy of history, and so on) is how the chain can begin or end. The issue is problematic for many because it is difficult to picture anything as arbitrary as a simple beginning or ending merely as such. If *a* is first or *z* is last then how can that be? Do *a* and *z* just happen, out of the blue? Are they just givens? Contingent "answers" like these simply do not convince reasoning beings, but invoking universals or predicates is logically only on this level. A philosopher such as Moore can invoke a universal like good or yellow and try to stare his critics down, but surely not Plato. But then what is Plato's view? He attempts to reason about the first causes. Some things should be such as to cause themselves. As I argue, Plato's answers are of the forms *zRz* and *zRR*. For example, in the *Laws* Book X God is self-caused (see Chapter 6), the self-moving psyche of the *Phaedrus* is self-caused (see Chapter 11), and the Forms are self-caused throughout this book.

Pedagogical Version. In the *Meno* Socrates famously teaches a slave boy by asking him questions (see Chapter 9), and educators have long celebrated this method. Following Socrates' lead they question their students instead of preaching or lecturing them down. The students learn to solve problems and not to parrot authorities.

But the same picture can also be reversed in an interesting way. For another famous fact is that children themselves tend to ask questions. They may be small philosophers (see Lipman and Bynam eds. for some examples; also consult the Introduction to my 2015 book), and some of the childish questions quite resemble ℝ. For especially the young child will at times refuse to stop asking *why*. If you give your answer, she will ask why about that, and again about your next answer, etc., much like Socrates. I think it is no accident that, at least in my teaching experience, children master ℝ quite universally based on but a few examples. The children plainly understand the regresses in questions and causes much in the same way that logicians distinguish between levels or orders, that is by means of recursion (there is the x of the x of the x: x^3, x^2, x). Of course, they do not define any of this, just as Plato himself does not. Their grasp of the structure is evidenced rather in the colorful examples that they generate: *this school* IS IN *Berlin* IS IN *Germany...* and where is the *Milky Way?*, or: Does God believe in God?, or: Am I inside me? They are small Platos.

Yet how can this be? What makes it possible that Plato's speakers and real children master certain rules this quickly? And how can the slave boy, any modern child, or indeed Plato himself generate coherent patterns in such abundance without copying anyone? This is what any rationalist will of course need to ask. Plato himself does his best on this question in the *Meno* and the *Phaedo* (see Chapters 9 and 3). In our time Chomsky tackles it—but the major Plato scholars do not. They prefer easier questions. For their logical riddle is only how a universal gets to be abstracted from particulars. But minds that small are found already in Locke. They do not require Plato's grandeur.

1.4 VERSUS OWEN, GALLOP, CASTAÑEDA, ETC.

In 1.2 we encountered one type of hostility to Platonic idealism and in 1.3 another. Now in 1.4 we meet with yet another way to oppose him. This third type is like the second in that it does not involve self-conscious opposition to Plato. The hostile implications are not drawn. Unlike the second type this third type is about relations, and in this sense it comes closer to $\mathbb{R}$. The difference between this third type of anti-Platonism and $\mathbb{R}$ is mainly in the size of the unit of evidence that is considered. The recent relationalists focus on a short wavelength, that is on microstructures, whereas $\mathbb{R}$ operates with macrostructures and larger waves. But why exactly is this a problem regarding Plato's idealism? This is best explained in response to the particular things that the scholars say.

I will now first distinguish between three ways in which relations have recently been studied in Plato, (A)–(C):[17]

(A) In 1957 Owen takes Plato's relational argument for the existence of the Forms ("argument from relatives") to be semantic in its basis (whereby Owen's focus is on *kath' auto* and *pros ti* in Plato and Aristotle) and such as to aim for a conclusion in which the Forms are particulars. Fine's *On Ideas* is a recent source to dispute Owen's claims, holding instead that Plato's Forms are universals and not particulars and also that the purported foundations are metaphysical and epistemological and not semantic (see Fine, *On Ideas*, p. 160 for a summary of the issues).

To clarify, this debate is not about whether the *Forms* (and/or Gods) could be relational, which is my view. More generally, Owen and Fine cling to particulars (Owen) and universals (Fine) in interpreting Plato, so the philological details they consider (*kath' auto* and *pros ti*) cause no alterations in the vocabulary with which they interpret Plato. Owen and Fine seem to be convinved *a priori* that Plato must fit into these Aristotelian slots. The error in this is the same as in 1.3 above, so I will not repeat the points here.

The fault in (A)—from my relational point of view—is that it is relational only on the surface. Relations are not really made use of to see reason in Plato in a deeper way. This error recurs in (B):

(B) Through the decades Anscombe and Geach, Matthews and Cohen, Armstrong, and Fine (in her 1978, Chapter 13) have considered whether Platonism in a rather standard form may as such be relational. To illustrate this with a simple example of my own, the possibility is that for Plato Socrates and his manhood stand in a relation because Socrates then relates to a separate entity, the Form of Man. By contrast, in these terms there is for Aristotle no separate Form of Man and so if Socrates is a man then Socrates does not *relate* to anything in being a man. For on the Aristotelian view there is no manhood out there for Socrates to relate to, and all the manhood there is is only *in* him, or in him and in other men. (These scholars (in (B)) are led by this to confront diverse other issues, such as whether a relationally understood Plato would have to see individuals as bear of properties, like the *Timaeus'* receptacles.)

Now in (B), as in (A) above, it is not the Forms themselves that are viewed relationally. Rather, the Forms seem to be pictured again as separate universals (or properties). What is relational on this interpretation of Plato is the relationship between a particular and a separate universal. But this is to operate with universals and particulars once again, just as in (A) and 1.3 above. Hence, relations are not actually allowed to influence the basic Aristotelian scheme for making sense of things. (To put this point in one way, the deep *symmetries* that Plato seems to me to be after are not possible to register or capture in these terms. Relations make this possible and the Aristotelian dualism makes it impossible.)

(C) In the 1970's Castañeda and Gallop debate whether Plato distinguishes relations from qualities (the focal point being *Phaedo* 102B2–D2).

(C) does not belong to the same type as (A) and (B), because Castañeda's bold move is to argue that *Phaedo* 102B2–D2 is to be interpreted relationally and *not essentially*. Castañeda thus makes the decisive contrast, using relations *at the expense of* Aristotle's basic logical categories. As such this is promising, but there are two unnecessary errors in Castañeda, and these make it too easy for Gallop to criticize him.

The first of these errors is that Castañeda says, needlessly, that *Phaedo* 102B2–D2 contains a *general theory* of relations (Castañeda 1978, pp. 39–40). This is clearly a mistake because *Phaedo* 102B2–D2 is explicit only about *one* relation (e.g. IS TALLER THAN, IS GREATER THAN, or OVERTOPS, so that *Simmias* OVERTOPS *Socrates,* see 3.11; it is the *Republic* that may have the total doctrine of relations, see 5.6–5.7). Thus what we find in *Phaedo* 102B2–D2 is an example, not a general theory. This makes it easy for Gallop to deny that *Phaedo* 102B2–D2 in fact contains any general theory (Gallop 1976, p. 156). Moreover, Castañeda's miscategorization of *Phaedo* 102B2–D2 gives Gallop the opportunity to point out that Plato seems to be incapable of distinguishing between relational and non-relational concepts (ibid. p. 150; this same issue will recur between in 3.11). Castañeda should not have implied that Plato is *clear* about his own habits or longings. Rather, a relational reading of Plato stands a chance only if the relations are used and *not* theorized in Plato. Plato *does* more than he can explain, as I argue. He plays a relational game without stating its rules (see Scheibe's spectrum of examples to see how various the textual foundations of relations can be in Plato; I will return to this variety soon below, still in 1.4).

Castañeda's second mistake is to not even ponder how relations could figure in Plato's overall economy of ideas. For, as I have already noted repeatedly, the very process of philosophizing seems to be relational in Plato. This is because his speakers so often form relational chains (as in $aRbRc...$). Moreover, the Forms (and Gods) may be interpreted relationally and hence self-consistently (as in $...zRR$ or $...zRz$). But Castañeda does not consider such wider connections and in consequence of this the larger philosophical point of his relational exercise is lost. In other words, what would it matter if Plato were found to be a relationalist? What would that do for the reality and value of the Forms and Gods, for the immortality of the psyche, or perhaps for the possibility of utopia, etc.? To be sure, if these matters are considered then it is not insignificant to assess a passage such as *Phaedo* 102B2–D2; but surely one should not expect to find everything of importance to be represented in that (or any) individual detail. One might as well attempt to squeeze an entire symphony into a single note or study Aristotle's logic by seeing how he uses the word "logic" (which he does not do, as noted; Kneale and Kneale p. 23). Platonism is not made of tiny Platonic particles any more than symphonies are made up of tiny symphonies or logics consist of uses of the word "logic." (Traditionally Plato's smaller particles have been studied mainly to settle issues about *chronology*. One gets a general impression of how this works from Lutoslawski's wide-ranging survey, see his pp. 74–193.)

However the careful scholars mentioned in this section (1.4) would not automatically agree with my message, so thus far I have made things too easy for myself. For scholars like Owen and Castañeda clearly have a point in seeking detailed evidence as in *kath' auto* or *pros ti* (Owen 1957) and *Phaedo* 102B2–D2 (Castañeda). After all, this is the kind of evidence that we can find from the Greek texts themselves. Indeed, *all* the evidence we have from Plato consists of specific words in ancient Greek. But then how is it possible for $\mathbb{R}$ to be true about Plato to this background? Must it not imply definite statements about which Greek words come after which in Plato's corpus? For what other evidence is there? Must one not proceed like a scientist?

This overall situation is perhaps best interpreted by considering an analogy from the philosophy of science. Scholars like Owen and Castañeda zoom in on the evidence, and this is analogous to examining one's data closely in any science. Then one asks, what is really under the microscope? One does not want to rest content with a mere hazy impression, and whatever expectations or interpretations one may have should not get in the way of the actual facts, which are empirical, individual, often surprising, and potentially resistant to any generalized theory. On the other hand, $\mathbb{R}$ is a general theory. It is about the overall structure or intelligibilty of the entire collection of data. Thus it zooms out, not in. Now Owen and Castañeda seem like positivists or empiricists whereas my kinship is with scientific realism (cf. Losee for historical comparisons; on Plato's own (realistic!) philosophy of science see Gregory; Chomsky instances one form of realism in linguistics, and some of his concerns resemble Plato's, e.g. about innateness and syntax).

To this background it can seem that $\mathbb{R}$ should be equivalent merely to a *larger set* of detailed studies like Owen's and Castañeda's. For it can appear that the difference between these two interpretive philosophies is only a difference in scope. It is as if I attempted only to do much *more* of what Owen and Castañeda already do. But things are not so. To see this, consider first the kinds of things for which I need to find evidence—(I) and (II)—and then the many ways in which that evidence can be located in Plato's texts (i–v).

If we know that Plato says of x that x is

(I) the superlative member of its class (like c in $a<b<c$; see 1.3 above) and also
(II) the general standard for assessing what belongs to its class (like $<$ in $a<b<c$; see 1.3 above),

then we know also that he adheres to a view which is rationally explained with $aRbRR$, or $\mathbb{R}$. (I omit zRz for the time being. The following points could be made on its basis just as well, however.) But now consider how many different ways Plato has to get (I) and (II) across. He uses i–v:

i. comparative and superlative *adjectives,* saying that some things are more beautiful than others, or else more just, better known, "higher," etc. In these terms the generality of (II) is achieved by ranking a spectrum of items as in $a<b<c$. The superlative status of (I) is attained in c on the same scale (see e.g. *Hippias Major* 288E–289B, *Symposium* 210B, *Re-*

public 472B–E, 475E–D, and 476A–480A, *Timaeus* 53D; for discussion see 2.1, 4.1–4.3, 4.6, 5.6, and 10).

ii. external and internal *relations,* for instance so that knowledge is of many things other than knowledge or else about itself, or so that something moves diverse other things or else it moves itself. In this vocabulary (I) is self-relational and (II) is externally relational (see for example *Charmides* 166E–172B and *Laws* 894B–D, which latter passage is discussed in 6.13).

iii. *contradictory expressions* for (II) and consistent expressions for (I), for example so that sticks and stones are both equal and not equal whereas a Form is perfectly equal or self-equal (*Phaedo* 74A–E, see 3.3; it may also be absolutely or essentially what it is, *Phaedo* 75C, 76D) or else in the way that several things are both virtuous and not virtuous but some other things are only or purely virtuous (e.g. *Phaedo* 68D–69B, see 3.2; cf. *Republic* 583B–588A in 5.6).

iv. *causal chains* in which the intermediate links represent (II) and the ultimate links are (I) (see respectively *Laws* 893B–895C for efficient causes, *Lysis* 219C–220B and *Symposium* 210E for final causes, and *Republic* 510B–511C for formal causes, for example, and for discussion see 4.6, 5.7, 6.13–6.14, 7, and 10).

v. *models* for some things in terms of others. For instance virtue is modeled on the crafts in several of the earlier dialogues (see Irwin 1977 and Chapter 9), and in the *Republic* Good has some of the sun's features (507B–509C) and the psyche has a parallel in the utopian polis (368C–369B). In these terms something is a perfect version as in (I) or else a copy as in (II) (it is difficult to put this more exactly because Plato's models vary so much; on several of them see Chapter 5).

This is not offered as a complete list, but it suffices to indicate that (I) and (II) are independent of any particular grammatical detail. What exactly does this teach us? That Plato's wavelength is long. He could as well be taught in smoke signals or Morse code. He is so cosmopolitan, so thoroughly thoughtful, that he does not depend on any contingent, local, symbolisms. (The medium is exacly *not* the message!)

But who exactly is supposed to be so naïve as to think otherwise, and where? Which sources in fact depend so heavily on Plato's explicit linguistic details that they ignore the larger relational patterns? The best examples are *kath' auto* or *pros ti* in Owen and *Phaedo* 102B2–D2 in Castañeda. (The same is true of Gallop, Kirwan, Matthen, Tarrant, Anscombe, and diverse others. Scheibe seems to be the only Plato scholar to notice the limitations of this approach, but he does not make it an issue of principle. He merely looks at the different kinds of cases; see endnote 6.) This is a tendency to cling to a small, individual unit of evidence as a verifier or falsifier of any theory about Plato's philosophizing. The leash is so short, so to speak, that there is little room for the formation of theories; for the unit of evidence which is then thought to prove or disprove a view of Plato is always so small that all it can confirm must likewise be quite small. This means that there is not even a possibility of evaluating a pattern like $\mathbb{R}$ without supposing that $\mathbb{R}$ must inhere in some small representative unit. For then it has been decided *a priori* that nothing else can be evident! (How easy and comfortable that would be! Just report what you see, verbatim. There is nothing else!) But this supposition is as absurd as that a melody can be squeezed into a single note.

But perhaps this is too easy. For how can claims about Plato be *falsified* if Plato's wavelength really is as long as it is in $\mathbb{R}$? There seem to be three main possibilities. The first two are that either (I) or (II) would be missing from one of the crucial passages that I have selected. But it seems that no one will bother to dispute these claims, because the passages that I have selected are the ones in which Plato indulges in his characteristic hyperbole about the Forms and Gods, and there seems to be no source which denies (I) or (II) concerning them. The third way to refute $\mathbb{R}$ would be by finding some superior way to explain the conjunction of (I) and (II). This is a real possibility because $\mathbb{R}$ is not supposed to be analytically true of (I) and (II). There could be coherent alternatives to it. (How close $\mathbb{R}$ comes to being analytically true of (I) and (II) depends heavily on how we formulate (I) and (II).[18])

1.5 PLATO, ANTI-PLATO, AND TOTALITARIANISM

If *Plato's Logic* is correct then Plato's way of reasoning has been misunderstood quite dramatically for a long period of time. But this purported fact calls for some explanation. For why would so many go so wrong? And what is it that makes me so confident that I can be so right? This section (1.5) makes some brief conjectures about the recent past.

First let us make some generalizations about recent scholarly studies of Plato. Here are the main secondary sources discussed in this book, by chapter:

- Chapter 2: Woodruff about the *Hippias Major*.
- Chapter 3: Bostock about the *Phaedo*.
- Chapter 4: Nussbaum on the *Symposium*.
- Chapter 5: Reeve on the *Republic*.
- Chapter 6: Bobonich about the *Laws*.

These scholars have their many differences, but their commonality is that each of them defends everyday opinions against Plato's idealistic claims. Woodruff denies that humans can reach any divine type of fineness; whereas Bostock argues that everyday agents are capable of being virtuous enough already and that Plato's allegations against them are only misunderstandings or logical blunders. Bostock also holds that Plato's Forms are based only on everyday intuitions of normal speakers and that Plato does not have a real basis for idealizing anything beyond that level. Nussbaum finds fault in Plato's doctrines on love and beauty, holding that his is only an artificial attempt to escape from the contingencies of ordinary human life. Reeve denies that the Forms are self-instantiating or separate, so for him the philosophers' prime object, the the Form of the Good, is not good at all, let alone especially good. Finally, Bobonich's claim is that the late Plato actually agrees that non-philosophers are as capable of virtue and happiness as philosophers. In these ways the whole idealistic edifice appears to come tumbling down. However I argue that all of these influential scholars are biased. Only their false impression fails.

What explains this bias? Very briefly, in history the scholars of the Italian Renaissance (*Humanitas*) and German Romanticism (*Bildung*) were much more prepared to see reason in Plato's bolder claims (see e.g. Feibleman), but their own times were ones of great innovation in both philosophy and the arts. Now the climate has changed. The past enthusiasts did not witness the dystopias and world wars of the twentieth century, and these have perhaps contributed to the need of recent philosophers to want to side safely with the man in the street against all greater experiments or revisions. However this implies a dishonesty about Plato, because he is viewed as the origin of elementary logical fallacies (1.2) or else as a rather toothless utterer of banalities (1.3) or as a tinkerer with linguistic nuances (1.4). Contrary to such views this book argues that his idealistic efforts actually make good sense, so the honest story should be more optimistic about novelties and experiments. It remains to be seen if future humans may be prepared again to read Plato as the visionary that he really is.

NOTES

1. That "Socrates" of all people so often figures as the ideal philosopher in Plato's works is well known. This book never implies that the "Socrates" of Plato's works is the historical Socrates. For discussions on the historical Socrates see Fine vol. 1 p. 1. In the *Laws* "the Athenian" plays a similar role (see 6.1).

2. Compare these two series: (i) a IS CAUSED BY b IS CAUSED BY c, (ii) Q: *Why a?* A: b. Q: *Why b?* A: c. In (i) we have $aRbRc$ (R=IS CAUSED BY) but in (ii) we have $aRbRc$ again (R=BECAUSE). The difference is only that in (ii) the cause (or

the "because," the "why") is prompted by a question. Thus ℝ covers both types of series, the causal chain as in (i) and the dialectical search as in (ii). ℝ is the logic of both. This indicates that ℝ pertains to Plato's thinking rather generally, for ℝ is how Plato structures dialogical inquiries as well as purposes, origins, authorities, and elements.

3. I do not mean to imply that dialogical views like Gadamer's are only a waste of time. (Gadamer is representative of the dialogical approach because he takes its associations especially far. He thinks of the philosophical process as an ongoing negotiation between subjective perspectives, or "horizons.") They can be highly instructive, but they seem to do little against skeptical readers who doubt that sense can be made of Plato's idealistic conclusions. For it seems that one needs hard evidence for Plato's idealistic claims or they start to seem too much like pleasant fictions. However this is not a reason why *all* studies of Plato need to be concerned with convincing skeptics. For his texts have many levels. In this spirit, Wilamowitz writes a biography of Plato, noting already on his second page (p. X) that he is as free to study the biography without attention to the logic of Plato's philosophy as he would be to study the life of Goethe without attention to Goethe's ("scientific") theory of colors. To use a different comparison, just as Euclid has a geometry as well as a biography, Plato has a philosophy and a biography. It is coherent to say that there is room for many different studies. However, if there are not *also* studies to refute skeptics then something philosophically central is missing from our picture of Plato. (For further reflections on Plato's biography see Grene.)

4. The key premise now is that Plato's *own wordings* do not explain his meanings sufficiently. The original wordings are often sketchy or metaphorical, not definite. If one clings to them then one's results will have to be skeptical in the manner of e.g. Lutoslawski (who says on his p. 363 that Plato's expressions about the Forms' reality are so metaphorical than they do not license inferences) or Voegelin (who on p. 112 goes so far as to say that inexpressibility of "the Agathon" is fundamental to Plato's ethics).

Why would one need to rely on the author's own words to explain his meanings? Who says one should, and why? Michael Frede is a recent example. In his study ancient authors begin to have a "concept" of free will at around the same time as they begin to use words which translate as "free will." The assumption may be that an author thinks what she writes, which would sound reasonable enough. One has views about free will if and only if one says so. However there are often assumptions and structures in texts which their authors do not explicitly recognize, so this view is not generally true. For one thing, texts can have fallacious assumptions which escape their authors (see 1.2 on Platonic "self-predication" and 2.6 and 9 on the so-called "Socratic Fallacy"). I also mentioned verbs which are used without being announced explicitly as "verbs." More generally there are very many unrecognized grammatical and logical patterns in every text (not to speak of phonetics, morphology, possible rhetorical tropes, and so on). This is somewhat as in music, so that one can compose melodies and sing them without theorizing the intervals, rhythms, etc. For one does not sing *about* the notes (as in "C," "$C\#$," "D," etc.). One merely sings the notes. A musicologist friend of mine tells me that some of Bach's harmonies are still unexplained to this day. People can hear that they fit together, but no one has the explanations. This is how I view Plato. He is a "genius" who does far more than he *says* he does. He "sings" his philosophy (cf. 1.4).

5. Kneale and Kneale Chapter 1 summarize several of the often noted things about Plato's logical views, and in part they base on Robinson for their generalizations:

Plato's earlier dialogues are said to instance an "elenchtic" method in which, as in Zeno of Elea, views are refuted by finding that they contradict themselves. This is a negative, destructive tool and the motive for its use seems to be skeptical (this Chapter 1 denies, arguing against Woodruff).

Plato's transitional and middle works instance and defend a method of "hypothesis" according to which hypotheses are assessed by their implications (on this see Chapter 9 on the *Meno* as well as 3.6 on the *Phaedo*).

Plato's middle dialogues and later dialogues contain a "dialectic." This is a more constructive manner of reasoning especially in Plato's middle period. In the *Republic* it turns into something hyperbolical and mythical (Chapters 3–5 argue that it is quite sharp at least on some levels).

In Plato's later period dialectic is more modest. Then it is a method of collection and division, which anticipates Aristotle. (Collection and division largely falls outside the scope of *Plato's Logic* because that method does not generate Plato's idealistic results. Some of Plato's later works are here studied in a different light which is more compatible with his idealism. See Chapter 6 on the *Laws* especially, but also 12 on the *Timaeus* and 13 on the *Theaetetus*.)

Kneale and Kneale add to this that the *Theaetetus* and the *Sophist* contain logical insights which are only primitive and childish in the eyes of current readers. In general, if Plato's "logic" is viewed as in Kneale and Kneale then clearly it is only of historical and not of any serious philosophical interest. In contrast, I argue that Plato is *ahead* of us in several ways.

6. This need not be viewed as an either/or decision, however, because some relational studies of Plato could be general (and imprecise) and some others local (and precise). The types could co-exist and potentially even inform each other. Then *Plato's Logic* would be in the former group (alone as far as I know) and several microscopic studies could complement it.

So far this has not been the reality, however, because the local and precise studies of patterns like zRz and zRR are rare. The only obvious exception to this that I know of is Scheibe (1967). He explores aRa in the *Charmides* (on this see my *Socrates' Criteria* (2012) p. 44), notes how love in the *Symposium* and identity are relational (compare this book's 4.1 and 3.3 respectively), and considers whether the Forms may be relational (which is this book's view, of course). Scheibe adds to this book's view by thematizing more of Plato's later works, such as the *Parmenides* and the *Sophist*. He does not formulate more specific or definite, local versions of zRz or zRR, however. (In general Scheibe did not affect this book's views, because I learned of his paper so late.)

Another rather exceptional study, but without any explicit reliance on relational logic, is Jeremiah (2013). He finds reflexive patterns in ancient Greek philosophy and considers that these may mark the beginnings of self-conscious speculation in ontology as well as epistemology and ethics. He goes so far as to include Gods as well as regress arguments in his narrative, and at times he seems to come close to ℝ in his positions. However Jeremiah does not attempt to use relations to explain things, and he seems rather to embrace a kind of philological determinism according to which the words or phrases of natural languages (such as the Greek *auto*) determine the thoughts of the people who use them, which is a view I oppose in 1.4. (Also Jeremiah's article came to my attention too late to influence the construction of this book.)

Bailey (2005) is one of several recent scholars who study relations in Plato but without any seeming awareness that the questions can have deeper implications for rethinking Plato. Bailey's paper concerns the consistency relation in the *Phaedo*, finding that this relation is stronger than coherence and weaker than implication and that it can usefully be compared to patterns in music.

What relational studies of Plato have mostly done is something different from these three examples, because they bring up relations only superficially (e.g. Nehamas, Owen, Castañeda, see 1.4) and then proceed to interpret them as if they were one place predicates or Aristotelian universals (see 1.4 for more on this).

Lastly I need to mention Natorp, Robin, and Milhaud, all of whom write that Plato's philosophy is fundamentally relational. However I am thus far familiar only with Natorp; see endnote 12 below on him. Robin and Milhaud have been difficult for me to access because I do not read French.

7. One reason to think there is a minimum is that the role of relata may be to provide relations with meaning. For then too few relata will often imply ambiguity in relations. This is easiest to explain in numbers. *1:2:4* can be followed with *7* or *8*, for example, so the relation (*:*) is ambiguous. Adding more relata usually determines the relation more exactly. However there is no exact number of relata that will suffice in every case.

But why would relations need to be explained by means of relata? Why would one not go to relations directly (as in *child:parent:grandparent* or *cat* EATS *mouse* EATS *cheese*, where parenthood and eating are relations)? This is because in Plato's world the Forms and Gods are not empirical entities. For this reason they cannot be encountered directly. They must be learned about through other means, and it is series of relata which provide such means. The simplest example of this is Heraclitus' *ape:man:god*, which I will dwell on in 2.1 when discussing definitions in the *Hippias Major*. As Fränkel says, Heraclitus' meaning seems to be as in *ape:man:x*, so that god is initially an unknown, but then god comes to be grasped by means of the comparison between the ape and the man. For God is even more intelligent, more moral (or taller, less hairy, or what have you) than a man is compared to an ape. It is as if the ape and the man gave one the co-ordinates or directions for imagining god.

Plato himself uses very different numbers of relata. In the *Hippias Major* we have three, in the *Symposium* five, and in the *Laws* we find ten (see Chapters 2, 4, and 6, respectively). In the *Phaedo* we have pairs of pairs, as in *a:b::c:d* (see 3), and in the *Republic* we have quadruplets as well as triplets (see 5). 2.1 explains how this book's views derive from Fränkel.

8. The reason is that in Plato a series like *aRbRc* is often, though not always, a temporal series of events, so that *aRb* happens first, then *bRc*, etc. Then first *a* CAUSES *b*, and next *b* CAUSES *c*. This temporal order is reflected in *aRbRc*, but it would not

be in *Rabc* or *R(a,b,c)*. For in these two latter series of symbols were read as temporal series of events then they would both make *R* happen first, then *a,* next *b,* etc. But that is not the temporal order of events in a causal series. (A similar point can be made in terms of dialogue. For Plato's dialogues are not conducted by first pinning down a relation and then using it in all kinds of individual causes. Rather, the relation is in play *in* the sequence of cases. More radically, the relation is often not even *clear* before the sequence has unfolded, see endnote 7.)

Why is not every relational series in Plato a temporal series in this sense? First, converseness (see the fifth note in 1.1) allows us to describe temporal series backwards as well as forwards, so we can actually begin a series *aRbRc* with what happens last and end the series with what happens first (as in *Socrates' hand* IS MOVED BY *Socrates' psyche* IS MOVED BY *Socrates' grasp of a Form,* see 3.11). Second, all relational series are not temporal (think of e.g. hierarchies of formal causes, for in such hierarchies the relata do not actually *happen* at all: they are timeless structural patterns; see 2.3 and 5.6).

9. Quine's example of dogs seems in fact to illustrate why the using existential quantifier does not directly settle questions about existence. In Quine's example, the claim that a dog exists is confirmed by a collie and by a spaniel, so there are (at least) two different ways for the existential thesis to be true. This same thing can be said about God talk, for one can use the existential quantifier also on Gods, as on dogs, and one can be right in doing so if Zeus exists *or* Aphrodite does *or* else theos *or* a demiurge *or* Atman, or whatever else. In other words, if one uses the existential quantifier to say that God exists then there is still a lot of leeway as to which of the many possible Gods is in question. In my view this indicates that the existential quantifier is rather useless, comparatively. For what is much more useful is the demand to describe one's believed-in object exactly enough. But this demand is not linked to quantifiers. It is a separate ideal about the proper use of language. One needs to *explain* oneself instead of merely dropping names or suggesting vaguely. (Is this ideal Plato's? I think it would not be if he were not dissatisfied with his merely allegorical descriptions of the Form of the Good in the *Republic* (506D–E), for example, or with unexplained references to "good" (505C); but he is.)

10. See e.g. Quine for the minimalistic answer that a relation is an ordered pair (1960 § 53): for *aRb,* <*a,b*>. In 5.6 and 5.7 I argue instead that the Form of the Good is the paradigmatic relation-relation. Quine, following e.g. Peirce and Schröder, wants to identify relations with something other than relations, namely their extensions. LOVES is a lover plus a loved one, for example. In contrast, Plato's relations are unraveled *in relations,* so he piles intensions on intensions. More exactly he is in my view interested in relations that are scales or measures (like IS LONGER THAN and IS JUSTIFIED BY). The Good is then a scale of scales which ranks itself highest. It is a relation relating relations—including itself.

11. With Aristotle the emphasis tends to be more on immanent universals and empirical science, so the tenor is less idealistic than in Plato. Human thought cannot then move as independently, for it is bound to a lower order. With Kant, again, dialectics lead to the antinomies and paralogisms, so no archetypes, Gods, or souls can be accessed and we are condemned to ignorance on all the major issues of metaphysics.

Even Hegel, whose patterns are of course very bold, tends to hide behind the facts of history, writing that the philosopher is free to think only what history has instanced already (the Owl of Minerva takes flight only at dusk). In general, no one trusts or appreciates the independent power of human thought like Plato. Hence it is he, and not Kant, who really says *sapere aude!* (For this view of Kant see my *Dialectical Thinking* (2015) Chapter 3.)

12. In Krämer 1964 the liberal view that Plato's philosophy consists mainly of a method without results is associated with Schleiermacher and Jaspers. Krämer calls their view "existentialistc" and "positivistic" (on philological positivism compare 1.4 below). This combination of existentialism and positivism is intelligible because (as Krämer agrees) the Platonic texts are poor in results. They are rich in questions, in the main, and the answers that they provide are few and sketchy.

Jaeger's *Paideia* is a study of the individual psyche's education (in German *Bildung*) in Plato's Greece, and Jaeger, who heroically contradicts and then flees the Nazis, seems to downplay the value of politics in Plato (see e.g. vol. 2 pp. 354–357), unlike several other German scholars such as Wilamowitz who favors Germany's participation in the First World War. In my view Jaeger's emphasis is attractive also in our day (though the organic Hegelianism is not Platonic).

Natorp sees Plato's Good as a logical ideal (see especially Natorp pp. 194–201), meaning that the Good is not any special *use* of logic. It is a cognitive tool. On his pp. 424–425 Natorp contradicts Aristotle, who holds that Plato's Good or Forms are (superlative) objects of their own. Natorp is in this way a Kantian scholar, making Plato's Good look only like a mere *condition* for other things. (The Sun and Cave allegories make the difference vivid, for as 5.8 reveals, they feature the sun as the most illuminated object, not merely as the illuminator of other things like trees and seas. Natorp confuses the tools of inquiry with its purposes.)

Irwin, Rowe, and several other recent Anglo-American scholars are criticized below for making Plato's demands seem too moderate, see 1.3; but they deserve credit for making Plato accessible.

13. What would this option involve? And why is it not used here? The idea would be to make do only with particulars and without universals. For example, there would be individual large things but no property of large*ness* to unite them as a coherent group. Similarly, if there are only individual beauties, like Helen, a lyre, and a temple, then there is no general type or theory to explain or to justify why just these individuals belong in the group and not others. Problems for this view arise as soon as explanations or justifications are sought, as *Parmenides* 132E–133A says. For why exactly is a comedy by the Marx Brothers not beautiful? (Or is it? How can one tell?) The only possible answer based on individual examples seems to be that the comedy is not suffciently *alike* to Helen, the lyre, or the temple (*Parmenides* 132D). But this leads to a regress, the *Parmenides* says. How? Apparently because the likeness between the individuals depends on their mutual alikeness to some *third* individual, and these relationships require still further go-betweens, and so on without end. Without any regress the problem with particularistic Platonism is sometimes said to concern the ambiguity of the likeness relation. For what is not somehow similar to what? Individualism is too lax a philosophy (but for a defence of it see Campbell).

14. Cf. *(aRb) R (cRd)* to see the general idea. If R is a relation of harmony, as for example in a musical interval or in a poetic meter, then R can bind together different elements like a with b or c with d, as in the first and third instances of "R" in *(aRb) R (cRd)*. Then a is one musical note and b is another musical note, whereas c is a word and d is a different word. But in the same series R can also connect the complexes (i.e. *aRb* and *cRd*) with *each other*, as in the second instance of "R" in *(aRb) R (cRd)*. The use of parentheses enables one to distinguish between these two levels. The first and low level is that of the empirical base (bearing on sounds and words like a, b, c, d), and the second level is that of a higher and more theoretic order (cf. 4.6).

How are things different with conjuction? 1.1 mentioned that conjunction symbols (like $\wedge$) can be used alongside or instead of parentheses in some places. To see how, consider this expression: *((aAb $\wedge$ bBc) $\wedge$ (dCe $\wedge$ fDg) $\wedge$ (AEB $\wedge$ CED) $\wedge$ EE)*. Here the small alphabets are only relata, not relations, but the capitalized alphabets are both relations and relata. Moreover, each of the capitalized alphabets is a relation of harmony. Now, *AEB* and *CED* are higher order harmonies but only *EE* is a harmony with the self-same harmony, as in a Form (according to 4.6). In this pattern the base of the hierarchy is described in *(aAb $\wedge$ bBc) $\wedge$ (dCe $\wedge$ fDg)*, and then an intermediate level is described all the way from (and excluding) g to, but excluding, *EE;* finally, *EE* is the tip of the structure. (See 4.6.)

15. One reason is that it is never fully obvious that Beauty=harmony or Goodness=order, for example. (Plato simply does not present answers that plainly.) There could be other contents. A second reason is that even if Beauty=harmony or Goodness=order (to use the same examples for the sake of clarity), then there is still the further question what harmony is, and what order. My personal view is that no matter how we define these or other values and however glorious examples we manage bring forth to make them vivid, we will never reach complete accounts which would answer all philosophical questions about them. Due to this, philosophical speculation along Plato's lines can never end. Hence, there can never be a time in which the children of utopia simply immerse themselves in the official dogmas and everything is alright.

That said, *progress* can be made none the less, at least if we select charitable enough parameters. For example, we can keep learning *much* about beauty for a long stretch of time if we examine harmonies in various types of poetry and music (in or outside Plato), but we learn only *little* if we analyze an adjective such as "beautiful" (in or outside Plato), cf. 4.6. Similarly , if orders are understood to be linguistic structures like i–v in 1.4 below (or dialectic as in endnote 2 or $\mathbb{R}$) and the Form of the Good is the order of orders (cf. 5.6–5.7) then Plato gives us *much* to go on concerning the Form of the Good. But if we cling to, say, the small portion of the *Republic* in which Plato mentions that the Good is somehow beyond being (509B) and attempt to decipher some kind of a being of beings as the Good from this alone, then the evidence will allow us to do but *little*. We need to read Plato in such a way that he flourishes.

16. Especially Fine and Irwin seem to philosophize with the intention to *minimize their commitments*. A philosopher of this type aims to presuppose as little as possible. And why? To find acceptance from others more easily. Thus the name of their game seems to be more or less skeptical, for the main ambition appears to be to overcome

others' doubts. It is no surprise that the results then end up being quite thin, for there is not much that is acceptable to many in philosophy.

Nehamas' approach is a little more Continental and literary, but this does not seem to affect his analysis of Plato's Forms. It is nowhere as rich as e.g. Heidegger's. Thus, Nehamas is only very slightly Continental. The same could said about Vlastos: he admires the wit of Kierkegaard, but he never dares to say anything as radical. However I would not personally side, quite, with the Continentals either, because spectacular as they can be, their views are often difficult to believe. It is structuralism that seems to me to be called for, as in the rationalistic tradition.

17. The scholars I exclude here are Matthen, who responds to (C) and quickly gets lost in minor details (e.g. concerning tallness, see especially p. 308 in Matthen 1984); Kirwan, whose view adds nothing to Gallop's in (C) or Bostock's in 3.12; and Scheibe, whose views remain mere sketches, see endnote 6.

18. If we speak of the independence or immutability of the Forms and Gods then the bond is still comparatively loose. Analyticity is approached more nearly if we read (I) and (II) as descriptions of self-sufficiency or self-causation, because these seem like self-relations, and self-relations seem to have the form zRz or zRR. In saying this I do not imply that an analytical relationship between *explanandum* and *explanans* would be a good thing (cf. Chapter 9).

Chapter Two

The Hippias Major

The *Hippias Major* introduces two major Platonic technicalities. One is a word and the other is a structure. The word is *idea* or *eidos* (both appear), which is used for Plato's special objects, referred to in English usually as the Forms (or Ideas). These are the perfect things that demand our assent, as explained already in the Introduction. They are the end-points of inquiry, that is the ultimate answers to the questions of persistent critics like Plato's "Socrates." The other technical innovation in the *Hippias Major* is not terminological but syntactic, and this is what will concern us almost exclusively in this chapter (2) and elsewhere in this book. ℝ is, after all, a syntactical account of Platonic reasoning. As I keep repeating, ℝ is not a translation for any *word* in Plato. For the words change, but the pattern ℝ does not. For uses of ℝ can be made up of different words. Accordingly, in a discussion of ℝ no particular word or name in Plato will be given primacy. What matters is the structure of the process that Plato presents, and keywords are not essential. Such things as distinctions and analogies are essential, and series of them are even more essential. They are the types of thing which take us to the vicinity of ℝ.

Section 2.1 takes us directly to the heart of this syntax. For in the *Hippias Major* Plato's Socrates wants a definition of the fine from Hippias. All the other questions that he raises always lead up to this one. But this is a peculiar question, because it is after a general standard and a superlative instance at the same time. Yet ℝ accounts for this double function, and otherwise it appears to be difficult to account for. On most readings it seems to make little sense. But this is, implicitly, the said syntactical innovation, so in 2.1 we officially encounter ℝ for the first time in the Platonic corpus.

2.1 covers only a few passages from the *Hippias Major*, so there are still plenty of pages left over after it. How should they be interpreted? More specifically, are they to be studied in the light of ℝ or not? Both of these alternatives are uncertain, but in the sections 2.2–2.5 I defend the former one. Thus, when Plato's Socrates comes to speak of complexes, of self-causation, of his superego, etc., I argue that he is actually applying ℝ. If this is true then the *Hippias Major* is not only a work of a few highpoints. Rather, it makes a whole series of serious points, and with an overall consistency. But this implies also that my view must face up to objections, because it differs so much from the more conventional accounts. In 2.6 I attempt to refute Woodruff's esteemed interpretation of the *Hippias Major*. 2.7 summarizes the chapter (2).

2.1 DEFINITIONS (287B–289D, 291D, 292C–E, 293C–294D, 299D–300B)

In the *Hippias Major* Socrates says that the finest thing (288E–289C) is also the general standard for measuring the degree of fineness in any thing (287D–E, 289D–290B, 292C–E, 293D–E, 299D–E, 300A–B). This seems to mean that it is both c and $<$ in $a<b<c$ and so, given that $c=<$, and if we insert R for $<$, $aRbRR$. But therefore we get ℝ, and so we have some evidence for this book's thesis, which is that ℝ is Plato's characteristic thought pattern. (See 5.6 on whether $<<$ is nonsense.)

As noted in 1, this is not to say that the *Hippias Major* contains the symbols "ℝ" or "$aRbRR$" or "$a<b<c$." Rather, these symbols are used to articulate a structure in the light of which Socrates' utterances make sense. This is to imply that they do not otherwise make sense very easily. Why not? Because the roles of $<$ and c seem so different from each other. This is, illustratively, the difference between weight and the heaviest thing there is, or between money and the richest person. On an ultimate level Socrates does not observe such a difference, and I argue that this is best explained by the hypothesis that he is a relationalist.[1]

Now let us rewind and consider the details more closely. What exactly does Socrates say? Let us first take one side of the coin, that is the side about a general standard which serves to rank things in point of fineness. Socrates repeatedly holds that Hippias should say what it is that needs to be combined with things to make them fine or beautiful (289D, 289E, 292C–D, 293D–E, 294A). The meaning of this is illustrated by an early answer from Hippias, according to which beauty or fineness is the same as gold (289E). This answer turns out to be mistaken because gold does not always play a role like this. For instance, a golden ladle is not fine because it is inconvenient (290D). In that context a wooden object is better than a golden one. But we see from this what *would* logically count as an answer, *if* it were valid. Gold just is not always the decisive element for things of value. But if it were then it would mark the difference between valuable and valueless things. (I follow Woodruff in holding that beauty or fineness in the *Hippias Major* has a generalized value theoretic status; see 2.6 below.) All we would need to do to insert value to a thing, or to remove value from a thing, would be to add gold or to remove it. Gold would be the ingredient with which we would master value, as it were. Gold would provide us with a recipe for producing valuable things, and in this way we would have mastered something important in life.

The idea seems to be similar at 299D–E and 300A–B though Socrates' way of putting the point is a little different. Here Socrates no longer speaks of combining or adding something to things to *make* them valuable. Rather, he talks about something being shared by all and only beautiful or fine things. We do not necessarily need to imagine any logical difference between this and the views of the preceding paragraph. Only the tone is different, for now the property or universal in question is viewed rather as an object of discovery than of creation. We do not control it; we only find it. But logically the view is the same, and we can illustrate it with gold as before. If it were true that the *fine=gold* then gold would be the common element in all fine things, and moreover there would be no golden things that are not fine. As before, what matters here is not whether gold really is fine. What matters for our purposes, rather, is the logical status of gold in these patterns. The status is that of a universal or property. It is the same as the status of, say, heaviness in heavy things. Heaviness is what is common and specific to all heavy things and only to heavy things. Light things do not have that universal or property in them and so they are not heavy. (Aristotle would view this as a formal explanation, see his *Metaphysics* V 2.)

Now let us turn the same coin around and consider what seems to be a very different logical status. It is not like the status of heaviness but like the status of the heaviest thing there is. The difference is, of course, that the heaviest thing in the world is not heaviness in the abstract. To use a different comparison (from the Sun allegory in the *Republic*, which is discussed in Chapter 5 below), the brightest thing is not the same as light. Light is scattered here and there. But it is an utterly different thing to say that something is a particularly lit up or bright thing. That particular bright thing is not the same thing as the widely distributed element. The intensity is not the same thing as the extension, if you will.

But now, it so happens that Socrates repeatedly demands just this other logical type of thing as well. For he often asks for what is especially beautiful or fine (288E–289B, 289C). In other words, the fine or the beautiful that needs defining should not be fine only in some comparisons, but in all. It should be the superlative case, the extreme. If x is the fine or the beautiful then x is fine or beautiful no matter what it is combined or contrasted with. It is not put to shame by the presence of a beautiful maiden or even by a god (289B). No matter where you go its value should be compelling, because it is the one and only superlatively valuable thing that can be found.

Similar thinking recurs at 292D–E (and, in a more complex way, at 294B–D) when Socrates explains that the beautiful or the fine proper will seem beautiful or fine to all. This is to say that it can be combined also with whichever *perceiver*, not only with whichever object or context as in the preceding paragraph. That is, no matter which person you take to the beautiful or the fine, you will always find that the emerging complex will be positively valued. For any person will react as positively to that object. They will recognize it for what it is. They will be forced to, given the way it is. (Presumably, if they do not agree then they cannot be focusing on the object at all.)

Now all we need to know is to ensure that the Socrates of the *Hippias Major* does not distinguish between these two functions. We know this because he shifts between the two functions without drawing them apart in any way. Hence, Socrates is after both of the functions in this double function, at once, because he thinks of the two functions as one.

But now, how is this thinking explained? How can one believe that the two functions which were described above are actually one? In other terms, why would one not so much as consider the possibility that there may not be one thing to satisfy them both at once? If one thought in that way then how could one not be making a silly, elementary error in logic? The answer is in the relational pattern $aRbRR$, as above, for in this way the two functions are satisfied at once. This is a compelling answer (recall from 1) because this seems to be the only way to make both of the two functions explicit in a single structure: the *same* thing is to figure as both (a) an extreme (i.e. the first token of the relation "R," which is highlighted here: R$RaRbRc$...) and (b) the recurrently instanced organizer of the whole series (i.e. all the later tokens of the relation "R," which are highlighted here: RRaRbRcRd...). Drop eiher (a) or (b) from your formulation and you will be unfair to the text. (You need a "fine" thing which is both the dictator of the utopia's laws and the its most valuale citizen—at once.) Due to this we should assume that the pattern $\mathbb{R}$ is tacit in Socrates' mind, for here is an explanation which saves the appearances in the text.

Of course, this will still seem too easy for many readers. To reply to some of their doubts let us now turn to a few objections. (Throughout this book the objections are in quotation marks.)

i. "Plato could not have anticipated the developments in relational thinking which e.g. Peirce or Frege develops. The stretch in time between them is simply too long for that, and Plato is placed at the wrong end of the long historical series. After all, Plato does not come after Aristotelian logic but before it; and so he is not even nearly a member of that group of logicians who take steps beyond Aristotelian logic in the recent past, which includes Peirce, Russell, and Frege. Plato is not more sophisticated than Aristotle but less (thus e.g. Owen, Hamlyn, Zeller). He does not observe more distinctions but fewer, and so it is that he comes to confuse subjects with predicates."

But apparently relational thinking is instanced already before Plato, in Heraclitus, and Heraclitus is one of the earlier philosophers who influences Plato. (The technicalities of recent logic are another matter, and I do not attribute them to Plato.) Fränkel says this about Heraclitus: a thought pattern of the form $A/B = B/C$ prevails in Heraclitus' thought, so that there are three levels of things for instance in God, man, and child, standing respectively for A, B, and C (cf. Heraclitus's fragment 79 in Barnes; also see Snell pp. 218–223 for a view similar to Fränkel's). Hence the relationships are: God/man = man/boy. Here the degree of perfection decreases, and the degree of imperfection increases, as we move towards the right, so we begin from the top. The proportions are the same, however, so the same pattern extends to both pairs (A/B and B/C). But instead of proportions we can also speak of contrasts, which may be more in Heraclitus' spirit (given that he sees war and conflict everywhere). A different terminology for the same pattern is comparative, so that how something is or what something is depends on what it is compared with. If a man is compared with God then he appears in a different light, even in the very opposite light, than if he is compared with a child. Fränkel interprets Heraclitus' message as saying that human adults qualify as perfect enough on conventional standards but not at all in terms of philosophical truth (which coheres very well with this book's message, of course).

Fränkel of course considers more passages than fragment 79. In the position of C we find not only a child but an ape, someone sleeping, someone drunk, and someone deaf. B tends to stand for common humanity and A for God or the Absolute. Fränkel shows how the same pattern recurs with such variations in Heraclitus' writings.

This suffices as evidence that Heraclitus' thought is relational.

But we should also pay heed to Fränkel's interpretation of the deeper philosophical significance of Heraclitus' pattern. For Heraclitus' point in using his pattern is not only no humiliate humans but also to steer towards God. The key here is that C and B stand for familiar, everyday things, though A does not. A, God or True Reality, is not depicted, revered, worshipped, talked about with justice among humans, Heraclitus wishes to say. His own is the way to teach the gospel, because it is purer than the others'. They cling to merely human idioms but he goes beyond them; they are caught in the contradictions of everyday life but he points to a single and unified God.

How Heraclitus' pattern allows him to manage this is made more obvious by writing x into the pattern, so that A stands for x in x/B = B/C. Now what is x? What is God? How can we fill this blank (x) if God is so far above us? Accordingly, how can a drunken man become sober, and how are the sleeping to be woken up? How can children finally become proper adults? The answer is in A/B = B/C.

In reply to i the claim is that if Heraclitus can do this then so can Plato. This is so even though Fränkel's pattern is clearly not the same as $\mathbb{R}$.

Now let us briefly go through the differences and similarities between Fränkel's interpretation of Heraclitus and $\mathbb{R}$.

One minor difference is simply in the mode of exposition, because I prefer to begin normally with the low-value terms that are familiar from everyday life and to rise from there. Thus I would place god at C and not at A and begin at A. This reflects Plato's procedure, which is typically ascendant. We look at mundane situations first and only later come to what is divine or free, because the latter is explained by reference to the former, and not conversely. A second difference is that I adopt Russell's symbols instead of Fränkel's, saying not a/b = b/c but rather $aRbRc$, where R stands for a relation. This is more economical, being syntactically simpler. A third difference between Fränkel's pattern and R takes us beyond the realm of Heraclitus, however, for it is Plato, or Plato's "Socrates," and not Heraclitus, who says $aRbRR$ or $aRbRb$, and not only $aRbRc$, thereby economizing further.

The only major step from Heraclitus to Plato is this last, and every reader should agree that if this historical step is attributed to Plato then what is supposed to have happened in history is no miracle. For this step that is being attributed to Plato is, no doubt, an ambitious one to take, and it can at first seem surprising to many, but it is not outlandish as a human achievement. It is arguably just the general kind of thing which one often finds in intellectual history when humans innovate. For it often happens that one author takes over another's line of thought and simplifies it or exaggerates it in some way. But that is how Plato acts after Heraclitus.[2]

Now let us briefly note what is similar in Fränkel's Heraclitus and this book's Plato. As Fränkel notes, Heraclitus' relational pattern provides him with a tool for communicating about topics that transcend the bounds of the mundane. The trick is to compare and contrast, as Fränkel explains. This is vital to Plato because Plato's effort is to steer us to Gods and Forms which are for him not a part of the ordinary order of things. It appears that Heraclitus teaches Plato how to communicate about the extra-mundane by means of the mundane.

Let me briefly accentuate what difference this makes. Because Plato communicates relationally (that is in series much like Heraclitus') he does not need to depend on any private or familiar intuitions about Gods or Forms. Hence he is free to steer his readers to what is distant or utopian. But if that is so then we should expect that the utopian contents like "God" and "Form" should not be familiar, and for that reason keywords for "God" and "Form" should not be thought to directly communicate anything important. The graded series of symbols would do all the communicative work, and no individual symbol would. In this way Heraclitus' thinking is quite elementary to this book's discussion as a whole.

ii. "But all this *explaining* is always too easily possible. In the meantime the cold and decisive question is only: Does the text of the *Hippias Major* contain the symbols '$\mathbb{R}$' or '$aRbRR$' or not? If not then they are not in the text, and in that case they are false about the text: it is that simple. To illustrate this with an analogy, if there is no evidence of water on Mars then one should not say that there is. There simply is or there is not. To test the hypothesis Mars is screened for H_2O and the result is either/or, so we can confirm the hypothesis or we cannot. But for theses about symbols or human thoughts this is not otherwise. Similarly in historiography, if you say that Mao said a, then you must show that Mao said a, literally. If he said b instead then you need to report b, not a. If you would like Mao to have said a then that is another topic entirely, and it may have nothing to do with his true history. The evidence for a or b simply is there or not in Mao or elsewhere and all one can do rationally is to reveal it, for this is how we form hypotheses which can be proved or disproved. (This is the issue of positivism as in 1.4 above.)"

This objection ignores the possibility of structural explanation (for the view that *kalon* in the *Hippias Major* calls for a structuralistic explanation see Sider p. 469; however Sider does not develop the point). To use an analogy that was already used in 1, if a linguist accounts for the speech of users of a natural language and says they use nouns and verbs then she does not need to maintain that they ever use the words "noun" or "verb." Similarly, a logician can maintain that everyday agents use *modus tollens* without implying that they know what the symbols "*modus tollens*" mean, and everyone can see that individuals count every day though perhaps no one knows how to account for arithmetics in a properly foundational way. The fact is that Plato does not need to state or name to relations we attribute to him. Rather he needs to use them. Conversely, if he stated them then that would not mean that he uses them (any more than to say "*modus tollens*" is to perform a *modus tollens*).

However the specific structures encountered in the text of the *Hippias Major* are relational. It repeatedly uses comparative idioms when discussing the fine or beautiful, as above, and this entitles us to say that at least sometimes its meaning seems to be relational.

2.2 COMPLEXES (300E–303C)

The *Hippias Major* is concerned not only with a standard of reasoning but also with uses of the standard in measuring particular hypotheses. One of the hypotheses happens to be complex, saying that the fine does not reside in anything indivisible but rather in a pattern which holds between different things. But such a pattern is a relation, and hence the complex hypotheses provides us with some evidence that Plato's Socrates thinks in relations, at least at times.

Here is what the *Hippias Major* says at 300E–303C. Some things can be done only in groups. For instance, together Hippias and Socrates are two though individually each is only one (301E). The fine might be like this as well. In that case a complex formed of many elements would be fine even though the elements taken in isolation would not be (302C). Only some things require complexity in this way, Socrates points out (302B). Being tired or wounden or golden are not like this, for example (301A), because if both of us are tired or golden then each of us is too, and so on.

As such this may not sound like anything spectacular. But consider, first, that relational logic was first associated primarily with complexes, for instance by Peirce (see Kneale and Kneale pp. 428–434). Peirce was drawn to study relations like a IS A BROTHER OF b. Here a is relational in having IS A BROTHER OF only when accompanied by a particular other thing, b. a could not possibly be a brother alone. In contrast, a could be brown alone, or silent. Second, notice that relational thinking about complexes is very different from thought in terms of universals and particulars. Indeed, one of the reasons why relational thinking is said to have originated in modern times is that the Aristotelian idioms were too simplistic for more complex and relational topics (cf. Carnap for introductory observations regarding this, and see 1.1 for a richer set of associations and references about relations). But therefore we could not possibly use the Aristotelian vocabulary to interpret the passage about relational complexes fairly. Instead we would need to say that sometimes the *Hippias Major* is about relational complexes and not about universals or particulars. However, third, no such shift of gears is needed if we use $\mathbb{R}$. $\mathbb{R}$ entitles us to use the same relational vocabulary throughout. For the relational complex is very easily accounted for by relations, such as aRb, and yet the passage in 2.1 which the Aristotelian believed to evidence Aristotelian dualism was accounted for by $\mathbb{R}$ already. Hence, the Aristotelian explanation is needlessly clumsy. It uses one standard for one passage and another for another, but we can use the same standard throughout (for other readings see Morgan and Wolsdorf).

2.3 SELF-CAUSATION (297A–D, 303E–304A)

Self-causation becomes Socrates' topic in the *Hippias Major* due to a particular hypothesis about beauty or fineness (296E). According to this hypothesis the beautiful is beneficial and hence causative of the good (296E), but this implies that goodness and beauty are different things (which is denied at 297C) or that beauty causes itself (297A–D, 303E–304A). At first sight Socrates seems to oppose this hypothesis because of the impossibility of self-causation (297A–C); but we should look beyond this first impression, because Socrates' super-ego, which appears so often in the text of the *Hippias Major* (see 2.4 below), is not really a separate agent. The separation is put forth only as a tool to fool Hippias into thinking that it is not Socrates who criticizes Hippias. In reality the critic *is* Socrates, however, and the inner voice which raises standards so high is Socrates' own. Hence, the causal origin of the criticisms of Socrates and Hippias is in Socrates himself, and so there *is* self-causation, contrary to how things are made to seem to Hippias. But thus Socrates instances self-causation, so he instances a self-relation, and so he instances zRz, as in $\mathbb{R}$.

Here are some objections and replies.

i. "This is quite hypothetical, for Socrates does not *say* that he instances self-causation. He does instance it if his inner voice is his own, but he may not believe it is."

But some of Socrates' ironies are lost if he does not consciously deceive Hippias into thinking that the silent voice is not Socrates' own. For the text of the *Hippias Major* receives a very different air if Socrates does not know that he is deceiving Hippias in several ways. For in that case the text is not about Socrates the philosopher poking fun at the rhetorician Hippias but rather about two speakers, a philosopher and a rhetorician, who are (more) on a par—both being fools. But that is a highly artificial alternative, given that Plato seems so plainly to advertize the merits of Socrates the philosopher in this work as in others. Hence, it is more likely that Socrates knows well enough that he is his own internal critic and that self-causation is actually something that is thought possible and valued positively in the *Hippias Major*.

ii. "If Socrates asks for the fine, which has the form $aRbRR$, and self-causation has the form $aRbRR$, then he is supposed by this book's author to be implying that self-causation is the fine. But if then *causing* things is supposed to be *fine*, which is absurd. One might as well say that movement is beautiful, which seems quite false given that at most some movements are beautiful."

But, first, self-causation is a narrower category than causation. Note also that it bears nicely on positive freedom given that the positively free cause themselves to do things. They are their own generators, so to speak.

Second, 2.1 already noted that the cause involved in the *Hippias Major* appears to be formal, so the kind of causing that is fine is such as e.g. to define them or to know them.

Let us look at the wider implications that these views would have. The basic point is that on these premises self-causation turns out to be definitional self-knowledge or definitional knowledge about knowledge. But now, this should not count as an entirely surprising message coming from a man ("Socrates") who seems to identify all the virtues with knowledge and seeks self-knowledge as an end in itself (cf. e.g. *Meno* 77B–78B, *Protagoras* 358C, *Gorgias* 468C; *Gorgias* 460B–D and 509E, *Protagoras* 345E and 360D, and especially the *Apology* throughout).

We may express this view in a fairly direct way by saying that if R=KNOWING then we get such patterns as *Socrates* KNOWING *Socrates* and *Socrates* KNOWING KNOWING. In these patterns, which conform, of course, to $\mathbb{R}$, "Socrates" has self-knowledge or higher-order, epistemological knowledge. But it needs to be recalled from 2.1 that KNOWING in the second expression is first a noun and then a verb, though with the same meaning, so nothing in these expressions depends on finding that verbs can be nouns or vice versa (this same thing was explained in other words in 1.2 and 3.3). The same would go for *Socrates* DEFINING *Socrates* and *Socrates* DEFINING DEFINING. A more technical pattern without any verbs would be as coherent as a series of symbols and without inspiring any confusion between verbs and nouns: DEF DEF *Socrates* DEF *Helen* DEF *horse* DEF *spoon*. Here we have a hierarchy beginning from its top on the left-hand side. For there is first a defining relation to the relation itself, and this relation is the fine. Next towards the right is Socrates, who receives his instructions from the initial shape (which is on the extreme left). To Socrates' right, again, is the same relation applying to the beautiful Helen and then running from Helen to a fine horse, and so on. In this picture the philosopher Socrates is a mediator between the pure Form and its of uses in mundane life, and so in a mundane comparison Socrates' philosophizing is closest to being perfectly fine. However the Form still ranks above Socrates. Socrates is made to look like a kind of prophet. He is the medium, not the message.

Why am I using these technical symbols? The point is to make the coherence of Socrates' self-causative pattern explicit. For the same formally causative relation can recur through the entire hierarchy. There is no inconsistency or gap in the picture. This coherence is not brought out as plainly if we shift between talk of *kalon* or the Form on the one hand and then secondly move to talk of self-causation, third to formal causes, and so on. Using $\mathbb{R}$ we reveal that it is all one string. There are no leaps or incommensurables (cf. 5.6 and 5.7 on formal causes in the *Republic*).

iii. "But the above are operational idioms. According to them something or someone knows or defines something. And yet it is implausible to say that the fine in the *Hippias Major* performs any operations. It looks more like an abstract entity than like any active relation. *Kalon* is not a perfomance or a verb."

We do not need to cling to operational idioms, because we can also picture "dead" relations with the same patterns. For instance, if on the extreme left we have the most elementary order there is, then this is the most orderly order, and the most orderly thing, that there is. Then as we move towards the right from this order of orders, gradually complicating it by applying it to always more complex objects, then we move from perfect order to less and less perfect order, and consequently also to less and less order. Now, crucially for avoiding operations or activies, the elementary order on the extreme left does not need to *manufacture* any of the orders to its right to be their *formal* cause. Hence there is no moving process but still there is a standing relation. There is a relation because order is a relation. It is a pattern which things can instance. Socrates reads that relation, and he obeys it because it is valid. (The relation does not leap out and grab him. It cannot *do* anything, because it is a *formal* cause.)

(What relation order should be seen as is another matter and it is not important to explore here, but if there is a need to visualize it one might imagine a very simple arrangement of points. If the arrangement is multiplied the complexity grows. It may help also to imagine a pyramid with a small and simple tip such that the tip's structure is repeated in more and more complex and elaborate as one descends down the pyramid, as in 1.2. Then the tip by itself is a miniature pyramid which contains the code, if you will, for generating the whole building.)

iv. "But now there is no superlative instance on the extreme left. There is only a series which is only guided by its left-hand extreme."

There *is* a superlative instance, because the extreme left both is the most orderly thing *and* the guide to order elsewhere (that is towards its right). Hence, the elementary order has the double function. It guides to order *and* follows that guidance best. (This is just the kind of thinking which Plato needs according to this book, as 1.1 already explained. In different words, Plato's Forms and Gods are *both* perfect examples and general rules. Both of these birds should be caught with a single stone, and in relations this is possible.)

v. "But what is this to say about the fineness of Helen, the horse, and the spoon? Is it that *Helen* DEFINES *the horse* who DEFINES *the spoon*? Or that *Helen* KNOWS *the horse* who KNOWS *the spoon*? Or perhaps that *Helen* ORDERS *the horse* which ORDERS *the spoon*? Do these relations consist of thoughts thought by Helen and the horse? These are absurd associations, for surely the horse will not speak, for instance. Hence, perhaps a pure relation to a relation can occur and perhaps it can extend to a philosopher's thought or speech, but how is it supposed to spread downwards in the hierarchy from that point?"

That the Helen of the *Hippias Major* is not presented as a speaker or thinker at all but only as a pretty maiden does suggest that fineness is not inherited or mediated through a series of thoughts or speech acts. Rather, there are certain other properties which connect the series of objects into a coherent whole. These do not always need to be transmitted by thoughts (think of seashells, for example). But based on the text of the *Hippias Major* we do not know about their specifics, and yet this is not a point at which the intelligibility of Plato would be at stake so we will not present hypotheses as above.

Now let us take in more evidence.

2.4 IRONY (281A, 286C–E, 287B–C, 288A–B, 292C–E, 298C, 304C–E)

In speaking ironically one says the opposite of what one means, and the Socrates of Plato's earlier works employs irony often in flattering his interlocutors. Then the point is exactly *not* to think very highly of them, of course. Why then does Socrates pretend to flatter? At least he seems to get the *attention* of self-important persons like Hippias in this way. For such persons so often overestimate themselves that they like to be flattered to an excess, and due to this Socrates is wise to pretend to be their humble student. What he can then really, and as it were secretly, begin to do, of course, is to ask his characteristic questions, and the questions begin in time to get so penetrating that they serve to teach the answerers, so the student-teacher relationship is reversed. But if Socrates did not begin with his ironic flatteries then he would probably often be brushed aside by proud people like Hippias, as someone too irrelevant to be concerned with.

Let us first consider the foundations of Socrates' ironic practice. In the *Hippias Major* it begins with the very first sentence (281A). After that Socrates keeps praising Hippias throughout the *Hippias Major* despite Hippias' continually poor performance, and one gathers that the praise can never be sincere. For Hippias' level of achievement is so consistently bad in this dialogue that Socrates cannot in truth maintain any hopes of hearing from Hippias what the fine or the beautiful is. Socrates must be feigning throughout.

But the preceding is only the basic level of irony in the *Hippias Major* (or in several of the other early Platonic works), and there is more. For Socrates is ironic also about himself, so we get *Socrates* IRONIZES *Socrates* and hence *zRz* and ℝ. How does Socrates ironize himself? He continually belittles himself, saying that he does not have knowledge or that he lacks the special abilities of Hippias. Thus, the situation is not only that Hippias is made to seem larger than he is by means of irony, as in the preceding paragraph, but also that Socrates is made to seem smaller. Moreover it is Socrates who makes Socrates seem smaller, so the irony we find here is undoubtedly self-irony. In fact Socrates' most extreme self-criticisms are only made by him to *seem* like criticisms given by someone else (286C–E, 287B–C, 288A–B, 292C–E, 293D–E, 298C, 303E–304A, 304C–E), though in reality they are self-criticisms because their author is Socrates. Thus, Socrates says an unnamed man demands from him just the sort of definition that he demands from Hippias (286C–E). This man lives in Socrates' house (304D) and questions whether Socrates' life is worthwhile without knowledge of fineness or beauty (304E). But of course the humor here is due to the fact that only Hippias can believe that some other man lives in Socrates' house and criticizes Socrates. For why would Socrates no throw such a strange man out of his house? In reality he cannot throw the critic out, because the critic is Socrates' inner voice or superego. It is him engaging in internal dialogue: in thought (compare *Apology* 21B, *Charmides* 166C–D, *Theaetetus* 189E–190A, *Sophist* 263E–264B, *Philebus* 38C–E, and *Timaeus* 37B–C; cf. Sedley 2008, pp. 214–215 for a recent summary).

As noted, thus far we have a self-relation of the type *zRz*, where *z=Socrates* and *R*=IRONIZES or CRITICIZES. But we can go even further than this, namely all the way to *zRR*. For Socrates strives to act as an authority *regarding* some conventionally respected types of authority. Hence, he is not really ironic only about particular individuals like Hippias or himself, as above. The stakes are higher because he wants to affect how individuals judge anyone, or anything. He is a judge of judging.

Now let us have some objections once more to test what has been said.

i. "Now IRONIZING is assumed to be the content of Socrates' formal cause, and this makes him into a humorist and skeptic. Yet there is a clear reason why this must be false. If IRONIZING is fine and the horse and the spoon are fine then the horse and the spoon ironize, which is a ridiculous thing to say."

This must be conceded. Ironizing cannot literally be at the center of Socrates' project. But ironizing is still of significance because in the *Hippias Major* it is a lead up to something more serious, namely to knowledge, proof, or order, as in the preceding section (2.3). This is because Socrates is ironic and humorous about many kinds of authorities but he takes argument and truth very literally and seriously. Hence, he does not ridicule everything. Ironizing is only his way of introducing his game. The game itself consists of honest debate, and it is intrasubjective and not intersubjective (so, to use

Plato's terms from his later works like the *Phaedo* (discussed in Chapter 3), the Republic (Chapter 5), and the *Laws* (Chapter 6), freedom is in the *psyche* and not in the *polis*).

ii. "But if that is so then why must Socrates introduce his game by means of irony? Why does he not introduce himself to Hippias with a sincere intention right from the start? Why does he not tell Hippias consistently what he really thinks? Why waste time making jokes?"

This was already explained in the beginnig of the section (2.4). If that explanation is correct then the route to sincere infomation runs through humor and irony with persons like Hippias. There are necessary preliminaries before the actual game can be played because some persons are not as accessible as open books. They are caught up in a web of their own unrealistic associations (cf. Lear's psychoanalytically inspired view of Socrates).

iii. "But when is the phase of sincere informing reached in the *Hippias Major*? Is it ever? In fact we seem to have irony all the way through it, and Hippias never learns anything from Socrates. Does Socrates not notice this? Or if he does then why does he bother to converse with Hippias after the failed beginnings? Is Hippias' bad performance supposed to be a surprise and a disappointement to him? Does he mean to torture Hippias (cf. Beversluis)? Is the humor sadistic?"

The possibility exists that other people learn from this conversation even if Hippias does not. After all, Plato wrote it down and probably circulated it. (Moreover, other persons may have been present to overhear what Socrates and Hippias said, if the conversation reported in the text was real.)

iv. "Then what lesson are Plato's readers to draw? Where is the moral of this wayward story?"

Socially or dialogically Socrates' hopes are quite low, but monologically they are high. There is an inverse proportion between these levels. The proportion is not only between the low and the high value but also between the humor and the seriousness. Thus in a series $RRaRbRc...$ Hippias the star sophist is placed at the ridiculous end of things on the right. At the other extreme, the criticism that occurs *inside* Socrates is revealed as something utterly serious. In the words of the *Apology*, Socrates will obey God rather than men (29D). He is philosophical animal, not a political one.

2.5 DIALOGUE ABOUT DIALOGUE
(282E, 287E, 291D, 296B, 297D, 304D–E)

The *Hippias Major* is not only a dialogue but, at least sometimes, a dialogue *about* dialogue. For some things said in this work do not only say things: they also say how things can be said better. But this is more evidence for ℝ, for now dialogue is used to improve dialogue, as a relation R to R.

In what way or ways is there dialogue about dialogue in the *Hippias Major*? For example, Socrates says he wants brief answers (286C), and he tells Hippias not to boast (294E). But the major reform he wants to realize is the one we have already encountered in 2.1: Socrates aims to raise the level of his interactions with Hippias especially by requiring a definition from Hippias. It is primarily on this score that the interactions are being used to produce improved versions of themselves, as speaking briefly and without boasting would probably count for little in Socrates' mind if definitions were not sought or provided. If this is correct then the main Socratic lesson is logical and not dialogical, in which case it would pertain to thoughts more than to social relations as such.

Now let us consider objections.

i. "But the *Hippias Major* is clearly a work about beauty or fineness and not about dialogue or definitions, so the above view is false."

We can reply that this dialogue, like any dialogue, can have several overlapping topics. We can admit that the topic is beauty or fineness and say that the topic is dialogue as well. Likewise with definitions.

(To anticipate, in the later chapters of this book we will encounter overlap of this general kind many times. For example: *psyches* and virtues can approximate the patterns of the Forms in the *Phaedo*, so no one is asked to choose between for instance virtues and Forms because they come together. Similarly, the lovers of the *Symposium* seek beauty *and* immortality *and* happiness, the *Republic*'s philosophers seek utopia *and* God *and* the Good, and in the *Laws* God's patterns recur in thoughts, heavenly bodies, melodies, utopian laws, and so on. It is quite normal for Plato to combine many separable agendas in a single work or argument.)

ii. "But it has already been said that the *Hippias Major* does not produce any valuable dialogue. Socially it consists of mockery. Its achievements are in monologue."

However we need to note how dialogical structures inform monological ones. As observed before, Plato often associates thought with internal or silent speech or dialogue, meaning that what goes on in an individual's thoughts is similar in kind to what occurs socially in dialogue.

Let us reflect briefly what elementary things this analogy between dialogue and monologue teaches us. For one thing, Plato's works become thoroughly relational because of their dialogical character. This is because, rather banally, dialogues consist minimally of questions and answers, and questions are relational at least in being *after* answers and *about* topics or realities. Answers, in turn, relate back to the questions and to the same topics or realities.

52   *Chapter Two*

It is worth noting that thinking is not always portrayed in this relational a manner. For instance Heraclitus' and Nietzsche's writings often consist of fragments which are not made explicitly to bear on each other at all. Visually we may imagine an archipelago of isolated islands. Plato's works are not collections of isolated islands, because there are bridges everywhere. Concretely, his speakers draw inter-relations between things that are said. Some *a* is said to imply or to otherwise cause *b*, or a speaker can be reminded that she said *c* or she may be obligated to keep her promise that *d*, and so on. In Platonic thinking there is a lot of inter-relating.

A second unrealized possibility is also informative: the mythical or mystical. Books may be obscure to such an extent that readers can ask themselves whether they are about anything or whether they are coherent. But in Plato it is usually not difficult to maintain control, and this has again to do with the dialogical structure. For if someone's expression gets too unclear or too long then it is checked with the question what it means, or what it is meant to prove, or what proves it, and so on. This is to say that thought on Plato's model is never allowed to drift for long. External reference points are demanded and produced repeatedly. (I will return to this in Chapter 10 when discussing the *Protagoras*.)

2.6 VERSUS WOODRUFF (DEFINITIONS)

Woodruff portrays the *Hippias Major* very plausibly in several respects (i), and in this he has influenced my own discussion, but he seems not to account for the Platonic obligation to produce a definition (ii) or to perceive the double function or the ultimate philosophical importance of the dialogue (iii).

i. This is the general setting of the *Hippias Major: kalon*, or something variously translated as beauty, nobility, admirability, or fineness, spreads out to cover very different things, such as virtues, youths, laws, habits, fast horses, fighting birds, true statements, and progressive speeches.[3] Woodruff well explains how Socrates' evaluative ambition in the *Hippias Major* is too wide for any specifically aesthetic category. For *kalon* is not a special word. It is used like we would use "good" or "value." It can be applied across the categories, to commend all kinds of thing. This implies, for one thing, that Socrates' thinking needs to be interpreted as a generalizable piece of evaluative reasoning. Conversely, we do not identify Socrates' meaning by studying the philological nuances of the ancient Greek word.[4]

Another important insight in Woodruff's account is that Socrates and Hippias are playing different games. There is no known convention to bind them. For Hippias, a sophist, does not normally aim to do what Socrates aims to do.

Hippias wants money and fame but Socrates wants intrinsic truth. Hippias wants people to learn to speak in impressive and entertaining ways, whereas Socrates teaches reasoning. But this asymmetry does not change through the dialogue, so neither Socrates nor Hippias shifts to the other's game. They start apart and end apart.

ii. But then why would one think, with Socrates, that Hippias is obligated to play by Socrates' rules? Wherein lies the justice of Socrates' side to the dispute?

Woodruff begins his answer to this convincingly by denying that Socrates' authority depends on meaning: Socrates does not commit the "Socratic fallacy" (on which see Geach; for discussion see Benson pp. 112–63 and Dancy pp. 35–64), Woodruff says, because Socrates does not hold that the *meaning* of "fine" implies the advantage of Socrates' game over Hippias'.[5] The so-called "Socratic fallacy" would be committed by assuming that if one knows the meaning of x then one is able to produce a definition of x. This would be a bad reason to require definitions because meanings are often understood without definitions. Hence, if Socrates' reason to seek definitions is based on a definitional view of meanings then he does not have a good reason to seek definitions, and so he should have a better reason or his whole quest for defnitions is only a mistake. (Chapter 9 will return to the "Socratic fallacy" when discussing the *Meno*.)

But now if Socrates' basis for his defnitional quest is not in a bad theory of meaning then where is it? As noted, Woodruff writes that Socrates is after knowledge about value, that is its formal cause for every situation. If Hippias had this knowledge then he would be qualified to dictate about everyone's affairs, for then he would know what everyone ought to do or be. Woodruff holds this standard to be superhuman, saying that Socrates offers it for a destructive purpose. He wishes to tear down social authorities like Hippias. No human being really has the abilities which a Hippias feigns.[6]

But troubles arise with Woodruff if we consider something that is implied in this supposition that Socrates' standard is superhuman. The first of the troubles is this. Why would humans need to live by a standard which they cannot satisfy? How could anyone rationally be obligated to do a thing which she is unable to do? That does not seem like a promising foundation for any ethical authority, because it does not make good sense to demand the impossible. Thus, something is deeply amiss in Woodruff's view of Socrates' philosophy. We should expect something more constructive from Socrates or he is incoherent in his demands.

There is also a second way of presenting essentially the same problem. If Socrates' standard of authority is superhuman then who is he, a human, to act as an authority against Hippias? No one, of course.

A third way of stating essentially the same problem is that if Hippias' fault is that he falls short of the divine measure, and Socrates also falls short of the divine measure, then the superiority of Socrates over Hippias cannot be based on the divine measure. It is a game at which *both* lose.

The generalization I want to get at is that it does not seem consistent to read the *Hippias Major* in a manner that is as skeptical as Woodruff's. We need a standard from Socrates which Socrates *does* satisfy, or else Socrates' game is not superior to Hippias'. There must be something that is divine in a way that humans *can* reach.

iii. The solution to this should depend on the precise character of Socrates' definitional requirement. Here is Woodruff's analysis of it: fine things are "stricly" fine, that is, fine no matter what. To say that the fine itself is fine is to say nothing more than that strictly fine things are always fine. By contrast, things are less than strictly fine if they are fine only in certain settings, that is, under particular qualifications. The girl, gold, and so many other things that Hippias praises are less than strictly fine.[7] The appearance is that Woodruff sees Socratic evaluations as comparative, as in $a<b<c$ (or $aRbRc$). Here b is fine compared to a but not to c, whereas c survives all comparisons (if only a, b, c are compared), so of a–c only c is strictly fine. On this interpretation strict fineness is superlative fineness, and it contrasts with mere comparative fineness.

To this background it seems, then, that strict fineness is what anyone should have to qualify as an authoritative educator. But as in ii we should discover also that Socrates *has* strict fineness though Hippias lacks it, because this way Socrates would have an advantage over Hippias on Socrates' own criterion. (Socrates' criterion cannot be *impossible* to meet, after all, if it *is* to be met, see ii above. If Socrates' game is to be superior to Hippias' then we have to be able to see how to play it.)

The trouble with this way of setting things up is only that "strict" fineness is too thin as a criterion which we could relate to Socrates' actual behavior in the *Hippias Major*. It is not informative enough about Socrates' *activities* to show us how Socrates' way of doing hings can be superior to Hippias.

We attain a thicker criterion of this kind by interpreting Socrates' *kalon* as something self-relational, which we can then expand into something self-critical and self-causative, as this chapter (2) already documented. The logical difference is made by thinking of *kalon* not only as c in $aRbRc$, which seemed to be Woodruff's position (the "strictly" fine) but also as the yardstick, R. The assumption in this view is that $c=R$, as in 2.1.

But now this thicker conception of Socrates' criterion does lead us to see performative self-consistency in his philosophizing, and this shows us how he is able to play by his own rules. The trick is that the thicker standard leads us to positive data for interpreting Socrates' own behavior. For if *kalon* stands for *self-relations* (and not only for "strict fineness") then we can already connect *kalon* with some things which Socrates so characteristically does, such as his self-ironies, self-criticisms, and methodological reflections (see 2.3–2.5). But in this way we understand just how Socrates' game can be played. Now we can see what it is that Hippias is failing to do.

The more colorful way to summarize this is to say that Socrates is keenly aware of his own motions, and that he knows that what he does inside his mind is at least vaguely divine. The social comedy with Hippias is in inverse proportion to his internal seriousness, and the inversion arises because Socrates uses his insides to measure Hippias on the outside. Woodruff's interpretation exaggerates the importance of the comic half and ignores the serious center within.

2.7 SUMMARY

This chapter (2) on Plato's *Hippias Major* began with a long section on its definitional standard (2.1). Next we brought it to bear on complexes (2.2), self-causation (2.3), irony (2.4), and dialogue (2.5). Finally Woodruff's more skeptical account was criticized (2.6).

NOTES

1. I say "on an ultimate level" because of course Socrates recognizes the difference in other, less fundamental settings. If he did not then he would confuse, say, the ablest sophist with the art or skill of sophistry, which view would be absurd to attribute to him. *Of course* he distinguishes between talking about Protagoras, Gorgias, or Hippias on the one hand and their skill on the other. I do not think this should even be discussed.

I will be as confident below that Socrates recognizes relations. Even though relational logic is new (some remarks on it will come later in 2.1), Socrates' equality (see 3.3) or *eros* (see 4.1), say, are plain example of a relation even if Socrates never uses a Greek term for "relation."

2. See my *Socrates' Criteria* Chapter 2.
3. Woodruff pp. xii–xiii. See Woodruff pp. 109–111 for discussion.
4. For more on his topic see my *Socrates' Criteria*, Preface and Introduction.
5. Woodruff p. 139.
6. Woodruff p. 141.
7. Woodruff pp. 153–154.

Chapter Three

The Phaedo

In the *Phaedo* Plato's Socrates tries to liberate psyches. Psyches would be perfectly free if they came to resemble the "Forms," he says. Psyches in ordinary life are not perfectly free, however, and the process of liberation consists of philosophical dialogue. If the philosophizing is done well enough then perfect freedom will be its result. Socrates tries to show also that the philosophizing psyche would be immortal, but his arguments to that effect are not a success. The moral we can actually draw from the *Phaedo* is only libertarian, as in ℝ.

This chapter (3) consists of thirteen sections. The first eleven, 3.1–3.11, defend the relational thesis of this book based on specific passages in the *Phaedo*. The rest, 3.12–3.13, focus on attacking hostile interpretations of the *Phaedo*, namely Bostock's. If he is right about Plato then Plato's claims are too bold, whereas I argue that Plato is right to be as bold as he is.

3.1 PLEASURES (60B–69C)

The very beginning of Socrates' argument in the *Phaedo* contains a relation, because at 60B–C Socrates notes how pleasures are relational to pains. He says there that pleasure is felt only as a relief from pain. Hence, if there is no pain first then there is no pleasure afterwards either. We may capture this view with *aRb* if *a=pain*, *b=pleasure*, and *R*=COMES BEFORE or IS PRESUPPOSED BY.

Soon the *Phaedo* proceeds to build on this basis. At 64B–68C Socrates explains how bodily pleasures and pains are avoided by the philosopher. The philosopher's psyche is liberated from the body, he says. The psyche separates itself from its bodily and hedonic entanglements. Pleasures and pains mix with each other as opposites that depend on one another, but the philosopher leaves such conflicted things behind and attains purity and consistency in a different realm. Much of what the *Phaedo* says can be interpreted as an explanation of this process of purification or separation (on how this involves both epistemological and ethical doctrines for Plato cf. Baltzly and White 2006).

However, one needs to be careful already at this point so as not to get caught in the wrong interpretive track. One may easily be fooled into believing that the philosopher's psyche is an isolated, and hence a non-relational, thing. This impression can arise from the talk of separation or purification, as in the preceding paragraph. But this is not what Socrates says. Instead, already at 65D–66A he mentions that the freed psyche relates to justice itself, and beauty, and goodness. Hence, a liberated psyche is not isolated or solitary. It is relational. For it, too, relates to things, so not only the confined, bodily, or hedonic psyche is relational. But the free psyche is relational to things other than pleasures and pains. As we will see in 3.3, those other things are not mixed or conflicted in the way that pleasures and pains are, and that is the great difference. In other words, the process of liberation does not take one away from relations to isolated points. Rather it takes one away only from a specific class of *conflicted* relations. It takes one *to* other relations, namely to self-consistent ones.

Now let us introduce some more evidence.

3.2 VIRTUES (68D–69B)

A little later in the *Phaedo*, Socrates argues that the *virtues* are properly instanced only by philosophers. Non-philosophers are virtuous out of vice, he says (68D–69A). For example, they are courageous concerning something only because they fear something else even more. What they are not is purely courageous, or totally fearless. They simply exchange some fears for others, not fearing one thing because some other fear is even worse. Fear still rules in them, and they are not rid of fear altogether. To take another example, philosophers are temperate in the full-blown sense of not seeking any pleasures, whereas non-philosophers sacrifice some pleasures for the sake of other pleasures. Then the non-philosophers are still hedonists, and therefore they are not purely temperate. Only philosophers make a clean enough break.

What, then, are the philosophers' virtues like? The philosophers do not fear or seek pleasure, so what *do* they do? How do they act, and what for? Socrates gives two answers to this. The first is the less surprising one that philosophers make their evaluations wisely (69B). The second is the more unusual point that philosophers value wisdom the most as an end (69A). The first of these points is about how philosophers form evaluative scales, like $a<b<c$ (or $aRbRc$). Here $<$ (or R) is the scale that is used to rank different things, and Socrates is saying that the philosophers' scale has a content like IS WISE TO RANK BELOW. But the second point is that $c=R$, for wisdom is not only a scale for ranking things other than itself. It is also the top-ranked item on its own scale. But this implies $aRbRR$ and hence $\mathbb{R}$. In other words, Socrates' view of the virtues in the *Phaedo* takes us to pattern of reasoning which Plato's writings so often employ.

Now let us turn again to a critical question to assess what has just been said.

"This book connects $\mathbb{R}$ to free thought and $\mathbb{R}$ has now been identified in a passage about virtue or wisdom. Hence it is justified to ask, Is Plato's view of wisdom or virtue to be identified with some libertarian theory? Is virtue or wisdom supposed to contain an element of free will or to effect a choice in an incompatibilistic sense?[1] If yes, where is the evidence for that? Where does Plato make such a connection?"

In reply, notice first that Socrates was seen to advocate the liberation of the psyche already in 3.1. The liberation is from the confines and conflicts of the body, and this requires no reference to free "will" or any form of incompatibilism. Such references are unnecessary because freedom is not a topic only of believers in a special faculty of the "will," and questions about compatibilism and incompatibilism do not matter to all versions of libertarianism (Stenzel and Michael Frede see this differently).

But a deeper point is that Plato's view of liberation is not tied specifically to the hedonistic comparison made in 3.1. He describes the liberation he is for in *one* way by saying that the free philosophize and in another by saying that the free are virtuous or wise. The reason why we can translate between these different descriptions is that the point is really a structural one. The liberation is always from conflicts to self-consistency, and this is what $\mathbb{R}$ registers; but the conflicts and the self-consistencies can be portrayed in many different vocabularies. There are pleasures and pains: that is one way to flesh out the conflicts. One can speak of courage and fear: that is another. But these are far from being the only ones. One can also use epistemic terms about conflicting beliefs, ethical vocabularies of agents with purposes or practices which exclude each other, sticks and stones that are somehow equal and somehow not (as in the next section, 3.3), and so much more. The different vocabularies come and go in Plato but the structural argument from conflicts to self-consistencies keeps repeating. In other words, whatever topic Plato comes by he is bound to argue in the same pattern. Every time he will try to get people to "rise" "dialectically," to abstract and to idealize, and to convert to a philosophical lifestyle. Give him hedonism or give him virtue and this is the way he will shape *that* topic. Give him beauty (*Symposium*, see Chapter 4), justice (*Republic,* Chapter 5), theology (*Laws,* Chapter 6), or whatever else, and he will propagate the same program again. He is in this way a syntactical monomaniac. Notice, however, that he is very far from monomania in semantics, because his range of topics is immense. He does not always talk specifically about hedonism or virtue, for example. Nor does he always defend religion, because sometimes he also attacks it (*Euthyphro, Apology*) and often he simply ignores it. He is not always even for the Forms, because in the *Parmenides* he opposes them and they are missing from the *Theaetetus*. Plato is not always about justice *or* beauty *or* God *or* anything else. There is no over-arching *content* in his corpus, and the continuity is structural.

3.3 FORMS (73D–75A)

A little later Plato's Socrates turns to the *Forms*, saying that equality is not only a relation between external things, like between sticks and stones. Sticks and stones are not the same as equality, or equal to it. Rather, equality is a relation also to itself. Moreover, it is the only perfectly equal thing, and such things as sticks and stones are never fully equal (73D–75A).

What does this have to do with $\mathbb{R}$? The first thing to notice is that equality seems very much like a relation. It is a relation like = is in $a=b$. It is not simply a one place predicate, for example, as in ...*is equal*. For rather it is a way to connect things. It is a liaison or a pattern, and not merely something like a lable or a property that can be attached to a thing. Next, this relation is applied primarily to itself, not to other things. Hence, aRb (i.e., as $a=b$) is a low-value use and zRR is a high-value use of R. But now we have reached $\mathbb{R}$, because if we picture the relation of equality first in its low-value use and finally in its high-value use, then we get $aRb...zRR$, which is a version of $\mathbb{R}$.

Before we move on I must concede that the preceding argument leaves a gap. For 73D–75A does not tell us why the equality of sticks or stones (as in the pattern aRb) raises the question about the equality of equality itself (as in zRR). In other words, why would a series of equations have to terminate in an equation about equation? Why are first-order questions supposed automatically to generate questions in higher orders? The reason why 73D–75A does not tell us this is that the context is too abrupt. We get the two extremes of the series, on the left and on the right, but we do not get its intermediate portions. For the *Phaedo*'s relation, EQUALS, takes us away from sticks and stones, which merely aspire to be equals and do not really fit the relation, and *directly* from there to a concern with the perfect Form of the Equal or Equality. Hence, Socrates leaps right away from backward experiences to central thoughts. He is, one might say, not the kind of teacher who would take his time to make things obvious and understandable to his students. (Beversluis argues that Plato's Socrates is often unfair to his interlocutors. For a more sensitive Socrates see Teloh.) But for this reason we do not actually learn almost anything about how EQUALS, being so different from sticks and stones, can be discussed positively and productively. EQUALS is given too bare, or too negative, a status. This is not an optimal basis for productive philosophizing. It is too austere.

But notice that this is a shortcoming specifically in the *Phaedo* at 73D–75A and that it should not be generalized. Plato is not always this abrupt and therefore he does not always leave a similar gap. We will see in Chapters 4 and 5 that in the *Symposium* and the *Laws* the dialectical progressions are more patient and graded, and the same will recur also in later chapters. They do not move as quickly as *Phaedo* 73D–75A. In $\mathbb{R}$'s terms, at *Phaedo* 73D–75A one has $aRb... cRR$ (or even $aRb... RR$), whereas in the *Symposium* one finds $aRbRcRdReRfRR$ and in the *Laws* $aRbRcRdReRfRgRhRiRjRkRk$. Plato's core message is always about a hierarchy, and the point of philosophizing is for him always to climb to the self-consistent top of the hierarchy, but it varies how many levels the hierarchy has. In aRR there are only two levels, for example, and in $aRbRR$ there are three. The *Laws* has ten.

Now let us turn again to questions.

i. "Is the equating of an equal thing not a nonsensical enterprise altogether? The basis for this allegation would be that the relation EQUALS requires *two* things to relate, namely what is related and to what, or a and b in a EQUALS b; but EQUALS is itself only *one* thing. And how is a single thing to be in a two-placed relation? (Thus also Castañeda's problem of dyadicity; further cf. Geach, Allen, Tarrant p. 125, and Matthen pp. 97–98.)"

1.2 answered this: there are informative equations (cf. Frege, Putnam).

ii. "Equality cannot possibly be made sense of purely in relation to itself, for this would lead us only to a repetitive series like EQUALS EQUALS EQUALS. (One way to formulate a similar problem that is well known among analytical philosophers is Moore's 'paradox of analysis', which says that an analysis must be trivial if it is true. In other words, it cannot be informative, and it must at least border on the tautological, or it is false. See Moore 1968 pp. 665–666 and Langford. The situation is as paradoxical for EQUALS if EQUALS is analytical in Moore's sense.)"

ii is wrong if the reply to i is right.

3.4 PSYCHES (73C–76A)

Now let us turn to a *psychic* relation.

In the preceding section (3.3) Socrates stressed the distance between EQUALS and such empirical and external objects as sticks and stones. The

62   Chapter Three

relation is not really *in* the empirical details, he said. It is outside, and it is imposed from outside. In this section (3.4) we discuss a different type of distance which he describes soon after. This is between the relation of recollecting and the external experiences which prompt it. We recall things quite differently than we experience things, he says. We see sticks and stones, and we can touch them, for example (75A). But if we remember things like EQUALS then we are doing something very different from seeing or touching. We are engaged in a psychic activity, not in an empirical one.

Let us first go backwards a little. At 73C–74A Socrates notes that when we are reminded of things by what we experience. The experienced things may or may not be alike to the things we are reminded of. For instance, one may see a picture of a lyre and be reminded of a human being (73E), e.g. because the lyre belongs to that human (73D). In that case the human being would not be much like the picture.

Soon Socrates generalizes this thinking to state that all learning is really recollection (75E), meaning that the things learned and recalled are not like the things that stimulate the educational processes (74D–75C). He emphasizes the distance and difference. To look at a specific case of this, we must have encountered the Form of the Equal in a previous existence, since we are familiar with it even though we have not experienced anything much like it during our material existence (75B–77A). This shows, Socrates says, that we were alive as pure souls before our bodily births.

Now let us turn again to $\mathbb{R}$. The first thing we need to note is that recollection is a relation from a to b, as in a RECOLLECTS b or aRb, such that b is a Form and a is something quite different from a Form. This distance between a and b serves to emphasize the active role of R, that is the psychic relation. The psyche is far from simply reporting experiences and from adapting to its environment. Its relation is that of an agent, not that of a patient. It forms a long bridge to something, that is to b or the Form, which is only vaguely suggested by something present (a). (Scott is helpful in explaining this distance.)

Next, objections.

i. "There is an ambiguity in the preceding use of $\mathbb{R}$ and this has implications for the purported freedom of the psyche. The ambiguity is between the relation of remembering and the relation of equaling. The first relation is psychic whereas the second is psychically accessed but real and independent of the psyche. The real, objective self-relation occurs in Plato (if 3.3 is right) but this does not mean that there is any psychic relation. But if there is no psychic relation then there is no positive freedom of the psyche either. But this is one reason why *Plato's Logic* is a misled interpretation of Plato altogether. In short, this book makes the error of trying to smuggle the Forms' (and later,

Gods') patterns into human minds, though Plato in fact distinguishes between these. He is a metaphysical realist."

In reply, I admit that recollections in Plato aim at the real entities, but the reader should observe that for Plato the one relation does not exclude or encompass the other. We can have both kinds of relation in tandem, the psychic and the objective. This point is important because Plato often says that free psyches *resemble* such external realities as Forms and God (see 3.9 below). His message would be impossible to understand if we could not have parallel patterns which none the less remain distinct from each other.

ii. "It should be noted how much the *Phaedo* generalizes about recollection. It is what learning *always* amounts to, Socrates says (75E). Does this not imply that Plato's view of psychic activity is rather uniform, contrary to this book's repeated suggestions? Is there not here some uniformity in the content of Plato's philosophy? If there is then his continuity is not only formal."

In reply, this is *one* of Plato's generalizations, but he also makes many other generalizations which are not the same, and moreover he nowhere fits all the different generalizations together. There are many works in which he does not bring up recollection at all, and his concern is often not to make psyches focus on the past. Sometimes Plato holds that we need to plan *ahead*, as for instance in seeking perfect Beauty in the *Symposium* (see Chapter 4) or in forming the Kallipolis in the *Republic* (see Chapter 5). In those places Plato does not hold that we are *originally* from the perfect places that he wants us to steer towards, unlike in the *Phaedo*, and that is why our ascent to perfection cannot then be a process which runs *backwards* in time. Other variations about the psyche abound as well, as e.g. how emotional or rational it is (contrast the *Symposium* with the *Phaedo*), how complex or simple (contrast the *Republic* or the *Phaedrus* with the *Phaedo*), how poetic or argumentative (contrast the *Phaedrus* with the *Theaetetus*), and so on.

3.5 MATHEMATICS (75C–D)

Now I want briefly to invoke the *Phaedo*'s *mathematical* examples. Socrates says at 75C–D that the objects of philosophical cognition are, besides the equal, at least the large, the small, beauty, goodness, justice, holiness, and altogether all those things which are thematized in the method of question and answer. This list is not meant to be complete, and no close connection is made between the list of philosophical objects and the dialectical method which is supposed elsewhere to lead us to these objects. What is worth noting, however, is that the items on the list are relations besides values. Moreover, mathematically or logically we do not have much of a notion of what the values may be like, though Plato is among those philosophers who holds, at least at times, that values have a status that makes them *alike* to some mathematical or logical abstractions. *How* they are to be alike may seem mysterious. But in the list at 75C–D all the mathematical or logical items are precisely relations, and this suggests that the values that Plato classes with them might be relations as well. They are being listed together, after all.

Here are a few further considerations along similar lines. First, if one classes mathematical relations together with values then one must have some reason for doing so. In the passage at issue at least one reason seems to be that the items of this class are imperceptible empirically (cf. 75B–C). But why are they imperceptible? This is not explained exactly. Yet if they are a unified class exactly because they are relations, as I am suggesting, then the passage is no longer as puzzling. After all, it is often maintained by philosophers that empirically perceived objects are particular or individual and that the comparisons and other systematizations we shape based on them are not empirically based. We organize our experiences, Humeans and Kantians say, for example, and the experiences are not as such anything organized. Second, consider that Plato could have listed as mathematical abstractions, instead of the equal, the large, and the small, e.g. the point, the line, and the circle. If he had then the suggestion would have been that values are *geometrical* objects due to their association with *these* mathematical objects in particular. But it is not this geometrical association that is now being made. Rather, the mathematical objecs listed are actually relations, as in $a=b$ and $a<b$, where "=" and "<" are mathematical symbols that are so often used outside Plato to mark equations and differences in quantity (such as differences in size, as e.g. between the small and the large, or the smaller and the larger, cf. 5.6–5.7 on relations in mathematics).

But once again it is possible to react skeptically.

3.6 METHOD (63C–64A, 85C–D, 89D–91C)

The *Phaedo* contains numerous *methodological* reflections about the process of philosophical dialogue. Hence it does not consist only dialogical elements like questions and answers, which are relations at least to each other (and often also to other things, such as certain topics which they are about), but also of portions of dialogue that are about an idealized version of dialogue. These meta-dialogical portions are self-correcting formally in the sense of $\mathbb{R}$. They use dialogue to raise dialogue to a higher level.

What are these portions? The list is not long or complex.

At 63C–D it is noted how the dialogical philosophizing involves a *shared purpose*, for if Socrates succeeds in defending his own convictions then he will simultaneously have made those convictions the property also of others. In other words, the egoistic project of weighing one's values or beliefs is now said to overlap with the socially more inclusive project of giving what one has to others without any loss to oneself. It should be noted how this type of cognitive communism, as one might call it, is absent in many human situations, as in, say, athletics. If you and I play tennis and you win then I must lose. We cannot both win. That is just in the nature of the game. But in philosophizing dialogically we can both win, at once. Why is this? The aims of this type of activity are not exclusive or necessarily scarce (cf. Habermas for this general *ethos*).

At 85C–D it is said that an effort must be made to arrive at the *optimal results* in inquiry. One should not give up too soon. The point is to emphasize that doubts and questions should be expressed and not concealed. One should not settle for too little. At 89D–90A this same line of thinking is continued, for it is claimed that the worst evil to suffer would be to begin to dislike proofs. Perfect proofs may be rare, it is said, just as the extreme points on comparative scales will be rare (that is, if the scales consist of many enough positions), but this should never be thought to imply that they do not exist. They deserve to be sought even if they are rare or difficult to come by. This is just as with the large and the small, the beautiful and the ugly, the fast and the slow, and so on: one meets often with average cases and seldom with the extremes (90A). The point of saying this, however, is that the extremes must be sought even so.

90E–91C repeats many of the same points but also adds a few new ones. One should not doubt whether certainties exist, it is said, and one should seek certain results, nothing less (90E). But the point in the dialogical search should not be only to win against others (91A). Rather, the results should simply be true (91B). It is no matter who gets to the best results but what the best results are (91B–C). This is the properly philosophical procedure, Socrates says (91A), even though he does not claim to live by this ideal perfectly himself (91A–B). 101E–102A adds that professional disputers (presumably sophists like Gorgias and Protagoras, as in the *Gorgias* and the *Protagoras*, see Chapters 8 and 10) are not philosophical in this sense because they do not seek real results. Socrates may mean that if the reward of the search is money and not the cognitive result itself then the latter end will tend to be sacrificed for the sake of the former: one will try to seem like one knows, only to get paid.

Notice how much has now been done on a meta-level. We have seen philosophical dialogue about philosophical dialogue. Sometimes it is triggered by prior questions and at other times it is not given much of an external context before it is offered more spontaneously. It concerns both questioning and answering. The general emphasis of the remarks is communistc (one speaker's good is also another's), foundationalistic (only perfect or certain results will be do), realistic (truth is not a function of agreement), and self-ironic (none of the speakers personifies the dialogical ideal, not even Socrates).

Now what does any of this have to do with $\mathbb{R}$? In time, dialogical relations are first applied to external topics, such as Socrates' situation before his death, the character of psychic liberty, pleasure, wisdom, and so on. But at a later stage the dialogical relations are applied to the dialogical relations themselves, so the relations become internal. At this later stage the dialogical relations point also to further and improved dialogical relations that lie in the hoped for future. Thus first, in time, we have a dialogical relation, R, which relates a and b, as in aRb, such that $a \neq R$ and $b \neq R$ (and $a \neq b$), and then, later, the same R is directed at itself, as in zRR. But this is a version of $\mathbb{R}$. Hence, we once again have evidence of $\mathbb{R}$ in the *Phaedo*. (To clarify, zRR and not zRz is instanced here because there is dialogue about dialogue, and hence a relation to a relation, as in RR. There is not simply an instance of some group of speakers relating dialogically to itself, as in zRz.)

What may be objected now?

i. "The preceding is a weak argument because every time we have dialogue we also have words, and none the less Plato's arguments are not simply about words. Similarly, the fact that dialogues are always relational does not mean that their philosophical significance is relational. Relations, like words, may be an accidental by-product. The main philosophical affair can be some other. There is no argument above in this section (3.6) about what is philosophically serious and why. Verbal or formal regularities are not important *per se*."

In reply, it is true that this section (3.6) has not argued that dialogical relations about dialogical relations are crucial to the *Phaedo*'s philosophical message. But this argument is actually easy to make, as follows. The *Phaedo* uses dialogue to propagate a philosophical lifestyle which consists of philosophizing in dialogue. Hence, a low-value version of dialogue is used to raise the value-level of dialogue. But therefore dialogue is used to improve dialogue, and hence a relation is used to improve that relation. Things would be different if the *Phaedo*'s philosophical aim were not dialogical, but it is.

ii. "Plato may mean to propagate an improved version of dialogue to dialogical speakers instead of meaning to propagate improved relations directly to relations."

This is a misunderstanding. This book's argument is never that Plato uses relations in total abstraction from human individuals. Rather, the ideal patterns are brought to humans for their own good. Plato is a "humanist" bent on improving life, and not for instance a mathematician.

3.7 REINCARNATION (79E–84B)

Socrates says that psyches are reborn in accordance with their activities, so that for example gluttony leads to a rebirth as an ass (81E–82A) and violence and tyranny lead to a new life as a hawk or a kite (82A). The thought seems to be, as before (and as in Chapters 5 and 6 below), that one reaps what one sows, so that aRb and R=IS REBORN AS, DESERVES TO REBORN AS, IS REVEALED AS, ACTS LIKE, RESEMBLES, perhaps even EQUALS. Here b is a barer or more transparent version of a, so on the surface $a{\neq}b$ though on a deeper level $a{=}b$ and therefore zRz, as in $\mathbb{R}$. But therefore this is to confirm a portion of $\mathbb{R}$.

That the doctrine of reincarnation is relational is, I hope, obvious enough. The question to ask at this point would rather seem to be what it is supposed to show in any serious sense. Are we really to be that there are reincarnations? Does Plato's way of thinking depend on this? If it does then its prospects can seem bleak, because not many readers today will be ready to trust him that any person is actually reborn in a new body.

However there is a way to build around this by reflecting that the *Phaedo's* doctrine of reincarnation is both metaphysical and ethical. It is metaphysical because it is offered as a basis for establishing the immortality of the psyche (because a reincarnated psyche would be born again after the death of the body it was attached to, and so the psyche would be immortal though the body is mortal; see 3.10 below on this), and it is ethical because it is meant to propagate a lifestyle which leads to superior rebirths (because no one would wish to be reborn as an ass, for example). Now if we discredit the metaphysical baggage in a passage such as this then we will not take the argument for immortality seriously, but we may still be left with an interesting ethical message. In the spirit of Kant it would command us to act in accordance with a counterfactual. One would need to act in such a way as to deserve to be reborn in a valuable form. This is just as in Kant because in Kant one pretends to legislate (as it were spatially) for all the world even though one really does not legislate for anyone except oneself. Similarly, in Plato one would legislate (temporally) for all one's future lifetimes even though one has no such future lifetimes. In Kant the individual free thinker attains a reflective yardstick due to one counterfactual generalization and in Plato the effect would be similar even though the generalization is in a different dimension. (I am not aware of a Platonic ethic from any recent source

68   *Chapter Three*

with this type of a message. Magnus interprets Nietzsche in a somewhat similar way, however; 5.4 will return to this ethos.)

3.8 HARMONY (85E–88B, 92A–93D)

The *harmony* of the psyche is a recurrent theme in the *Phaedo*, and though harmony does not provide foundations for any very serious arguments about the psyche's freedom or immortality in the *Phaedo* it is significant to note that also harmony and the arguments depending on it can be formulated in relations. (The suggestion now is as before that Plato can be intuitively or implicitly a relational thinker, because so much of what he says is accountable relationally; see e.g. 1.1, 2.1, and 3.1.)

Harmony is a topic at 85E–86D, 87B–88A, and 92A–93D. Here Socrates seems to think of harmony as a weak consistency relation. It obtains between external things, so it does not involve self-consistency. His illustration of it is that of a lyre which, when played, makes a harmonious sound.

This is not much of a basis for an argument because the harmony at issue is such a frail thing. The melody which is played on the lyre would not survive the demise of the physical lyre. Hence, if we assimilated the psyche with the melody and the body with the lyre then the immortality of the psyche would require the immortal harmony or melody. In that case the melody would need to go on and on though different instruments for playing that melody would perish. But this kind of a melody is not heard. What happens in fact is, of course, that melodies are heard only from physical instruments. The music ends when the instruments perish. So there is a dependency on the physical in all music. This is why this analogy does not work for immortality claims but against them (93A–B).

In $\mathbb{R}$'s terms we can interpret this musical example as $aRbRc$, for what is at issue is, as noted, a relation that is formed out of external materials. R is then the relation and a, b, and c are the external materials. More exactly, we can picture R as an interval between the notes a, b, c (one note per lyre's string, on a three-stringed lyre). Then the point about mortality is that there is no RR because a melody cannot be played without external or physical instruments, and this is because the melody is not a note or a string of its own.

Socrates also uses a different metaphor to discuss harmony: the weaver of cloaks (87B–88A). The weaver may die though her cloak remains, but this does not show that the weaver's lifetime is shorter than the cloak's, he says, because in her lifetime the weaver makes many cloaks. Similarly, a psyche may wear out many bodies during its lifetime, Socrates suggests, so a body's death need not signal the end of the psyche. Where is the harmony in this?

It would be in the weaver's many productions and not in any single one of them. For she would make a series of similar products. She would stand above them, and keep doing the same thing (weaving). Thus we would again find the same pattern, *aRbRcR..*, where *R* would be weaving (literally e.g. IS WOVEN INTO) and *a*, *b*, etc. would be cloaks. But the metaphor of weaving is simply dropped at 88A, so I, too, hereby leave this comparison behind.

Let us consider a single objection this time: "There are many ways to explain harmonies and patterns of consistency, and these do not always require talk of relations, and Plato's interest in harmonies or consistencies does not therefore indicate anything about relations. For example, Plato's philosophizing may be based, rather, on a doctrine of types. Perhaps he pictures types of sound and interval, and constructs melodies and harmonies on this basis. As a different alternative, Plato may constantly speculate, actually, in physical terms. When he says something about equality, he may in fact primarily think of visible equals in length or weight, no matter how imperfect, such as sticks' and stones'. As a visually oriented mind he may only be groping, quite helplessly, after more abstract truths for which he has no theoretic status, be that the status of a type, a relation, or whatever."

In reply, I cannot claim that the passages considered in this section show that Plato must philosophize in relations, because it is true that he may have some other theoretic model or none. But at least the comparison with music seems to suggest relations, because we get chords and melodies and harmonies by intervals, which are relations (cf. Bailey, who interprets the *Phaedo's* consistency relations as orders or musical harmonies; also see Rothstein, who also describes how Plato was probably familiar with Pythagoras' views on music; cf. 4.6, 6.5).

3.9 OPPOSITES (70C–72E, 102A–E, 104B–107D)

Relations between *opposites* are a recurring theme in the *Phaedo* and their explanation is easy relationally but difficult otherwise (for discussions on them see Kirwan as well as Irwin 1995 Chapter 10; also see Owen; this same topic was considered already in 3.1; also see 4.5 and 5.6 below).

At 70c–72e Socrates attempts to generalize that all things originate from their opposites so that, just as we take turns being awake and asleep, we move back and forth between being alive and dead. Later Socrates clarifies his thinking in opposites by noting that only concrete particulars arise from opposites and that abstract relations are those opposites, invariably and eternally (102A–E; also see 104B–107D). The Forms are pure extremes which are unmixed with anything else. The particulars, meanwhile, are torn between the different Forms, as it were pulled in different directions at the same time. The particulars are conflicted and contradictory, but not so the Forms.

We can understand opposites in $\mathbb{R}$'s terms in at least one way. This is that in $aRbRc...yRz$ a and z are opposites. Then if R is a Form it stands for one extreme in taking the position of z at the extreme right of the series, as $...zRR$ or $...zRz$. What makes opposites natural to $\mathbb{R}$ is the fact that $\mathbb{R}$ consists of relations (besides terms or objects, like a, b, c, etc.) and opposites are some of the relations that there are. For instance, IS TALLER THAN is a relation that is suited for forming opposites. If we follow this relation to its extremes then on the left we have the tallest thing, as one opposite, and on the right we have the least tall thing, as the other opposite. It may or may not be the case that each Form can be interpreted as an opposite of some thing or other. That is not something one can easily establish based on the *Phaedo* because this dialogue does not strive to produce a complete list of Forms. (Cf. 65D, 75C, 75E, 100B, 104A–C, 105D, 106D.)

At any rate, not even Plato's Socrates seems to think that every Form has an opposite in another *Form*, for otherwise he seems to need, as the opposite of the Just, the Unjust at 70E–71A, and he does not seem to consider the option of having negative Forms. Forms tend to stand for things reasoned, free, and divine, that is for the good things that Socrates wants to reach as a philosopher, and not for the terrible or confusing things he seeks to get away from and which hold him back. Metaphorically, there is a heaven of Forms but no hell (see *Parmenides* 130B–D on this).

A different point is that Socrates does not seem to be entirely clear about how an individual psyche can *link* with opposites. For he may not notice that it is not of much service to an individual psyche's immortality if there are opposites or Forms as opposites. In terms of $\mathbb{R}$ we can make sense of the psyche's liberation as a movement towards the right, if at the right extreme of the series we have $...zRR$ or $...zRz$. Then the psyche can move towards its own self-relation by repeating a suitable relation in the appropriate order. But this as such would do nothing for the psyche's immortality. For the psyche's would always be only a *use* of R, that is of a particular content such as MOVES or EQUALS. The psyche could not possibly *become the same as*, or in any way for all times join, R (e.g. by becoming movement as such). Hence, the immortality of the psyche would not be helped if R or zRR or zRz keeps being tokened over and again. The later tokens may be those of *other* psyches. Once Socrates has died, Plato can think through the same patterns, and then Aristotle, etc. Thus, the patterns may live on without the particular individuals, so the patterns do not cause any of the individuals to be immortal (however the *Symposium* adds a twist to this, see 4.4).

Again let us consider an objection. "The passages about opposites can be explained also in other terms, not only in relations. For instance, we can use types and tokens, universals and particulars, predicates and subjects, and perhaps even numerical or adjectival accounts on which positions on scales are indicated either by quantities (as e.g. for weights or heights) or by comparatives (like *pretty: prettier: prettiest,* or *ugly: normal: pretty,* etc.)."

To reply, this is false, because types/tokens, universals/particulars, and predicates/subjects are binary distinctions and they do not allow for the formulation of distinctions of degree (see e.g. 1.1, 1.3, 2.1, and 3.3), and this is why they do not allow for the formulation of the kinds of oppositions which Plato mentions. To be sure, there are many binary oppositions, too, but those do not typically concern Plato, as e.g. above/below, in/out, parent/child, and so on. Plato's oppositions seem to consist of more several positions; and we can see why that is so when he argues from contradictions and to superlatives, because it is the mixed positions between the extremes that can be viewed as contradictory and it is the superlatives that are free from such mixtures. If the possible positions are only two then there is no mixed or conflicted intermediate, of course, and then also the superlative aim must fall away. But therefore the binary vocabularies will not do, of course.

Here is an especially blunt way to state the central point against the preceding objection. In *aRb* there is no compresence of opposites. If e.g Jin is taller than Jan then there is so far no reason to say that Jin is both tall and not tall. The logical reason for this is very simply: nothing is ever torn between two opposites unless at least three terms or objects are related. Two do not suffice. But universals and particulars or types and tokens cannot be used to formulate series like these. What is required are relations. (As 1.3 noted, many-termed predicates can be much like many-termed relations. However the difficulty of self-predication arises if predicates are predicated of predicates, as in Vlastos 1954, and meanwhile relations seem to face no similar problems, see 1.2, 2.1, and 3.3.)

Numerical and adjectival scales suffer from a different shortcoming from a Platonic point of view. They do provide us with grades but they fail to provide us with something else that Plato also needs, namely *self-consistent* extremes. To illustrate, the heaviest weight is not the same as weight in the abstract, and the most beautiful horse is not the same as beauty itself. In other words, simply to use numerical scales or adjectival scales is not to explain how anything can be perfect by its own standard. But such a need is precisely what motivates this book's relationalism (cf. 5.6–5.7 for a more inclusive view).

3.10 SIMPLICITY (78B–84D)

At *Phaedo* 78B–80B Socrates tries to build on the *simplicity* of the psyche. The psyche's immortality can be defended based on its simplicity if death is decomposition. For to die may be to break up into smaller parts. But if this is what it is to die then what is partless cannot die. Partless things cannot be split into parts, after all. So on this theory of death it is crucial that the psyche is partless.

Now as before one of the stakes in the argument is the psyche's affinity to the Forms. For the simple and hence immortal psyche would be like a Form. This is because in the *Phaedo* the Forms are simple and eternal (cf. Silverman). This is, of course, a recurrent theme in this book, for we find repeatedly that Plato wants human psyches to rise to the level of the Forms. A different version of this view is that humans should grow to resemble God or the Gods (cf. Sedley 1999 and Snell Chapter 7). In colorful language the overall meaning of this is that humans should shed their animal skins and act in more reasoned ways. Formally the point is again $\mathbb{R}$, as we will soon see below.

We should interpret this at least ethically and materially. The ethics of this section's topic says that a free psyche should be something perfectly self-contained. For the soul should be ruled only from within, not form without (83A–B). But, now, this ideal may be impossible to meet for any complex thing. If this is correct then the ethics of psychic liberation may involve the metaphysics of the material cause. I may illustrate what Socrates can have in mind with an example of my own. If my psyche has two parts, or as it were two personalities within it, an extraverted one and an introverted one (as in Jung), then I am not self-ruled if the extravert rules the introvert. Nor should the introvert rule the extravert. Rather, the introvert should rule itself and the extravert should rule *it*self. That would be freedom. Nothing would rule over anything but itself. But this would now be to say that the self-ruler must be simple. It is difficult to be fully certain that Socrates makes this association between simplicity and psychic freedom, but the possibility is worth noting in passing because it makes ample sense as just explained.

A more important aspect of psychic simplicity is its status as a first material cause. A simple psyche would be first material cause because it were one of the basic elements of reality. We can communicate this in $\mathbb{R}$'s terms if we give R the content IS MADE OF, CONSISTS OF, or HAS THE PARTS. Then the series is that a IS MADE OF b IS MADE OF c..., and so on, until ultimately ... z IS MADE OF z. Here z is atomic, so it cannot be split. It is an *Ur*-element and it is immortal.

Now what if anything does the *Phaedo* say about this material simplicity? Three portions of it are crucial. The first is an irony. For it may sound paradoxical that the *Phaedo* itself describes the psyche in so many different ways. In it the psyche seems at least to believe, to desire, to feel, to perceive, and to be alive (cf. Bostock pp. 22–30). But one may feel that a thing that is this heterogenous cannot be simple.

The second crucial portion to consider is that the Socrates of the *Phaedo* may himself have the means to determine that the psyche is actually simple, that is contrary to any initial appearances of complexity (as in the preceding paragraph). It seems he has the necessary means for this in his dialectic of questions and answers. For he may ask, for example, what a psyche IS MADE OF. Then, if he receives fitting answers to this question many enough times, his process produces simplicity at its extreme on the right-hand side. In other words, Socrates' own dialectical process may be exactly what one needs to determine the (or perhaps a) psyche's simplicity. This would be exactly as in ℝ, of course.

We may have a short interlude to visualize this. Picture a tree which is climbed upwards, beginning from the trunk. Then as time passes different branches shoot off in various directions, each of the branches consisting of what is inessential to the psyche. This process of climbing upwards and dividing further is then continued until the very top of the tree is reached. Here there are no more divisions and the psyche comes to a standstill. Now it is confronted with itself in its bare simplicity.

The third and last portion that is relevant now involves a distinction between the pre-philosophical and post-philosophical psyches of the above process. The former is the term a in the series, and the latter is z. Now, the *Phaedo* portrays both of these, that is all psyches as they are already (93A–94C) and the ideal psyches as they should be, at their freest and most philosophical (67C, 79C–80B, 80E–84D, 107C–D). Thus, Plato provides us with views of both ends of the series, and this suggests that he understands how important their differences are. But in this light of this his message is not that the psyches at a are immortal. Rather, the psyches at z are. Accordingly (and contrary to the first portion above in this section, 3.10), psyches can be complex and colorful at a without the same being true of psyches at z. But therefore there is really no irony in the *Phaedo's* basic position about immortal psyches. Rather the situation is, as it often is according to this book, that Plato distinguishes between everyday appearances and utopian realities (this is very different from Descartes' *Cogito* or Kant's "I think," both of which are present in everyday affairs; see Scott again on this difference; Penner is especially far off the mark).

Of course, many questions still arise, but that is always so with the great questions which Plato is so apt at raising. All he gives us are their main lines or frames. What does he leave unexplained this time? For one thing, and as in 3.3 above with the Form of the Equal, the *Phaedo* is short on intermediate steps. Thus it says things about psyches in position a and psyches in position z, as above, but not about psyches in positions like b, m, n, and so on. It leaps from the starting line to the finishing line and leaves us to guess what might happen in between. But this is to leave open the possibility that psyches in real life are actually more schizophrenic. For, as in the picture drawn above, the branches shoot in so many different directions. How can one be sure which one is one's own? A soul can ask, which am I? Where is my true home? (Think of Kierkegaard's *Either/Or*.) She can get lost. Plato does not save us from such troubles, for rather he is one to generate them for us in the first place.

Here is an objection:

i. "This cannot be right. For if the simple psyche is discovered simply as the product of a process of division into parts as above then the simple psyche is not attained only by converting into a philosophical asceticism as the *Phaedo* clearly requires (cf. Seldey 1999 pp. 310–311). That ethical purpose is served only if the immortal psyche is attained only as a result of certain philosophical activities. But that picture is impossible to draw if such the utopian psyche (z, above) is construed merely as material part of the ordinary psyche (a, above), for a part is present already in the whole. In other words, logical consistency requires that something must give. One must let go either of the material cause or of the ascetic *ethos;* for they do not mix."

A possible reply to i would be that only a philosopher would learn to *identify* with her simple and immortal part. For only a philosopher who goes through the dialectic of ℝ with the content IS MADE OF learns, step by step, to view herself more and more simply. (After a she learns to see herself as b, then as c, and so on.) Stated conversely, non-philosophers will see their simple and immortal portions as mere strangers. But therefore they will not recognize themselves in their new lifetimes or recall their past lives. Rather they will cling to what is *not* continuous between the biographies or reincarnations. Put differently, their *self-identities* (or they on their own self-conceptions), will be mortal, whereas the philosophers' will be immortal. (Sedley 1999 p. 320 makes a similar connection but without considering the performative awareness of the speakers in Plato's text. Gadamer's focus is on the perfomative selves at play in the text, but he does not attempt seriously to see reason in Plato's aim of immortality.)

Here is a second objection.

ii. "If we say, with Plato, that a psyche is at its freest when it is most like a Form and a Form is a simple and motionless abstraction which exists in a totally cold and indifferent way through all time, then we are saying that the freest persons or agents are simple and motionless abstractions. But freedom cannot be like this, and psychic activity cannot be this simple or bare (also see 73D–75A). After all, ascetic and austere persons can be free only *from* bodily obstructions, just as the poor may be said to be free from the concerns of wealth, but their positive and *internal* wealth, or the vivid and insightful and innovative sides of their mental lives, would seem to demand problems, metaphors, and other types of complex content. For is not a lively mind necessarily complex and unstable, and is it not therefore a mistake to aim at simplicity and eternal stability?"

In 4.4 I will argue that a living, human psyche cannot ever make it *all* the way to the Form. The distance between the psyche and the Form should become as small as possible without ceazing to exist.

3.11 CAUSALITY (94A–95A, 96A–99D, 100B–102D, 105B–D)

Causal relations are the final relation-type that I will consider from the *Phaedo*. They come up many times in the later portions of this dialogue.

At 94A–95A Socrates seems to consider a self-moving psyche as an initiator of actions. For the psyche can oppose the bodily impulses and rule the entire person, he says. A psyche may even punish the body to which it is attached. Hence, the psyche need not only depend on the body in the way that the harmonious melody depended on the physical lyre in 3.8; for the body can also be made to depend on the psyche.

Socrates continues along these lines when he suggests that causes are actually mental and intelligent and that material environments amount only to conditions and not to causes at all (99A–C). For instance, Socrates needs his bones and sinews to do what he thinks is the proper thing to do, he says, but the bones and sinews do not make him do the proper things which he decides to do. Clearly Socrates here wishes to defend a world in which minds rule over bodies. He only shifts between different terms for making his position understandable and plausible to his interlocutors, but he has no doubts about the mind's causal powers.

Somewhat confusingly 100B–102D turns for a time to formal causes (provoking questions whether Socrates sees how different they are from efficient ones, see this section 3.11 below). Some scholars have made a number of the seemingly relational claims in this passage (cf. e.g. Castañeda, Gallop, and Matthen again), because it appears to view the formal cause of height in a comparative way. The example is that *Phaedo* OVERTOPS *Simmias* OVERTOPS *Socrates* (102B–D). In this example the formal cause of Phaedo's or Simmias' relative tallness cannot be in any particular size (such as that of a head), Socrates says, because that size can make one taller *or* shorter than someone else. However at least outside the *Republic* (see 5.6–5.7) Plato does not seem to be entirely clear about geometric relations, because he has the tendency to think of e.g. a Form of the Large as the largest thing (cf. 102D) and not only as a comparative scale. (This is the reason I do not rely on 100B–102D.)

At *Phaedo* 105B–D Socrates comes back to what are recognizable to us as efficient causes. Here the psyche is presented as the cause of life, just as fire is said to be the cause of heat and fever of disease. Apparently the thought is that the psyche is so intimately linked with the project of causing life that you cannot take life away from the psyche, just as you cannot have a fire that is not hot. Hence the death of the psyche should be impossible, and this is one of the *Phaedo*'s arguments for the psyche's immortality.

A final aspect of causal relations in the *Phaedo* is that the Forms are, as causes, logically independent of their effects (105B–C). There would be a logical relation between cause and effect if for instance heat caused a thing to be hot. Plato's view is that the cause is not heat but something especially hot, as for instance fire. The hottest thing heats up the other heated things, he seems to say, and the hottest thing is the Form. The extreme case affects the less extreme cases, and the extreme case is the Form.[2]

All but one of these five scenarios seem to be about efficient causes, and this allows us to interpret them collectively by inserting a single relation into the pattern $\mathbb{R}$. The relation is that of an efficient cause (e.g. EFFECTS), and the first causes are either Forms (such as fire, or Fire) or psyches which resemble them (like Socrates' psyche when he makes his decision). Besides the first causes these four passages in question bring up the effects of the first causes, as for instance heat for fire and Socrates' bodily movements for Socrates' psyche. The general order thus formed is a string $aRbRcRd...$, e.g. such that *fire* EFFECTS *heat* EFFECTS c EFFECTS d, and so on, or, by replacing the terms, *Socrates's psyche* EFFECTS *Socrates' walking* EFFECTS c EFFECTS d, etc.

There are a few obvious shortcomings in this account. One is that the formal cause makes its appearance amid efficient causes; more on that soon below. Another is that the passages in question do not actually allow us to attribute any self-caused structure to the first causes. For the passages do not say that Socrates' psyche EFFECTS itself, or that *Fire* EFFECTS *Fire*. Due to this we do not find evidence for all of $\mathbb{R}$, but only for a part. (The evidence is for $aRbRc...$ but not for $...zRz$ or $...zRR$.) A third shortcoming is that one of Plato's basic associations is left out of the account. For how can fire (or Fire), which most of us now think of as a material or physical thing, seem to Plato to have a soul? But this is something I will not be able to explain in the *Timaeus* or the *Laws* either, see Chapters 12 and 6, and I must pass this problem by.

Here is an objection to my own view: "Socrates' causal picture is backwards. For now Socrates wants the *final* results of inquiry, that is for instance the perfected psyches or the Forms, to operate as *efficient causes* in processes of inquiry (thus Vlastos 1971 section I; however, for Vlastos it suffices that in ancient Greece this would be *called* an *aitia,* which is usually translated as "cause," so Vlastos is not concerned with the quesion whether there *really* are causes like these, and he refers to Davidson for further discussion on this). We know that he wants this because he wants his self-relations to be, first, the ultimate causes and, second, the endpoints of inquiry. But if the endpoints of inquiry cause the earlier (successful) steps of processes of inquiry then in those processes the final events cause the prior events, and this is backwards because it places effects before causes. Ordinarily, of course, we tend to think that a cause comes *first*. It is the effect that comes last, not the cause. For example, if the boxer performs a knockout then the blow must come *before* the victim hits the canvass. Similarly, if the lightning causes the forest fire then the lighting must *precede* the forest fire. One cannot cause things after they have occurred. But Socrates is implying that a series of questions and answers would come by the ultimate cause only at its end. In a temporal series *aRbRc a* would happen first, then *b*, then *c*, but, for Socrates, *c* would be the cause of *b* and *a*. How can this make sense?"

Here is a reply. First we need to shift gears. We should not try to interpret Socrates based on materialistic examples like the preceding paragraph's. We should consider situations which lie closest to Socrates' own interests, which are psychic and not material. In this vein, Socrates appears to be thinking that something self-relational, like a Form, as an optimal end-point of a thought process, can have a kind of pull on us even before it is instanced in our minds or speech in any transparent way. That is, he seems to imagine that free thinkers search for Forms which they trust to exist but which they do not understand fully until all their free thinking has been fully performed.

But now, this seems quite rational. For Socrates' thinking on this score seems to be no different than that of many researchers and artists, who use certain techniques to arrive at novel results. The results they are after are not familiar from past discoveries and creations. They are supposed to be new. But they are the reasons and causes why the agents in question act. The pioneers want to arrive in the new territories. They act so as to reach and reveal those territories. It is the pull of the new territories that makes them act. (Penner says such thinking is "utopian.") It is not about everyday meanings but about the optimal results of unforeseen actions. I am now not saying only that this thinking may be common among pioneering thinkers and researchers. I am suggesting also that it is not optional. It appears to be mandatory to believe in the pull of the utopian results if one operates as an agent in a utopian type of inquiry.

How is this? We can explain this best in graded terms. A group of artists may be after beauty and they may, at a certain stage, be familiar only with moderate versions of beauty, which are not entirely beautiful. Then it is understandable if they want to find extreme beauty, and also if they hold that the search for extreme beauty motivates their creative search (cf. Murdoch). Similarly, if scientists characteristically seek exact truth and find only approximate truths then it is fitting for them to be dissatisfied and to seek more exact results. But in such circumstances they would be rational in saying that what draws them to take up their research projects in this perfectionistic direction is the perfectionistic aim itself. Conversely, we would not accept that the scientists act out of rational causes if their main motivation is something external to their aim (say, the way they were treated as children, or what their diets have consisted of). But this utopian result now appears as a Form in the *Phaedo*, and this is a way to interpret Plato's theory of Forms with charity. If this is correct then Plato's thinking about causes is not backwards at all, contrary to the objection.

This concludes my survey of the *Phaedo*.[3] Next we will compare this book's account to some of its competitors'.

3.12 VERSUS BOSTOCK I (FORMS)

Bostock's account of Plato's *Phaedo* contrasts with mine in denying that Plato's philosophical rebellion against common sense or ordinary language is sensible. For Bostock holds that Plato's Form of the Equal does not need to exist separately from many equal things like sticks and stones. The mundane examples from everyday life suffice, and Plato is wrong to demand a separate "heaven" (Hades) in which the purities can exist timelessly. Hence, Platonic philosophers can think they get off the ground in their dreams, but in reality they are bound to the same earth as everyone else all the while.

Why does Bostock say this? He holds that at 74D–75B nothing is actually said, in the Greek original, about perfect or exact equality. There is nothing about degrees of satisfaction. Hence, the Form of the Equal is not a superlative case of equality. It is not the most equal of things. There is no hierarchy of lesser equals and superior equals at all, Bostock says. So the Forms are only universals or standards, not superlative instances, even if Plato does not fully understand this. Due to this, one finds equal enough things in ordinary life, and there is no call to leave ordinary norms behind and to begin a new life as a philosopher. For nothing more equal would be come by in that way.

But Bostock goes further than this and argues that, independently of what Plato says, it does not even *make sense* to say that empirical or material things do not ever appear equal. For instance, two boxes of matches *can* seem equal, Bostock says (p. 87).

I have four reasons to question Bostock's account, A–D.

A. As Bostock concedes, at 74D–75B non-Forms, like sticks and stones, seek and strive to be equal. This implies that they *do* have some kind of a shortcoming, and one suggestion is to explain this by reference to degrees. But for Bostock this means only that these non-Forms do not manage to be the same as *the* Equal. The sticks and stones are never the same thing as the relation ...*equals*... But the sticks and stones manage to be cases of equals, in pairs, in just as perfect ways as anything else. Hence, there is still no rational motive here for becoming an otherworldly philosopher, Bostock implies.

B. As Bostock admits, there are hierarchies of cases elsewhere in Plato. But he insists that there is no hierarchy at 74D–75B. His point is based on the textual details of this passage in particular. He thinks that he is free to have other views about many other passages. Plato does not need always to be of one mind.[4] Perhaps Plato can defend a philosophical *ethos* in some other work or passage, but not here, according to Bostock. In my view this is quite artificial of Bostock, but this suspicion does not suffice for refuting him.

C. Bostock admits also (p. 89) that for Plato the Form of the Equal *is* equal (74B–C). So Plato does self-predicate when he discusses the Equal in the *Phaedo*. How does this square with Bostock's interpretation? Apparently for Bostock it is only a negligible blunder of Plato's, because Bostock does not even try to explain it. This is troubling, because it is flatly to leave Plato's syntactical innovation out of the discussion. It is to omit exactly that portion of the passage which calls for a philosophical interpretation in the first place. Everything else is in keeping with ordinary language.

D. The most serious reason to doubt Bostock's interpretation is that he makes a rather ridiculous assumption about equality. For he assumes that by equality Plato means equality in size. It is equality in size, clearly, that stones and sticks and matchboxes (to use Bostock's own example) can seem to have and have. But it is flatly absurd to assume that Plato means equality in size when the possibility to consider is whether an abstract thing such as a Form can be equal. For of course an abstraction like a Form cannot have a size at all. Thus, what tells against the possibility of self-instantiation in Bostock is not anything in Plato but only something in Bostock. Bostock's own imagination limits equality to the most mundane cases. There is no justification for assuming that Plato's meaning is as mundane.

3.13 VERSUS BOSTOCK II (VIRTUES)

Bostock also objects to the *Phaedo*'s view of the virtues, and as before Bostock defends common sense against Plato's attacks. For Bostock, there is nothing illogical about being courageous out of fear or about being temperate for the sake of pleasures, because it is coherent to abstain from some pleasures so as to attain others. Socrates only makes things seem strange by using contradictory descriptions, so that among non-philosophers virtues are combined with their opposite vices. Apparently Bostock holds that there is a deeper level on which there is no incoherence and that revealing this takes us to see the underlying consistency. On the deeper level there seem to be, instead of opposite virtues and vices, homogenous pleasures or preferences. Bostock says that ordinary men are temperate not so as to avoid pleasures altogether but so as to avoid the wrong kinds of pleasure. In the meantime everyone is driven by pleasures, Bostock asserts, so even the philosopher is hedonistic in her motivations, contrary to the idealist Plato (Bostock pp. 31–32).

But Bostock seems to beg all the questions against Plato. If Plato says something against ordinary views of courage or temperance or pleasure, then Bostock simply states the ordinary views as if these were evidence against Plato. What Bostock then assumes is that the ordinary views are correct, and this is an assumption Plato would reject. For Plato attacks the ordinary views. Bostock appears to maintain that Plato must seek to philosophize in a manner that does not violate norms of common sense, but no basis for such an obligation is given in Bostock's book.

What Bostock fails in fact to do is to interpret Plato's actual arguments about virtue. As we saw in 3.2, the *Phaedo* holds that ordinary versions of the virtues are contradictory, and that the only route to self-consistency is by aiming at the same things which one uses more generally as one's standards. For instance, wisdom must be its own standard and its own reward. Both its measure and its purpose need to internal to it. Why so? For Plato, the psyche must reach positive freedom, so it must rule itself, but this demands that it has *internally* driven standards and aims. For Plato argues that philosophical principles come from within. In contrast, our objects of fear and pleasure come from without, and such forces threaten our self-consistency or integrity. In what sense do they come from without? Pleasures and fears are external in that they come to us through our senses, Plato says (cf. *Phaedo* 82E–83E). What comes from within are the principles which drive philosophers (see 3.1, 3.3, 3.4, 3.10, and 3.11 above). Bostock does not refute this view but ignores it.

Bostock might ask what such ideas about positive freedom have to do with *virtue*. Does one need to be all that strict in distinguishing internal drives from external forces to qualify as courageous, temperate, or just? And is one not therefore justified in studying Plato's views of the virtues independently of Plato's views on the self-ruled psyche? But this is not a very problematic point. One should consider how difficult it would be to call a puppet on a string virtuous. It would seem strange to say that it is courageous or just or temperate, because its "actions" would not be up to it. The *puppeteer* might be virtuous, if it is indeed the puppeteer who pulls the causal strings, or the director who directs the play which the puppeteer enacts, or the playwright who tells the director what to do, and so on (Chapter 6 will find this example from the *Laws*). But in any case it is relevant for the ethical evaluation to know who or what is causally powerful in each case. Hence, questions about freedom do seem relevant to questions about virtue. This does not seem like a weak link in Plato's position.

From the angle of the Socrates of the *Phaedo*, ordinary virtues are not based on a strong enough conception of the self or psyche. It is ordinarily not reflected adequately how certain principles and purposes come to us from without and how others come from within. But if such a matter is considered deeply enough then it is noticed that the properly virtuous must be philosophers. For only philosophers focus on what is internal to the agent. Everyone else is like a puppet by comparison. It seems that Bostock does not try hard enough to take this argument seriously, but the effect of this is not that Plato is refuted. Bostock misses his target.

Now let us consider a different aspect of Bostock's criticism of the Platonic virtues. This aspect is moral: Why would a Platonic philosopher care for others or be kind to them? Would helping others aid her search for the Forms? Would her search lead her also to be forgiving, considerate, and loyal, for example? Bostock doubts this because the Platonic philosopher is so egoistic. Others will be distractions to her, just like her own body. She cares only for her own mind. Bostock allows that there may be some self-regarding virtues which are instanced by being so self-centered but emphasizes that morality requires other-regarding virtues, and these the idealistic philosopher does not have (Bostock pp. 34).

This deserves two different responses.

First, the virtues can be more personal more often that Bostock admits. For virtues may quite often be highly personal. For example, a temperate agent must control her *own* impulses. She should not focus on others' impulses, and even if others control her it is not *she* who can possibly be made temperate in that way. To take another example, to be wise is to think in some way, perhaps, or to know something, or to typically have certain feelings, to have certain priorities as opposed to others, etc., and again it would seem that others are not essentially involved. It does not seem to be very important to one's wisdom whether one's company is wise. It is conceivable that a wise person is among fools (like Socrates in the *Hippias Major* or the *Apology*) or alone: those are not the key questions to ask about her wisdom. As a third example, courage is the virtue connected to fears, but it may be that fears are at their most extreme, at least for many people, in confrontations with death. But death is typically confronted individually, because it is not usual for humans to die in groups. But therefore courage would seem to be a personal virtue in the main. (In the *Phaedo* it is, of course, Socrates who instances courage before death. The other speakers are not about to die.) One should not assume too quickly that the virtues are generally or essentially social and moral. Some are and some are not.

Second, Bostock ignores the *Phaedo*'s procedural communism, as I called it, and the morality that this may involve. Being virtuous in this dialogue is about philosophizing, and philosophizing is portrayed in it as a communal affair. Each participant in the discussion respects and learns from the others and benefits from their gains and suffers from their losses; and no one tries to manipulate or control anyone, etc. (cf. *Phaedo* 91A–C, and see 3.6 for further aspects). One should note that every human pursuit is not like this, because in many areas of life one person's gain is another's loss. Such competitive pursuits are often targeted at material goods, and it is not absurd of the *Phaedo* to say that it is material greed that leads to the worst of social evils, war (*Phaedo* 66C).

3.14 SUMMARY

This chapter (3) contained, first, sections which located relational patterns in the *Phaedo* (3.1–3.11) and then sections which argued against other, non-relational, interpretations of that dialogue (3.12–3.13). The relational pattern was found in surprisingly diverse contexts, as e.g. ones concerned with virtue, wisdom, the Equal, recollection, dialogue, opposites, simples, causes, etc.. But every time the pattern's use seemed to be libertarian despite this diversity, because every time it had a separate and self-sufficient aim. The non-relational intepretation considered in 3.12–3.13, namely Bostock's, was less sympathetic to Plato's ambitious aims than this book's is. In the next Chapter much the same story will be told again, though many of the names and points of comparison will be different.

NOTES

1. For these uses of "libertarianism" see Watson, ed., and Kane, ed. For some other uses see Chomsky and Nozick.

2. In passing we should note that 105B–C contradicts 73D–75A unless EQUALS at 73D–75A produces logically independent effects. It does this if in *a* EQUALS *b* *a* and *b* are logically independent of each other. I argued that they are in 3.3. This implies that EQUALS EQUALS *c* could not read "EQUALS" at *c*. Rather, *c* would need to say something new.

105B–C also contradicts many interpreters' accounts of the *Phaedo*, as e.g. Penner's. Interpreters often assume too quickly that a Platonic Form must be a universal which ordinary particulars have. This assumption is also Bostock's in 3.12 below, but my discussion of Bostock focuses on other questions.

3. The last pages of the *Phaedo*, 107B–118B, are not considered here.

4. Bostock, pp. 91–94.

Chapter Four

The Symposium

The *Symposium* portrays a hierarchy of beautiful things. Lower down in the hierarchy we have beautiful bodies. Further up there are things with more beauty, such as beautiful souls, beautiful poems, and beautiful laws. At the top of the hierarchy we have the most beautiful thing of all, the Form of Beauty. In accordance with this hierarchy, human activities, too, may rank low or high, because the activities can aim at different things in the hierarchy. One may have bodily interests and hence live like an animal, or else one can be active as a soul, as an artist, or as a political animal. But the only way to live in a fully satisfying way, and the only way to achieve perfect liberation, is as a philosopher, Plato argues. As before I explain his view by means of $\mathbb{R}$.

This chapter begins by collecting textual evidence for this book's thesis from the *Symposium* (in 4.1–4.7). First we encounter love as a relation in 4.1 and then the further relation of creation in 4.2. Both loves and creations can evolve, we find in 4.3, crucially for Plato's argument. This takes us to the problem of satisfaction in 4.4 and to the curious gap that exists between lovers and their ultimate satisfiers in 4.5. Next, the Form of Beauty is best interpreted relationally because it has the same double function as the fine in 2.1 and the Equal in 3.3 (4.6). For the Form of Beauty in the *Symposium* is both perfectly beautiful in itself and also something to be used as a model or blueprint for causing and explaining lower degrees of beauty in other things. Section 4.7 briefly addresses the more complex and literary issue of how to interpret the non-Socratic portions of the *Symposium*. For Socrates' speech is presented as the highpoint of a series, but the earlier points do or do not make for a consistent progression towards that highpoint. This in 4.7 is a more hypothetical basis for $\mathbb{R}$ than those of the sections before it.

Later in this chapter we will turn to confront Nussbaum's (4.8) interpretation of the *Symposium*. Nussbaum is skeptical about Plato's message, but I argue that she misrepresent him. Broadly, her error is to think that Plato philosophizes so as to account for the human condition in general or to express everyday intuitions. If that were Plato's aim then she would be right that he is unsuccessful, but it is not. Nussbaum overlooks that Plato's attempt is not to clarify the commonplace (who needs that?) but to reveal something superior to it, and in this, I argue, he succeeds well.

Section 4.9 summarizes the chapter.

4.1 LOVE (199C–212A)

Officially the topic of the *Symposium* is *eros*, which is usually translated as love. The *Symposium* contains six or seven speeches on this topic (depending on whether Alcibiades' is considered a speech; e.g. White 2008 and Nussbaum view Alcibiades' contribution as significant) but only the sixth speech, Socrates', discusses it in a way that is interesting philosophically. The other speeches are not by philosophers but by a comedian, a doctor, and so on (for some overviews see Dorter, Levy, Rosen, and Sheffield).

Let us survey the main things that Socrates says.

First, love always has an *ulterior object* (199D–200A). This is illustrated by comparing love with for example fatherhood (199D). One cannot be a father alone, for if one is a father then there must be someone whose father one is: one's child. Conversely: no child, no father. But just as one cannot be a father without a child, one cannot love without some other thing, Plato is saying. One loves someone or something out there. It cannot be in here, that is in the loving or the lover alone. There must be an ulterior object or loving is not taking place. But this is, of course, to say that love is relational in a certain way (cf. Scheibe pp. 32–33). It is a relation from a lover to a loved, as in *father* LOVES *child*, or if *father=a*, LOVES=R, and *child=b*, aRb, as in a portion of $\mathbb{R}$.

Second, love has the aim of *attaining* or possessing its object (200A–B, 200D). One may wish for and have for example such things as tallness, strength, swiftness, and health (200B). Clearly there is in each of these cases a difference between the wishing and having, because wishing to be tall is rather distinct from actually being tall, for example. Hence, loving is not only a matter of wishing.

Third, in loving *a* one *lacks a* (200A–B, 201B–C, 203C–D, 204A). One cannot seek to have what one already has. One must sense that there is a defect in how things are or one will not long for change (204A). In this way the lover's drive is always for something more, so satisfaction and rest are not for lovers. Lovers are restless, always moving, endlessly ambitious. In different terms, they are incomplete and they seek completeness from ulterior objects (as in the first point above). Is the point, then, that they cannot ever attain completeness, that is, that they will always have their lack as long as they exist? Would the love vanish if the lack vanished? This issue will concern us in 4.4.

Fourth, lovers seek to *reproduce* themselves (206B–C, 206E, 208A–B). Animals produce offspring, poets produce poems, politicians produce laws, and philosophers produce philosophies. This is, for one thing, to say that the kind of love which Socrates means to discuss is not passive but productive and creative (the next section, 4.2, is about this). It is not about simply admiring things that exist already. Loving of the type which he means to discuss is a doing and not a sensing. It is a drive to make things, to bring them into existence. But next, this making, producing, or creating is self-relational, as in zRz, because what lovers strive to produce copies of are themselves (208A–B). At first the easiest way to understand how this is so is in the shape of biological reproduction, so that lovers want to have children so as to be reborn. Yet this model will not carry us very far with Plato because this model does not contain the kind of idealizing element which he so often brings into his doctrines. His actual view is that the lovers seek to reproduce their *best* parts or aspects. For instance, a poet's children, that is, her poems, are the best things the poet can create, and if she lives on then it is due to the reputation of her best poems among a future readership (208C–E, 209C–E). Hence, the poet does not reproduce *all* of herself, or what is statistically most typical of her. One might say that she reproduces her "ideal" or "higher" self. An illustration of my own would be of a sculpture, which is made of someone at their best. The statue eternalizes the model's best qualities. The statue does not show her embarrassed or bored, for instance. Athletes are shown breaking records, and so on.

Fifth, and again crucially for what Plato wants ultimately to communicate in the *Symposium*, there is *variability* in lovers' objects or aims (202E–203A, 208E–209B, 210A–E, 211C–D). However perhaps the more adequate term for his meaning would be perfectibility. For it is not only that lovers do not always stay the same, as when a person can devote time to loving her children for a time and then turn to focus more on art, for instance, or vice versa. For the *Symposium* shows absolutely no interest in declining changes, so all the changes mentioned in it are improvements. Lovers can "rise" from animal interests to mental or spiritual ones, from those to the artistic, from these again to political ones, and from there eventually to philosophy, as we will see in 4.3. This upward mobility is worth dwelling on for a moment already now, however, so as to get the tone right from the start. Most clearly, unlike Hobbes Plato does not view human life as incorrigibly brutish. But unlike Aristotle he does not hold that a human being is essentially a political animal either, for there are human loves both below and above the political level in Plato's hierarchy. He is closer to saying that our drives really are those of philosophical animals, or with (one of his so many later followers) Pico della Mirandola, that we humans have something divine in us. But notice that Plato's people do not *always* philosophize either. We are not philosophical animals at birth. Philosophy is where we would reach our peak. It is what we should be doing, not what we most usually do.

Sixth, love comes in *degrees* of intensity (e.g. 210B–C, 211D). But when is the degree high? Is there to be a more intense emotion or a more strenuous activity on the side of the lover, for instance? Or is the loved object different? If it is, how? There is more to love in an artwork one has made and/ or in the younger artist who is somehow touched by it than there is in one's physical children, Plato says at one point (209C–D), and he seems to mean that there is more of a personal connection. But this cannot be generalized as his standard, because the philosophical climax which he ultimately aims at seems so impersonal (Nussbaum will criticize this below). So what explains the differences in degree? How is there "more" love somewhere than somewhere else? References to beauty as such do not seem to answer this, but in 4.6 we will begin to make headway by identifying something logically separate as the content of beauty, as for example harmony. For then it is plausible to hold, with Plato, that there is more beauty in a psyche than in a body and also that there is especially much of beauty in a simple and immutable Form. On this approach the perfectibility of human aspirations is an objective topic, so we do not study the subjective relations of lovers as much as the objects they relate to when we want to understand the degrees of love. The thought in this is that the higher objects pull up the subjects, so the objects are the causes.

Seventh, lovers seek happiness or satisfaction (204D–205A, 205D–206A). This appears as the ultimate final cause at 205A. But eighth, what lovers are after is also said to be *beauty* (201A, 204B–D, 210E–211E), or else they are after reproduction or creative action somehow in the context of beauty (201A, 205E, 206C–E, 212A, 209B–C). Moreover, ninth, and lastly, lovers strive for *immortality* (207A, 207C–D, 208B–209E). This is ultimately *why* they seek to reproduce, Socrates reports Diotima as saying (206D–E, 208A–D), seemingly meaning that *this* is the final cause. This variety in answers about the ultimate final cause may prompt one to ask which of these it really is. Is it happiness, beauty, or immortality? In fact Plato's thought seems to be that happiness, beauty, and immortality overlap and do not compete with each other. More strongly, they seem to overlap with necessity, that is in such a way that none of them can properly had without the other two, and this despite despite the fact that they can obviously be described, thought about, and even loved separately (as above in the list of this section, 4.1). The ultimate *telos* is attained only by combining them, and so the lover needs to be properly informed about the complete character of her end. However I will not be building on this complexity below, and rather the focus will be on beauty, as in the preceding paragraph (4.4 will explain why).

This is, no doubt, not the only list one can compile of love's properties in the *Symposium*. Let us now consider some objections.

i. "If lovers reproduce their *ideal* selves then they do not produce themselves, or their actual or most typical selves, exactly, so zRz is not instanced as above. For instance the poet at her most typical is not the same as her best poems. (In Kierkegaard's words, "Is he himself *sub specie aeterni,* even when he sleeps, eats, blows his nose, or whatever else a human being does? Is he himself the pure 'I am I'?"[1])

This must be conceded. The *Symposium* cannot simultaneously speak of self-propagation and of the propagation of ideals without conflating selves with ideals.

ii. "Love is never the only object of love in the S*ymposium*, so in this work love does not instance the pattern $\mathbb{R}$. Other loved things include at least happiness, creativity, beauty, and immortality."

But neither the text of the *Symposium* nor $\mathbb{R}$ implies anything this exclusive. In the *Symposium*, we saw, lovers are after many things (satisfaction, beauty, and immortality), so these overlap. As for $\mathbb{R}$, a relation R need not be *only* to R for $\mathbb{R}$ to be instanced. Lovers can love each other as well as loving to love, and to boot they can love sunsets and wedding cakes also. All the other loved things are also welcome to the package, so long as love itself is also on the list. (This is just how $\mathbb{R}$ is defined.)

iii. "$\mathbb{R}$ cannot apply to love if loving *a* implies lacking *a* (200A–B, 201B–C, 203C–D, 204A), because this implies that the lover of love must lack love. But lacking it she cannot have it or relate to it."

This is mistaken because loving *a* implies lacking *a* but it does not imply any failure to relate to *a*. In this way loving is similar to wishing or hoping. One precisely *can* wish for, and hence relate to, what one does not have. Indeed, and as already noted, it would be odd to wish for something that one *does* already have. But we can apply this also to love, so that in loving x one lacks x and x=love.

iv. "But now the lover loves something she herself does (namely loving) and does not have it. How does one not have what one does? How can one lack something one produces?"

This oddity disappears if we recognize degrees of love, as above. Lower degrees aim at higher degrees, see point six in the above list (in this section, 4.1).

v. "Love is never loved most of all in the *Symposium*. It is loved more than some things but not more than all other things. Hence, love does not carry itself to the highpoint on its own scale. But therefore ℝ is not instanced through the LOVE relation in the *Symposium*."

This needs to be admitted.

Thus we see that none of the claims for ℝ made above in this section (4.1) has survived. For not one was exact.

4.2 CREATION (206B–207E, 208B–209E, 210C–D, 211C, 212A)

Now let us inspect the many ways in which the relation of creating is described in the *Symposium*.

First, creation happens in a very basic sense when things persist despite the changes in their parts or aspects. For instance, all of the parts of a body may change and the body can still retain its identity through time (207D–208B). In such a situation the body "creates" itself anew periodically, as in a CREATES a, or aRa. But the same happens with a person's manners, pleasures, and other more mental or spiritual traits as well, so she remains the same individual although she goes through so many changes in different aspects (207E). Hence we seem to have multiple ringlets of aRa in the *Symposium*, for many different material and mental beings will continually be "creating" themselves anew according to it.

Second, in the *Symposium* we encounter biological procreation, which is associated with animals (207A–B). Many animals and humans instance the *eros* relation in seeking to reproduce. As in 4.1, this makes them restless and driven. But what the animals and humans reproduce then is themselves, so, if a=animal, a REPRODUCES a as in aRa.

A third type of creation is artistic (208C–E, 209C–E). But here the same pattern applies once more (aRa), because artists produce themselves. (Ignore for now that this was refuted in 4.1 i.)

Fourth, we also have political creations, as of laws and institutions (210C, 211C), and once again the same pattern may hold, aRa.

Fifth, there are philosophical creations in the *Symposium*, for philosophers produce things when they contemplate the Form of Beauty (210D, 212A). This takes us to aRR at least if philosophers propagate their own philosophical activity in this way. If so then we would have philosophers CREATING CREATING.

Now it is time for objections again.

i. "4.2 was written as if 4.1 never happened. In fact aRa and zRR are not instanced in creative relations in the *Symposium*, because creative relations in this work always aim at something beyond themselves, that is at certain ideal things which the creators themselves do not exemplify, such as immortablity or Beauty. In other words, Plato's ultimate meaning is not conveyed by any autonomous creating any more than it was conveyed by any autonomous loving in 4.1."

This needs to be conceded. Despite this the reader should note that the *approximations* of the self-relations abound in the text of the *Symposium*, so it seems quite likely that Plato intends to produce self-relational patterns at least suggestively even if he does not adhere to them to the letter (on the *Symposium's* literary allusions see Rosen).

ii. "But philosophers do not create the Form of Beauty. Hence the self-creating decreases, instead of increasing, as we rise to the top of the *Symposium's* hierarchy, and this implies that $\mathbb{R}$ is not being instanced. Thus it is not creativity that there is steadily more of as we evolve. But therefore creative activity is also not something self-contained in the *Symposium*. It is not internally driven and so it is not free either. Rather it is subservient to something real that awaits above it: the Form."

This must be conceded. Plato's realism about the Forms (and elsewhere about the Gods) puts a limit on the extent of human creativity. Accordingly, in Plato we are ultimately discoverers and not creators, and so talk of human creativity can never take us to the heart of his philosophy.

4.3 EVOLUTION (208E–209B, 210A–E, 211C–D)

Loves and creations evolve, it was already noted, but how exactly? What are the stages and the relations between the stages? There are three passages on this in the *Symposium*, 208E–209B, 210A–E, and 211C–D, and we will now inspect their commonalities and contrasts (see Wedgwood and Irigaray and Kuykendall for different ways to organize this material, and see Griswold and Gerson on the wider interpretive issues).

The first one says that the lowest type of love is after bodily procreation (which we hereby symbolize as a, 208E). Somewhat superior are the pregnant souls, whose love is of inventions in the arts and crafts (now symbolized as b, 209A). Third we have the love of politics (c, 209A–B). Now a EVOLVES INTO b EVOLVES INTO c, as in $\mathbb{R}$.

In the second passage love is first of a single beautiful body (a, 210A) and secondly of several, indeed of all, beaufitul bodies which share the same beauty (b, 210B). Third, love is of beautiful souls (c, 210B–C); fourth, it is of customs and laws (*d*, 210C); fifth, it rises to love different kinds of knowledge (*e*, 210C–D); and sixth it ends up loving an ocean of beauty as a philosopher and as a thinker (*f*, 210D–E). Here we have an evolution from *a* to *f*, consisting of six points or stages. Thus we have a series much as in the preceding paragraph but with six levels instead of three.

The third passage is a little different from the second. This time *a* is a single beautiful body (211C), *b* is a pair of two beautiful bodies (ibid.), and *c* is the set of all beautiful bodies (ibid.). Next come beautiful customs again (*d*, ibid.) and learning (*e*, ibid.). *f*, finally, is the study only of the Form of Beauty through philosophy, which object will clearly outshine all the ones below it (211C–D).

Now let us compare these three passages to each other. The first (208E–209B) seems to be no more than a sketch of the later two, that is a way of indicating the general direction of the evolutionary progression before individuating its steps more fully. The main difference between the latter two passages, again, is clearly that the second inserts a pair of bodies where the first has a soul. Beyond that difference the two latter passages appear to be intended as conveying exactly the same message, so that the relation of love becomes increasingly intense and more rewarding as it evolves. Its lowest version is animal and the highest one is philosophical.

A interesting implication which Plato himself does not dwell on is that probably each stage in the evolutionary process involves a type of metamorphosis of *eros*, as perhaps especially the second of these passages (that is 210A–E) seems to suggest. For in it *eros* is said to interact with other things in different ways in its different stages, and it is natural to assume that the manners of interaction must accord with their objects. To illustrate, one could not philosophize with an animal or growl like a brute at a philosophers' symposium. Rather, Plato's meaning seems to be that the bodily lover will engage in bodily intercourse, and that among souls *eros* operates as a soul (ibid.). But if so then *eros* may need to be seen as some kind of a force which can assume different shapes according to its evolutionary stage, which thinking coheres nicely with the doctrine of reincarnation which Plato describes in for instance the *Phaedo* (see Chapter 3). The coherence is due to the fact that the same thing (the *eros* or *psyche*) can outlive its various shapes (body, soul, art, politics, and so on). It is as if it dispensed with forms of life in roughly the same way as humans now dispense with their clothes. The humans do not cling to the clothes inseparably, of course, because they can purchase new ones and change according to the season and to the fashions. Just so, *eros*, too, sheds its skin and keeps being reborn in different shapes.

What also seems to fit well with the *Symposium's* thinking as it was interpreted above is Plato's frequently expressed *ethos* according to things should be repaid in kind. Among animal bodies one should act as an animal body, for example, and among philosophers one should philosophize, as noted. This norm goes against many different possible others, such as the very different *ethos* that everyone or everything should be treated the same (whether they are animals or philosophers, for instance) or that one should cling to a particular manner of living independently of one's environment, as if one were a solitary being. For in Plato the Gods and the Forms are solitary, but human beings are not. This fact comes up over and again in Plato's works, and the implication would seem to be that humans need to adapt to their environments until they reach their divine peaks where they can be as independent as the Forms and Gods. This again should not be interpreted to mean that they need only to adjust to the environments, because their effort to rise is supposed to be continuous. Among animals, say, the advised way to act would not be animal quite, for it would involve pressures to rise up the scale to the psyche. This would seem to require that there must be ways to prefigure the psychic life from within the animal life (the only source I know for this is Schelling, who says metaphorically that spirit "sleeps" in physical nature), and so the steps a–f would need to form a smooth continuum. This implied fluidity or absence of sharp margins in the evolutionary process does not appear to receive attention in the *Symposium*, however.

Also the highpoint of the *Symposium*'s evolutionary process raises a crucial question. For on the one hand the text seems to say that the completed evolutionary process ends with the lover's immortality (212A), that is as if *eros* could somehow join the Form of Beauty which culminates its quest; but on the other hand 207C–D and 212A–C suggest that philosophers, too, must remain among humans and propagate *eros*, Beauty, and philosophy in this lower realm, in effect never rising above the limitations of their own species to join the Forms and Gods. But then which of these two competing perspectives is true? They exclude each other because there either is or is not the former, superhuman possibility for humans. In this discussion this latter alternative is trusted over the former one because the mystical unity of the former is too sketchy to explain. The difficulty is specifically that humans, or human loves or thoughts, can at most model themselves on a Form but not melt together with it in any way. What can be humanly done is this: if a Form has the pattern P then our relations of love or philosophy may also instance P, at least roughly. But it is not imaginable how we might become one with P, and so P's eternity and immutability does not appear to make us immortal no matter how me mimic it (cf. 3.9). If this is correct then the evolutionary process aims at a Form which it cannot reach, and this will lead to some issues in the next section (4.4).

Now let us turn to interpret these views in terms of this book's program, that is by means of ℝ. We already noted that we clearly have an evolving series from a to f such that a EVOLVES INTO b EVOLVES INTO c EVOLVES INTO d EVOLVES INTO e EVOLVES INTO f. Now on one level each of a–f is equal to *eros*, so *eros* is continually there in the proces from beginning to end, but on a more differentiated level a=*body*, b=*psyche*, and so on, so *eros* keeps changing its shapes. (This is another situation in which a thing changes though it also stays the same in Plato. For *eros* extends through time though it changes its shape from a body to a psyche, an artist, and so on. In Chapter 3.3 we discussed something similar in terms of EQUALS (or MEANS). Also see Chapter 9 on the "paradox of inquiry" and its solution. As in 3.3 and 9 one may here think of Frege's and Putnam's recent distinctions to make Plato's commitments understandable in the terms of contemporary philosophy.) Now to complete the pattern ℝ we would need a terminus for the series, as in zRz or zRR, but this we do not seem to get for a reason that was already given. This is that the evolutionary progression is not purely self-relational. For it is modeled on the Form of Beauty which is above it and independent from it and which it never joins or melts into. Thus, Beauty lifts us upwards to our freest peak but we cannot rise all the way to its perfect freedom, which is after all superhuman. It lifts us, but only so high as we are able to rise. In one way this spells trouble, as we are about to see.

4.4 LACK (200C–204D, 206A, 207C–D, 212A)

A philosophically interesting relation which recurs in the *Symposium* is one of *lacking* an object (a LACKS b, thus aRb), that is of not having it. There are three main passages about this. First, at 200C–D lovers seek but do not have what they love. Second, at 200C–204D *eros* is represented as a kind of intermediate being which exists somewhere between the higher region of the divine Form and the lower region of animals. This implies that *eros* is not a part of the higher region, even though it strives to be there. Third, at 207C–D humans are said to seek immortality but not to attain it, and 212A may also signify as much. These are three ways of saying that *eros* will always lack its object, so that it is bound to want what it cannot have.

Plato appears to perceive a kind of philosophical dilemma involved in this, because at 200C–D he seems, through Diotima's mouth, to consider the possibility that *eros* can never be satisfied. For would the satisfaction of *eros* not simultaneously spell its annihilation? For is it not impossible or at least irrational to wish for something that one already has? We may now first formulate this apparent paradox—call it the "paradox of ends"—and then inspect the two solutions which the *Symposium* offers to, the first of which is invalid and the second valid (these points are not reflected in the recent literature on Plato or the *Symposium;* cf. Chapters 7–8 and my *Socrates' Criteria* Chapters 2–3).

The precise paradox of ends can be formulated as follows. Happiness consists of wanting what one has, but wanting is rational only when it is of a thing *not* had. Hence, nothing is ever had *and* wanted, so there is no happiness.

We can alter the terms in the paradox of ends so that it concerns a different relation from wanting, such as is wishing or loving, and instead of having we can speak for instance of being. Happiness may as well be termed satisfaction or fulfilment, and despite these variations the paradox will make its appearance in the same way. For example: if fulfilment is wishing to be who you are and one can reasonably wish to be only something one is not then fulfilment is impossible.

How $\mathbb{R}$ pertains to the paradox of ends is seen if R=STRIVES TO BE and the series starting from a and running to b, c, and so on is infinite. So we get a STRIVES TO BE b STRIVES TO BE c, *ad infinitum*. There is no prospect of z STRIVES TO BE z, so there is no terminus.

There are some logical ways out of the paradox that are not philosophically interesting, and we can note a few in passing. It is possible to want to have a because one is not aware that one already has a, which would happen for instance if one sought one's eyeglasses while wearing them, being absent-minded. But though this possibility is logical it does not address the real issue.

What is the real issue? We perceive it by considering some of its philosophical cousins. Social critics sometimes call the quest for social success a "rat race," meaning that one cannot win the race. Like the rat in the wheel, one will forever be running without reaching any external endpoint. More existentially and less socially there is for instance Camus' *Myth of Sisyphus* and Schopenhauer's pessimism. Schopenhauer in particular seems to philosophize rather often in terms that resemble the *Symposium's*, so that his *Wille* is alike to Plato's *eros* and his *Idee* is similar to Plato's Form (I will quote Schopenhauer below). Also the earlier Nietzsche's dichotomy in *The Birth of Tragedy* of the Dionysian will, which breaks all barriers of individuation, and the Apollinian mind, which individuates things or is the principle of individuation, is similar, and probably due to its debt to Schopenhauer. Schopenhauer inherits some of his thinking from ancient India, and we may no doubt identify similar strands of pessimism there. But Plato, from whom Schopenhauer's philosophy also partly derives, responds to the problem in a way that is optimistic and not pessimistic.

Now let us examine why Plato remains an optimist by considering his two solutions to the said paradox, first the worse one and then the better.

The worse answer in the *Symposium* is that even the perfectly satisfied, that is the individuals who have all that they wish for, can still wish for something more, namely to *keep* what they already have (200C–D, 206A). How this is an error is noticed by comparing the following four possibilities:

a) Trump owns one skyscraper and wishes to own one skyscraper. In this event Trump already does own the single skyscraper, so he has no need to wish for it. (This is, so to say, a "dead" utopia.)
b) Trump owns one skyscraper and wishes to own two. In this situation Trump's wish makes sense but in it he is not satisfied, so this is not a portrayal of contented wishing. (In other words, this is not a utopia in the first place, so it is not a "living" utopia either. It is a living place, but not a utopia.)
c) Trump has made sure that he will get to keep his one skyscraper as long as he lives. In this scenario he cannot sensibly wish to keep his skyscraper, because he has already secured that aim. (Here is another dead utopia. Everything has been achieved and only death awaits.)
d) Trump has *not* made sure that he will get to keep his one skyscraper as long as he lives. In this scenario there is room for further wishing but there is no satisfaction. (Thus here there is again no utopia at all, and hence also no living utopia. The aims that have been set simply have not been met yet. Notice also that nothing is different if it is *impossible* for Trump to be absolutely sure that he can own his skyscraper for the rest of his life, for then there would again be no utopia.)

Of course, the logic of this situation will not change if we picture one hundred skyscrapers instead of one or two, because the points concern whatever wishes there may happen to be. Also, we can insert whatever we like for the skyscrapers and for Trump and nothing will change. What this scenario reveals is that the aim of *preserving* something which one has does not take one out of the nihilist's circle.

Before we move on to the true solution let us take note how there is also a second, though a lesser, reason why the option of keeping an attained object is not a suitable aim for the lover. Such a prospect erases the picture which Diotima paints so well at 202C–204D. In that picture *eros* is a seeker for beauty and an intermediate between the beautiful and the ugly, somewhat as a philosopher, seeking knowledge, is midway between ignorance and knowledge (203E–204A). There is no necessity to this picture if keeping an object is a lover's valid aim, for then it is coherent also to paint the lover as someone beautiful who wishes only to never lose her beauty. That picture is not even remotely as interesting as the one which Diotima actually paints. (Why not?

Perhaps because the tension between *eros* and Form makes for the suspense and the real-life interest of Diotima's picture.)

Now let us turn to Plato's better answer. This is that the maximally though still imperfectly happy humans aim to resemble the Form of Beauty as closely as possible without ever managing this exactly, being merely human. For philosophers cannot join the Form in any way in the *Symposium,* and so the run of Gods will always be distinct from the run of humans (207C–D, 208A–B; cf. 4.3 above). On this view all talk of a perfectly happy utopia is not a Platonic prospect, at least in the *Symposium*. It is only regulative, as Kant would say (*Critique of Pure Reason* A312–A320/B368–B377, A508–538/B536–565, A567–571/B595–599).

In closing of this section (4.4) let us consider two objections.

i. "But now we have learned that the liberation of *eros* is impossible. For on the one hand it reaches for the Form, which would kill it, but on the other it cannot love itself either (see 4.1), so it cannot be autonomous or perfect by its own lights. It is doomed to serve what is ulterior, but it can never unite with that ulterior thing. But this is tragic picture of human life, not at all a liberating one. Plato should be categorized as a pessimist like the Hinduists, Schopenhauer, Camus, and the rest."

This ignores the differences of degree. In its lowest versions *eros* is wild with desire and dissatisfaction and very far from the contentment of the divine Form of Beauty (which we will come to in 4.6). At that stage it is virtually blind because its conception of what it is after is still so vague. But it soon grows eyes, evolving to stages of more competence. Its activities gradually receive more definite guidance from the Form, and the closer it gets to the Form the more it finds serenity and satisfaction. Therefore, the situation is not black and white. One is not only *either* perfectly happy *or* else a blind idiot fumbling in a chaos. There is evolution.

ii. "Yet is also remains a fact that humans strive for the Form which they can never quite reach, so we are doomed to be disappointed."

True.

4.5 OPPOSITES (199D–200A, 202C–D, 203E–204A, 206C–D, 207A–C)

The *Symposium* draws a number of oppositions, and perhaps the most significant one in its Socratic portion consists of *eros* on the one hand and the divine Form of Beauty on the other. The Form is perfectly self-contained, simple, unchanged, and eternal (210E–211E), just as the Gods are forever happy, beautiful (202C–D), and knowing (203E–204A). But *eros* is very different. It is dependent on things outside itself (199D–200A) and its relations with those ulterior things are unstable and changing, so it is exactly not self-contained or simple. It is vulnerable and fluctuating. It is the motor of change in the *Symposium*'s world, and in contrast Forms or Gods have no urges to change anything at all (203A). They merely stand there in perfect tranquility. In the meantime, *eros* lives like in another world: it flourishes at one moment, dies at the next, and then it is suddenly reborn once more (203E). It is mortal, not eternal. It is exactly *not* serene and symmetrical, Plato seems to imply. It is prone to *deformity* (206C–D), which contrasts again with the Form. *Eros* is bent out of shape by its wild and insatiable needs (207A–C). It strives to live with the Forms and Gods, but that is not where it lives most of the time. Its life is normally far away from them.

Thus far we might be tempted to think that the setting is black and white, so that *eros* and the Forms or Gods are always opposites. But as already noted several times in this book, it is typical for Plato to recognize numerous shades of gray between these two poles. In the context of *eros* the point is that *eros* strives to come as close to the Form, apparently so as to approximate the Form's perfect independence as closely as possible (212A, also see 210D). Hence what we have is a graded scale as in $a<b<c<d<e<f$, or $aRbRcRdReRf$, where $f=Form$ and $a=eros$ in its lowest version. If *eros* ascends from a then it becomes b, next it is c, etc. But this is to say that we have interpreted the *Symposium*'s meaning by using $\mathbb{R}$ once more, which provides support for this book's inductive thesis. (For the time being we are omitting ...zRR and ...zRz.)

What is wrong with this?

i. "This topic of opposites is forced, because Diotima does not make *eros* into an opposite of the Form of Beauty or of the Gods. Rather, she says that *eros* is intermediate between two poles."

This is so in some respects but not in others. In point of restlessness *eros* is an extreme, not an average. Relatedly, nothing is as intense in desires or as driven to seek *change* as *eros,* whereas—at the other extreme—nothing could care less about reforming anything than a God or a Form (203A). Again, *eros* is dissatisfied, but in the meantime the Gods have beauty, knowledge, and happiness (202C–D). The generaliation is that on some scales *eros* is not extreme but on others it is.

ii. "It is true that Plato's picture in the *Symposium* contains the restless character of *eros,* so the picture is not all about eternal tranquility and sunlight. However the moral which Plato wishes to communicate is not friendly to the unsettled figure of *eros.* On the contrary, the teaching of the *Symposium,* or at least of the portion in it which is narrated by 'Socrates', is that one should get *away* from the unstable life of *eros* as soon as possible. A Nietzsche might value the instability as an end in itself, but Plato is Nietzsche reversed. For

Plato the dynamics and acrobatics of *eros* are only an ill. (This is a further objection that is inspired by Nussbaum. On her views see 4.8 below.)"

This calls for several replies. First, in Socrates' picture it is exactly the mobility (and hence also the instability) of of *eros* which makes it possible for animal-like agents (or patients) to transform themselves into more elevated beings. Stated conversely, if Socrates' world contained no elements which could change radically then he could not advocate a major transformation. But he does advocate just such a transformation, and *eros* is the mobile and unstable agent he elects for that purpose. True, ii is correct that this unstable *eros* is not an end for Socrates. It is but a means. But iii is mistaken none the less in suggesting that the mobility is not *valued* by Socrates or Plato.

A second reply builds on the Kantianism of 4.4. If the attainment of the perfect Form can never be secured in a way that is more than gradual or comparative, then it follows that the instability of of *eros* will never be entirely eradicated. In that event humans will always have to do battle to find their higher selves.

A third reply to ii is that the difficulties involved in securing one's immorality are so severe that *eros* can never die. This is because Plato's Socrates and Diotima seem to say in the *Symposium* that human immorality can be attained *only* through works. For example, an able poet will have a new life through her followers in the next generation (see 4.1–4.3 above). Conversely, the possibility that one could somehow merge with a perfect and eternal Form and attain immortality by that means seems to be denied as well as doubted (see 4.4 above).

4.6 BEAUTY (210E–211C, 211D–E, 212A)

In the *Symposium* the Form of Beauty is presented both as a supremely beautiful end in itself (211A–E) and as a means for propagating beauty in other things (209B, 212A). Accordingly it is to be contemplated as such (211D–E), but it is also a means for ulterior effects (209B, 212A). This is the familiar double function once more (cf. 1.1, 1.2, 1.3, 2.1, and 3.3), and it will now be explained largely as before (for a very different view from mine on the Form of Beauty see Nehamas; I will direct my arguments specifically against a more explicitly anti-Platonic scholar, Nussbaum, in 4.8; Chen and Murdoch are closer to my own view in different ways).

The central point in this book's account is this. There is no intrinsic duality or division in the Form of Beauty itself despite the distinction between the said two functions if we interpret the Form relationally as in $\mathbb{R}$. For in the pattern *RRaRbRcRdR*... the Form of Beauty is first and foremost a relation *R* to R at the extreme left of the series, and in this use R is satisfied in a superlative way. Next the same R also applies further down, that is to a, then to b, c, and so on, where a is less than perfectly beautiful but b is even less beautiful, and so on. Hence, these lower grades of beauty are to the right of the Form in the series $RRaRbRcRdR...$ But now there is nothing dual about the Form of Beauty itself, even though it is both an end and a means, because the same R that is applied first to R itself and then to other things (a, b, ...). But for this reason Plato does not need to be confused between any two meanings. He can have two functions for a single thing in full consistency, so there is no logical blunder.

Now let us compare this view with the *Symposium*'s passages on the Form of Beauty in a little more detail.

The text of the *Symposium* describes the Form of Beauty in two main passages, 211A–B and 211D–E. In the first the key element seems to be that the Form does not inhere in other things (211A–B), and we will do well to focus on this first.

The Form itself is not, for example, *in* a body, *in* a piece of knowledge, or *in* the sky. Lesser beauties are in such other places, as the earlier passages of the *Symposium* have already taught us: there are for instance bodies with *some* degree of beauty, and souls with some, and so on. But *extreme* beauty has no location in any place ulterior to itself. This is to say that the Form is separate or independent, which may be identified as the standard "Platonic" doctrine in metaphysics (cf. Jubien Chapter 3).

Now how does this square with $\mathbb{R}$? Can $\mathbb{R}$ explain this separation or independence in the Form? It can because the separate, Platonic entity is then seen as a relation (R) to the same relation (R) such that the relation is satisfied to a superlative degree in such an application. Why is this an explanation of separation or independence? Because then R relates to R and nothing else is needed, so R is instanced without the aid of anything ulterior such as a or b. In contrast, there would be ulterior entanglements if the only (or else the optimal) way we could have R would be *with a* and *b*, and *not without* their likes. Then R would be a beautiful relation and a and b would be its relata, inevitably. It would need them in order to be anywhere at all. But then the Form *would* be in a body and a psyche, so it would *not* be separate or independent. Thus, by contrasting RR with aRb we actually explain the difference between separation and participation, or in other words the difference between independence and dependence. (In Plato's more colorful language, RR is divine and aRb is polluted by the dirt of this earth.)

Why is separation or indepedence the key element at 211A–B? What is primary about it? It seems to explain the other things said in the same passage (211A–B): that the Form does not change, that it does not perish, that it is not partly ugly, and that it does not seem to be anything but extremely beautiful to anyone. The first two of these four features are intrinsic to a separate, "Platonic" entity precisely because such an entity exists on its own. It cannot be affected by outer things. Nothing will make it rot, for example, because nothing, no rot, can touch it. Nothing will burn it, blow it to pieces, and so on. For it is alone. In terms of $\mathbb{R}$, this point is that Beauty is in a relation purely to itself, as in RR. Relations to externals like a and b could in principle lead to burning, smashing, and so on.

How about the third feature? It is explained by the same RR as above if a relation purely to a relation is partless. If R is to R purely then R is not to anything but R, but this implies that there cannot be any part of R (call that part S, and $R \neq S$) to which R would also apply, and so R must be simple. In other words, R cannot carry any additional luggage or it loses its independence, but if it does not carry any additional luggage then it cannot have parts.

Finally, the fourth feature of not appearing other than extremely beautiful to anyone is explained by $\mathbb{R}$ if we consider that *those who go through the entire evolutionary process* ($aRbRc...$) cannot notice any fault in the Form and that no one can notice the real Form for what it is without going through that process. This is a very different affair from saying that no man in the street would sincerely call or think the Form ugly if he somehow happened to encounter the Form without approaching it to the right background of comparisons and contrasts. For then he would not be appropriately adjusted to "read" it at all, that is to notice it for what it really is. He would mistake it for something else, like for instance for someone's bothersome effort to be provocative by means of an outlandish work of modern art, or for a symptom that he is about to lose his mind (viii–ix will expand on this, still inside 4.6).

How about the second of the two passages on the Form of Beauty, 211D–E? 211E repeats that the Form of Beauty is not mixed with other things, and 211D says that it outshines everything else. The first of these descriptions seems to repeat the Platonism again, that is the claim that the Form is independent of other things, which has here been explained as RR. The second claim, again, appears to be either an assertion of the extreme degree of the beauty of the Form again or else a new way to state that the Form will not appear ugly to anyone (or both). In any case 211C–E does not seem to add anything to 211A–B except colorful imagery.

Now let us have objections.

i. "But Plato's procedure for identifying Beauty seems empirically inductive. For is this not a procedure of collecting cases and then abstracting to a commonality? Socrates notices beautiful bodies, beautiful souls, beautiful artworks, and so on, and then he aspires to say what they share—what beauty is. And indeed it would be strange if his procedure were any different from this, for who would ever intuit beauty spontaneously out of their own minds? Surely one needs first to view paintings of landscapes, ballet performances, and other things. There is no hope of *a priori* answers in aesthetics. Hence, it is sensible of Socrates to proceed inductively, that is by generalizing from cases. But if he is that sensible then we have no need of special symbols like ℝ. Then Plato's lovers simply generalize based on their experiences like everyone else. Everyone is out to out-guess experience, and that is why we generalize. There is no need for anything more exotic."

This objection is mistaken because, as we have already seen in 4, first, the procedure of the *Symposium* implies a constant rise in the degree of value whereas induction does not. In induction the cases collected are of equal value, because they are all equal members of some group (say white swans). Second, the Socrates of the *Symposium* envisions, and engages in, a search for a self-sufficient highpoint, which is not an element in ordinary inductions. Hence, one may have different views about whether Plato's procedure should be the standard inductive one as in i, but in the meantime fact is that it is not (thus also 5.1 about the *Republic* on justice). But none of this implies that Plato's philosophizing is *a priori*.

ii. "Does the *Symposium* ever *actually say* that Beauty is a relation? If it does not then there is no textual basis for that connection. Plato's Socrates says that love is a relation (as in 4.1), and perhaps it would be odd not to view creation as a relation (as in 4.2), but neither of these relations was of a thing to itself as in aRa or RRa, so they did not confirm ℝ. But with Beauty the prospects are only worse for *Plato's Logic*, because we do not even have evidence that it is a relation at all (let alone that it is a relation to a relation). It looks either like a property (a universal), that is something which is had by a spectrum of different individual things or particulars, or else like an individual instance (a particular), that is some individual thing which is especially beautiful. That is how Plato himself portrays things."

One piece of textual evidence for the thesis that Beauty as a relation is at 212A (also see e.g. 209B): Beauty guides the philosopher to propagate Beauty realistically in her environment. But this makes little sense unless Beauty is a model of some kind, and if so then it is a relation. For it needs to be the ideal *for* the environment, somewhat as a stop sign in traffic is a rule *for* the driver to follow. The stop sign is not simply an autonomous work of art. If Beauty did not have such a normative relation to the environing world, and if it were only to be contemplated in divine isolation (which Plato also of course prescribes, at 211C–E), then the philosopher's ambition to use it to change the world around her would be only misled and not especially enlightened. Her reformist project would be ulterior and artificial to the matter at hand. She would be twisting an autonomous object into an external instrument. But this is not how things are in the *Symposium*. Rather, Plato clearly views Beauty *itself* as having a normative relation to a very wide range of things in the world, remote though it is from them, and especially from many of them (such as bodies). Thus, it is not the philosopher's work artificial and external labor that makes Beauty concern so many things. Rather, that relationship derives from Beauty itself.

However the more specific type of relation which the *Symposium* operates with seems to be aesthetic, and this brings us to harmony. Harmony is no doubt a relation, most obviously in music. For as everyone knows since Pythagoras, ratios between different notes make for chords or melodies, and it makes no difference whether the notes are high or low (or played on trumpets or skulls, etc.). But likewise with rhythms: it is the recurrent ratio that makes them. Outside music, take poetic metaphor, which is often seen as an implicit analogy. *The wind blows:* it is as if someone blew. There is a similarity, a recurrence. Rhymes are another structural example. Plots and motives recur between different productions. Architecture is also known to obey forms: such an such for the temple's roof, such for the posts, etc. (3 above and 6 below go into some of Plato's own musical examples. Jaeger is in general a rich source on these matters in Plato. Snell Chapter 9 is a widely ranging introduction to the verbal arts in ancient Greece.)

Now how would one seek to convey a progression of harmonies in terms of $\mathbb{R}$? Without verbs one might write: HARMONY WITH HARMONY WITH *philosophy* HARMONY WITH *politics* HARMONY WITH *art* HARMONY WITH *psyche* HARMONY WITH *animal body* HARMONY WITH *physical entity*. This is a pyramid structure like *((aRb) R (cRd))*, to use its simplest version. (A more complex version which is truer to the text of the *Symposium* is *(((aRb) R (cRd)) R ((eRf) R (gRh)))*; for the different types of things which figure in beautiful or harmonious relations in the *Symposium* are several, not merely two: there are at least bodies, psyches, artworks, political laws, and philosophemes.) Here a and b are e.g. musical notes in which case the first R on the left is the melody or chord which the musical notes form, that is a musical harmony. c and d again are e.g. two terms in a poem, so the third R in *((aRb) R (cRd))* is a poetic harmony, not a musical harmony. Lastly, the middle R in *((aRb) R (cRd))* is the harmony between the first and the third harmonies (i.e. Rs) in *((aRb) R (cRd))*. Thus the middle R is a harmony of harmonies. It is a harmony purely on the level of harmonies, so it does not have the sounds or the language of a *Gesamtkunstwerk,* that is of an artwork which consists of sound *and* words *and* many other things in conjunction). The Form of Beauty is a soundless and wordless harmony, a harmony purely with itself.

iii. "A harmonious relation obtains between *many* things, so one simple thing cannot be harmonious with itself. A symphony can be harmonious because it has many instruments, not one, and a melody can be harmonious because it has many notes, not one. Colors can be in a harmony because they are several, but a single color does not instance harmony. But similarly it is impossible for a simple Form to be in a relation of harmony with itself (more on this in 5.6 when the Forms of the *Symposium* and the *Republic* are compared)."

One reply is to say that if several different colors fit together then they are unified in a whole, and so they are "one" in a certain sense. But what is "one" or unified in a more direct way is simply a single color with no variations or contrasts. Now it is arguable that what is here stated about oneness can be stated also about harmony. If this is correct then a simple can had especially much harmony.

A second reply is that the arts may usually happen to be as in iii but that the perfect, philosophical beauty would be a harmony purely with harmony. The philosopher would learn about pure beauty by studying the different arts, but the apex would take her above them. iii assumes falsely that there is no higher beauty above the arts.

4.7 SPEECHES UPON SPEECHES (ENTIRE WORK)

The *Symposium* is somewhat unusual as a work of Plato's because it is not strictly a dialogue. It is rather a series of speeches. This is not completely outlandish in the sense that the corpus also contains the long speech of the *Apology*, letters, myths, and so on. None the less, most of Plato's productions are dialogues, so we should take that as his standard pattern. Speeches are an exception. But if so then how should we interpret this work containing speeches?

It is easy to assume that the speeches before Socrates' anticipate his because certain motifs recur (this is registered by all readers of the *Symposium*, it seems; see Rosen as an example). Moreover, Socrates enters the stage last and wins the competition that arises between the speakers. But if so then it is natural to seek a progression in the *Symposium*, and if Socrates' speech provides a self-conscious summary of the entire series then the overall structure of the *Symposium* just might be $aRbRcRdReRfRR$, as in $\mathbb{R}$. Here a=*Phaedrus*, b=*Pausanias*, c=*Eryximachus*, d=*Aristophanes*, e=*Agathon*, f=*Socrates*. What would be R? I do not know the answer to that.

4.8 VERSUS NUSSBAUM (RISK)

For Nussbaum Plato's perfectionism is something artificial. If beauty is uniform, she writes, then it is the same whether it is encountered in a body, a soul, an artwork, or elsewhere. And if it is also graded on a single scale, she continues, then it follows that there will no indeterminacy between its instances, for everything will rank in a definite relation to everything else (pp. 178–179). If value is uniform and quantified then all one needs to do is maximize it: one simply chooses whatever has more of it. Conversely, choices cannot be rational if there are incommensurable "islands" of value, as one might put it. If there are only so many separate islands and no ways of comparing them fairly (no "bridges" between them) then choices become arbitrary. Then choices cannot be reasoned or rational.

Nussbaum holds that Plato's Socrates only pretends to "discover" that beauty is this uniform. In reality he only decides to view things in that way: it is Plato's own artificial choice. For Plato indulges in wishful thinking in the hope that the anxieties and uncertainties of human life can be escaped by means of a utopian philosophy (p. 109). But Nussbaum wishes to suggest that things are that irrational in reality, and inescapably. Beauty is not really like Plato wishes it to be. Rationalistic philosophizing provides the thinker the illusion of being in power. Meanwhile the philosophers always remain as powerless as everyone else in the real world. The philosophical fictions are only so many fables told by the insecure. The story-tellers believe in their own stories and thereby lull themselves to sleep (cf. Chapter 8 on the *Gorgias* for more allegations along these lines; Freud and Nietzsche have popularized views like these in modern times, and they have been inspired in part by Schopenhauer, see 4.4).

These are stimulating allegations, but they are mistaken in three general ways. Let us take the matter of *risk* first. It does not seem true to say that the perfectionistic aspirations of artists, politicians, and philosophers are taylored to *avoid* risks, whether in the *Symposium* or in real life. Rather, they appear to engage in risky efforts so as to locate or to produce something fully paradigmatic even at a high cost. In such projects the risk is enormous at least because in them the emotional investments run so deep (cf. Murdoch and Jaeger). For example, if the monument you construct means virtually everything to you then it will be a highly serious affair in your eyes whether it is a success or not. If faults are found in it by worthwhile critics then you will be devastated. Conversely, if you do not invest your energies in any project, *then* you are safe. Then you are satisfied that there are no higher things to reach anyway, and life becomes easy. But thus you avoid risk. You simply conform to a low world of dust and dirt. But it is often the case that artists, politicians, and philosophers aspire to things in idealistic ways, and consequently there is evidence to support the generalization that they, or many of them, risk things. Yet this general fact is misrepresented in Nussbaum. She does not see the crucial role of "higher selves" (Jaeger), but Plato does (cf. especially *Symposium* 206B–C, 206E, 208A–B, 208C–E, 209C–E, and see 4.1–4.3 for discussion).

A second point has to do with Plato's *motivations* for his perfectionism, which Nussbaum seems to by-pass entirely as if they did not exist. For are there no good reasons to seek perfect objects? Is it all just a mistake, a kind of artificial escape, as Nussbaum would seem to have it? In this chapter (4) we have mentioned for instance musicians, architects, mathematicians, and philosophers as persons who may more or less instance the *Symposium's* Platonic thinking in this regard (many of them have been inspired by it as well, e.g. in Antiquity, the Renaissance, and Romanticism; on English examples see Baldwin and Hutton, eds.). Now one frequently finds that persons active in these fields do wish to do something exactly right. Nussbaum is naive to brush all this aside so as to protect the mediocrities and insecurities of everyday life (are they that great anyway?). More than this, Nussbaum herself seems to be unable to advocate feminism (see her pp. 3–4, for example) unless she favors reform. *She* needs a foothold somewhere above the everyday run of things—a Platonic ideal to set above the Aristotelian actualities. (It is not accident that Plato is the feminist.)

Now let us come to the third and final issue, or really a group of issues, which is logical. This has to do with the uniformity of beauty which Nussbaum claims to find in the *Symposium*. Several points need now to be distinguished:

(i) Nussbaum does not *show* that there is no scale for beauty: she only assumes and states that conclusion. But this is a catastrophic assumption for any interpreter of Plato to make because it begs the most central question against him.

(ii) Nussbaum seems to go wrong also in representing Plato's scale in *quantitative* terms, for it is not obvious that the *Symposium* actually implies any numerical values for the gradations of beauty. (It seems that Nussbaum would like to be attacking Bentham and not Plato. She does discuss the *Protagoras*, which is much closer to Bentham, e.g. with quantities of pleasure, see Chapter 10. But it does not follow that the *Symposium's* perspective is the same.)

(iii) The uniformity of beauty should not sound too *threating* if we interpret with sufficient abstractness. For as in $\mathbb{R}$ the picture is that almost nothing except the Form of Beauty literally has beauty at all, and this makes the allegation of hellish uniformity quite exotic. For Beauty is perfectly instanced in the Form, but it is barely recognizable in animals or physical entities (see 4.3). But hence these things are *not* very much like each other. Again, human bodies and souls have beauty only in an approximate or comparative sense, not strictly, because they are only vaguely beautiful. But if so then how homogenous a set are these things, the physical entity, the animal, the human body, and the human soul? Not very. For all of them instance beauty only in such a rough or distant way. But in this way the uniformity which Nussbaum envisions is simply not there in the text, and so her dreaded dystopian vision is her own nightmare, not Plato's dream.

(iv) Things are not drastically different even if we assume that the *Symposium does* seek a quantitative scale, contrary to the facts. For all things with *weight* are not very similar though they are certainly ranked on a quantitative scale, for example, so it would be strange to think of them as something depressingly uniform. Again, in an economy all goods and services have *prices,* but this does not make them similar to each other.

4.9 SUMMARY

This chapter (4) began with sections interpreting the *Symposium* on love (4.1), creation (4.2), evolution (4.3), lacking (4.4), opposites (4.5), beauty (4.6) and speech-making (4.7), and after this we compared this book's views to a major scholar's in 4.8.

NOTE

1. *Concluding Unscientific Postscript*, p. 271. Of course, Kierkegaard's challenge is not to Plato but to the Hegelians of his time.

Chapter Five

The Republic

The *Republic* defines justice as a relation of a just person or psyche *a* back to *a,* as in *aRa* (and hence ℝ). The surprising thing about this is that now the just are just to themselves, not to others. They are not moral, kind, or fair to others. But how can it then be appropriate to call them just? Plato's thinking is that the just flourish according to their own talents. Justice in this sense is reaping what one sows, as the Bible says. Long before Jesus also Hammurabi had a similar ethos: "An eye for an eye, a tooth for a tooth," and Pythagoras is among the further ancient sources. Armed with this view of justice Plato constructs his utopia, the Kallipolis. There everyone lives by this measure, attending to her affairs and not meddling with what is not properly her own. The second main topic of the *Republic,* namely the Form of the Good, is also primarily an internal affair, I argue. In the terms of the Sun Allegory, the sun does not only illuminate all visible objects for the eye to see, because what it illuminates most is itself: it is after all the brightest object by far. The Cave Allegory is plain that the sun is itself the most worthwhile thing to see. Thus, it is not for the lakes and the trees that one escapes from the cave, though they are also worthwhile: the ultimate object is the sun. Without metaphors, the Good is a model for other things too, yes, but especially it is a model for itself. Hence it is the first formal cause in a hierarchical series of formal causes, *RRaRbRc..*, as in ℝ.

This chapter (5) consists first of four sections about justice (5.1–5.4), then of a single one about God (5.5)—which operates as a bridge between the topics of Justice and the Form of the Good—and then of three sections on the Form of the Good (5.6–5.8). This approach is taken because justice and the Good seem to be the two main topics of the *Republic,* and other topics are discussed only as aspects of these two (justice or goodness). For instance, the analogy between psyches and cities is here taken to be a feature of justice, not an independent theme. Similarly, questions about knowledge or mathematics are only some of the many that arise in connection with the Good, but in the *Republic* they are not objects of interest for their own sakes. However, both justice and goodness *are* of independent interest. Neither is a function of the other. They are separate at least logically, that is because of the difference between *aRa* and *RRa*, as in the preceding paragraph. But in Chapter 6 I further clarify their apartheid by arguing that justice is the first *efficient* cause (Good being the first formal cause, as noted; see endnote[1] on this complication).

Throughout Chapter 5, and especially in section 5.9, I argue against the prevailing view that justice and goodness are properties or universals. This is a clumsy analysis of Plato's logic, but it is popular. Especially mistaken are those views which think of either as a simple property, for this makes the topics inexpressible and mystical. However also the complex properties of recent scholars like Reeve are irrelevant. For justice and the Good need to qualify as intrinsically compelling, and as very different from other things. Otherwise the whole idealistic edifice of the *Republic* crumbles to pieces. Reeve is too concerned to make Plato seem like a normal American philosopher of the twenty first century. If he were that then he would not be the great idealist that he is.

5.1 SIMONIDES (331C–332C)

Early in *Republic* I, Socrates evaluates Simonides' definition of justice. Simonides' view goes in the right general direction, Socrates implies, but it is too imprecise to be exactly true. Now let us first (A) inspect the key difference between Simonidean and Socratic justice, then (B) consider how vague, initial intuitions like Simonides' can be sharpened into precise accounts like Socrates', and finally (C) reply to an objection to this perspective.

A. As 331E and 332B–C note, Simonides *means* to say that it is just that one gets what one deserves, but he has a clumsy way of phrasing this. The discrepancy is not only between the bad language and the good intentions, however. For also the thought contents are amiss: Simonides' grasp of justice is not essential or principled enough, and its associations are too superficial, arbitrary, and conventional.

An image of my own design will help to see what is involved in this logically. Picture that the target lies northward from Simonides and that Simonides shoots roughly northward but that his arrow still misses the bull's eye by several meters. Then Simonides is not *wholly* wrong, so it would be false (or misleading, or uninformative, or clumsy) to say merely that his definition is simply false. For he could do much worse. He could shoot west, or indeed south, or he could straight into the ground or upwards into the sky. He could even fail in some manner to shoot at all! But this imagery is *graded,* of course, in the way that Plato's thinking requires according to this book (see 1.1 for the simplest generalization). For in his works there is not a simple binary evaluation as in *true/false*, *black/white*, *1/0*. There are several different levels, as in *1: 2: 4: 7*, *black: gray: white*, etc.

But in what sense is Simonides off-target at all? Why is he not right on the mark? He is naive about the *kinds of things* that each person deserves, Socrates teaches. For he says that justice amounts to giving to people what they *own,* and this implies that one should pay one's debts (and also e.g. that one should not steal). But as Socrates notes, the debtor could be insane and the debt could consist of weapons. For debtors and debts can be like this. Yet it would not be just to pay the debt in that situation, Socrates implies. (Why not? We are probably to imagine the debtor hurting people arbitrarily, because insane persons do not in general know what to do or why, and weapons give a person the power to inflict physical harm on others.)

But then what would be *on* target? As we will see in 5.3–5.5, Socrates defines justice roughly as reaping what one sows (5.3–5.5 give the references). Now, this is clearly different from having what one *owns,* for one may own things one has not "sowed," or produced (and conversely). I personally did not make this computer or any of these clothes, for example, and yet I own them. In utopia there are only symmetrical or reciprocal relations everywhere. Criminals are their own victims, doctors cure themselves. Socratic justice is *purely* reciprocal, as we will see by comparing it with other conceptions of justice in B (5.3–5.5 and Chapter 6 will elaborate on this same view of justice in the *Laws;* cf. 7 and 8 on the *Lysis* and the *Gorgias* and 3.7 on reincarnation in the *Phaedo*).

B. The way in which Socrates comes to find fault with Simonides' view of justice can seem at first to accord rather badly with ℝ. For the logic of Socrates' argument may appear inductive. For it is easy to take Simonides to say that it is *always* just to pay back one's debts and the above scenario with insanity and weaponry looks like a *counter-example* to the generalization. This logic would consist of something general and then also of the many particular things of which that generalization consists (or which it implies). If this is how Socrates reasons then his reasoning would be on a par with inductive generalizations like *All swans are white*, which generalization is refuted if a non-white swan is found. More widely, if this is what Platonic philosophers are to do then they resemble empirical scientists in a rather general way, because empirical science is known to be inductive (cf. Losee).

Things are quite different with ℝ, however. If ℝ is the pattern of Platonic or philosophical reasoning, as I argue that it is thoughout this book, then the way we philosophers should reason is not so much aligned with the empirical sciences. For then reasoning is not inductive. It is more exotic. Why so? $\mathbb{R}$ is not made up of universals and their instances but of hierarchies (this suffices as a description of $\mathbb{R}$ for the time being, though it is not the full story). If $\mathbb{R}$ is used then a view (e.g. about justice) is not simply a generalization about individual cases which generalization is flatly right or wrong depending on whether it covers a given spectrum of individual cases (which is the situation with *All swans are white*). Rather, a view is more or less adequate; there are degrees.

Let us consider now how this graded perspective makes sense with regard to justice by comparing some different standards of justice. I and II are familiar from above:

I. Socrates' view (from A above and especially from 5.3–5.5 below) according to which one reaps what one sows. The simplest version of this is that you do everything to yourself: aRa. You=a, your deed=R. (For simplicity I omit the difference between is and ought until 5.2 and 5.3.)

II. Simonides' view from A above, i.e. that it is just to pay one's debts. This is that aRb requires bRa. What a donates to b, b should donate back to a. Now DONATING is more narrow and arbitrary a relation than in I, and moreover the complex is social, because $a \neq b$.

III is an interesting variation which resembles both I and II:

III. At 332A–B Simonides' view is said to be that one should be friendly to one's friends and hostile to one's enemies, paying each back in kind. This is that aRb requires bRa. What a does to b, b should do back to a. This III is an intermediate between I and II because III's relation is not aribtrarly restricted as in II and yet III is social like II.

IV and V are some famous relatives of Socrates and Simonides from the mainstream of moral philosophy:

IV. Jesus' Golden Rule and Kant's Categorical Imperative tell us to treat others in the way that we wish to be treated by them (though already Confucius says this, and so may several other ancient East Asian sources). Thus aRb if a wishes that bRa. This is social and reciprocal again. (However there are a few differences, chief among them that harm may now be excluded if one would not wish to be treated in a hostile way by one's enemies. Additionally, some self-sacrificing Christians and Kantians may *not* wish to be rewarded for their kind actions, because such rewards would make their kindness impure.)

V. Contractarian conceptions of justice say that persons should *negotiate* with each other concerning how they should treat each other (cf. *Republic* 358E–360D). Hence *aRb* if *aSb* such that *S*=SIGNS A BINDING CONTRACT WITH and *R*=ACTS ACCORDING TO THE CONTRACT. This *R≠S* complicates the formula further. The contracts need to come to have force *outside* negotiations. (Additionally, in IV each *individual imagines* what might be just, but in V there is collective bargaining about this, and this may or may not mean that the reciprocation goes deeper. That depends on where real reciprocation is. Is it easier to imagine alone or to negotiate with another? Both can deceive.)

Finally, VI is an influential position which is already quite remote from Plato (outside the *Protagoras,* at least; see Chapter 10 on that book):

VI. Utilitarians say that happiness is to be maximized, and this does not per se involve *any* reference to reciprocation or symmetry. For if you produce coats, for example, then for the utilitarian you deserve a maximal amount of happiness, but likewise if you are a flutist. Shoemakers get: happiness, gold diggers get: happiness, teachers get: happiness, etc.: *aRh, bRh, cRh.* This is in general a very *non*-reciprocal way of defining justice.[2]

I–VI are not, of course, the only conceptions of justice in or outside Plato. (At *Charmides* 161B–162B the just do everything for themselves, so their lives are entirely self-sufficient. They make their own food, write their own books, etc., somewhat like the yeoman farmers idealized by Thomas Jefferson. At *Republic* 359A the conventional view of justice is said to be that to obey the law of the land is just, whatever it be. This is "legal positivism" as in Bentham or Kelsen. Thracymachus says law is based only on physical power, 338D–339A. Cf. 7 on the *Lysis* and 8 on the *Gorgias.*) But from I–VI we can already tell that if Socrates is right about justice (with I) then II–VI, which differ from his view (I), are not all *equally* false. For, minimally, each of II–V is closer to I than VI is. In other words, if pure reciprocation (as in I) is ideal, then any impurer reciprocation (as in II–V) will be less ideal and total non-reciprocation (as in VI) will be non-ideal. Socrates' *Ur*-logos is at once elementary and extreme.

C. Here is an objection to me (in quotation marks).

"The procedure for determining that a hypothesis has the precision of Plato instead of the imprecision of a Simonides is not ℝ but the familiar conception by induction (familiar from Aristotle's generalizations about the pre-Platonic Socrates). For if one needs to determine whether some hypothesis x is a specific enough or/and a general enough to cover only and/or all of *j* (for justice), hence equating *x* with *j* as in *x=j*, then all one can do is consider a series of cases. Is *x* just also if... such and such? Is it if someone is insane? Is it if someone is cruel, or if someone makes a mistake?, etc. But this is an inductive process, and ℝ is not, so ℝ is wrong."

This deserves three replies.

The first is that arguably *both* ℝ *and* possible worlds are involved in Socrates' philosophical method, because it consists of aiming at a maximum of self-consistency (as in *zRz* or *zRR*) *by* reflecting on possible scenarios (e.g. that the debtor be mad). This would imply that Plato's text allows for several different interpretations all of which are true (which would count as no surprise given that Plato's texts are often so rich in associations; a simpler source would not permit of as many alternative explanations because it would not involve as many overlapping phenomena; cf. 3.4 and 4.7).

A second reply concedes less. For it is not exactly *alternative possibilities* that Socrates' philosophizing requires. What is involved is really the *internal coherence* of the just agent (thus 5.2–5.5 below). The whole method circles around this central aim. Accordingly, the mad weapon owner needs to be seen as lacking this ideal integrity. He is *disintegrated* in a way that a competent shoemaker in action is not. After all, the mad weapon owner will not know where to use her weapons or what for, and her injustice may stem from *this*. (To illustrate the point, one might compare her to an ape seated at a computer, the ape not knowing how to use the machine properly. It does not know how to spell words as commands or to type, how to select between different windows, or in general what a computer is good for. Consequently the ape might use the computer simply as a building block with other pieces of furniture; but if so then the ape would not realize the computer's function. It is not a great chair, for example, but it is excellent for processing texts or pictures. But this is just to say that the ape would be badly adjusted to the machine, somewhat as the insane debtor would be badly adjusted to the proper use of any weaponry.) 5.2–5.5 expand on this.

Third, it does not sound right that equations can be weighed only as inductions, for sometimes relations between terms are more intimate. Conceptual analysts know this from analytical relations: one need not make a survey to discover whether all bachelors really are unmarried. In a different vein, logicians since Zeno of Elea know the negative method in which one proves *p* by assuming *not-p* and deriving a contradiction. This does not require any survey of everything (at its simplest the course is run already if *not-p implies q*, and *q implies not-not-p*, for then we know that *p*). But it could be that Plato's formula for justice is like this, and the objector is not entitled to assume that it is not. We can study it further with an open mind.

5.2 INTERNAL AND EXTERNAL (357A–368C)

The *Republic*'s Book II opens with a distinction between means and ends, but it soon associates rather many things with both halves of this dichotomy:

A. 357B–C: Justice should turn out to be *intrinsically* valuable (like health, sight, knowledge; cf. 358C–D). The speakers clearly hold that justice is valuable intrinsically *and* instrumentally (like exercise or medication for the sick, 357D–358A), but these two claims are here divorced from each other, because the intrinsic claim is seen as the more interesting one. It is contested in ordinary life, for it is conventional to think of justice as a socially necessary pain (358A–367A).
B. 357A–B, 358C–D: Justice should also qualify as *more valuable than* injustice, and in *every* situation or in *every* way (357A–B). Thus the end is not simply valuable as such or in *isolation* as for instance in Moore's *Principia Ethica* Chapter VI. Rather, it is juxtaposed with an opposite. Moreover the end should rank above its opposite in every world. (Notice that this contest is among unequals, because if the opposite of an end wins in *some* world, then the opposite wins altogether. The opposite does not need to win *half* the time or *all* the time, but the end does need to win *all* the time. In numbers, the end's success rate must be perfect, at a 100 per cent, but the hurdle for the opposite is set at a mere 1 per cent, or more exactly at 0< per cent, so even e.g. 0.001 would suffice.)
C. 359C–361D: *Real* justice differs from *pretended* justice, and in general only the latter pays off in *external* rewards. For the Gods as well as humans reward those who pose as just, but no external rewards, and various punishments, can be expected by the authentically just (361D–362C). Due to this, real justice comes at a high price, because it involves no external rewards at all. Conversely, injustice is by comparison very useful, if injustice is only made to seem like justice. For no one in power will look behind the masks. To them the surfaces suffice. This accounts in a way for A above as a version of the means/ends dichotomy, for now ends proper (such as justice) are not means to *any*thing. They must be entirely pure.
D. 366E–367A: Justice is instanced inside the individual's *psyche,* whereas the outward benefits described in C are material. For justice is an inherent force in the just person's soul, and it is not detectable to other humans or Gods (366E)! Thus, as in Chapter 3 there is a rough suggestion here that the psyche is private and that material affairs are not, and this would explain the association in C above that others are not likely to detect how just one is (on psychic justice in the *Republic* see Krämer 1959 pp. 91–96 and Jaeger vol. 2 pp. 354–357; also see Santas and Lear; 5.7 will return to this).

We may summarize A–D as a series of dualities:

- ends/means (A above).
- always/sometimes (B).
- real/apparent (C).
- psyche/body (D).

Plato sides, of course, with the first member of each of these four pairs. Why? His overall object seems to be to bring about a sweeping moral change. For if it turned out that justice is intrinsically rewarding as a real presence in the individual's psyche, then individuals would have reason to stop monitoring *each other* to make sure that *others* are acting justly, and their interest would rather be in ensuring that they *themselves* are just (367A). Thus justice would become each individual's internal affair and the social pretensions and policing of others would become superfluous.

We may, once again, analyze Plato's meaning in terms of $\mathbb{R}$. For Plato seeks the purity of an extreme. He wants to identify a as justice such that a has as little in possible in common as possible with its contrary, z, and a and z stand at opposite ends of the spectrum R as in $aRbRc...\,...yRz$ (cf. especially 361B–D as evidence for this view). On this way of thinking, one may be either entirely intrinsic and pure in one's motives or else at least a little tarnished by outward or superficial motives and forces. In the latter case one would already concede at least one's little finger to the devil: to opportunism, to contingency, to bodily powers. But one would then have given just so much way to something other than proper authority. (It is a matter of tilting scales.) Yet not so with the pure a. For such an a would consist of an honest relationship with oneself (as in aRa). In such a relationship there would be no one to fool, and nothing to purchase, and one would only be faced squarely with oneself. (The reader may consider this a kind of anarchism. But it is a *spiritual* anarchism, for now the presupposition is that each individual *has* a private conscience. Moreover, this conscience cannot tell one to do just any old thing: it says only that one reaps what one sows. It cannot tell one to trust Ron Hubbard or to buy cocaine. It is not lawless.)

5.3 JUSTICE (370A–B, 374A–D, 397E, 430E–431B, 441C–442E, 443B–444B)

The *Republic*'s definition of justice requires a political comparison:

A. 370A–B: Individuals' abilities vary, so some are more suited for some tasks and some for others (370B). Moreover they should specialize accordingly, tending to their own affairs (370A).

B. 374A–D and 397E: A cobbler is to stick to cobbling, a farmer to farming, a soldier to soldiering, and so on. Hence, a pilot should not do cobbling: the pilot is for piloting. Similarly, the soldier should stay away from money-making.

However these seemingly political generalizations are only so many metaphors or similes for what really occurs only inside the individual psyche (368C–369B):

C. 441C–442E, 443B–444B: Just as the professionals of A and B above specialize in the utopian city, the utopian psyche has specialized parts. But the psyche's labor is internal, not external (443D). It masters itself (ibid.) by making its different parts focus according to their abilities (443D–E). By contrast, an unjust psyche's different parts would meddle with each others' affairs (444B), just as a political utopia would be ruined if individuals did not devote their energies to what is proper to them. Thus the psyche must impose an order on itself.

Is C paradoxical? Consider:

D. 430E–431B: Here Plato seems to say that self-mastery is unintelligible because then a MASTERS a. At first sight one might take this for a protest against the logical pattern aRa; but that would not really be charitable, because aRa is obviously sensible in many versions, e.g. (to use banal examples for the sake of simplicity): a TALKS ABOUT a, a KNOWS THE NAME OF a, a IS THE SAME AS a. Thus the issue seems to be with the specific content for R, i.e. MASTERS. This content may be in fact be nonsensical for aRa in the way that OVERTOPS was in 3.11. For a IS TALLER THAN a and a IS MORE POWERFUL THAN a may be gibberish in exactly the same way. For no a IS GREATER THAN a in any way. Thus the problem seems to be with the content and not the form. Plato seems to concede this in relating the soul to itself without qualms at *Republic* 409A. (Cf. 5.6 for the *Republic*'s coherent way of treating relations which do not satisfy aRa, and 6.1, 6.13–6.14, 7, and 8 for more on self-mastery.)

Now it should be plain that in the *Republic* justice amounts to reaping what one sows and that its logical pattern is aRa. (I do not maintain that the *Republic*'s tripartite psychology coheres with this well. Rather, my suspicion is that it is confused.[3])

What is questionable now?

i. "It is ironic that Plato, the universal genius, should defend specialization (says Jaeger vol. 2 p. 223). It is as if the libertine set up a dictatorship, making rules for everyone but himself. For Plato writes poetry and myth freely, but he forbids it of others (in *Republic* Book X). He speculates about politics (*Republic*) as well as nature (*Timaeus, Laws*), language (*Cratylus*), and everything else that he can find: but others must specialize."

Contra Jaeger this book does not find Plato to be a universal genius. The generalization is rather that he *thinks* about much, and *speculates* a great deal, so his *mind or psyche* is multidimensional (because he studies all the first causes: origins, purposes, elements, authorities). He is in general *the intellectual,* and he ranges very widely in *that* way. But that does not make him into a universal genius: he is not the engineer and visual artist that Leonardo da Vinci is, for example, and he does not study colors, plants, minerals, literatures, and so on like Goethe. He is not the representative, well rounded human being but the boldest idealist. (He has two left hands, as someone said about Emerson.)

ii. "In the *Republic* Plato sets out to show why one should be moral, but all he ends up showing is why one's psyche should be orderly (see Sachs for this view; Annas' reply to Sachs in 1978 and Vlastos' "Justice and Happiness in the *Republic*" in 1981 differ from my reply below). Hence, though the *Republic* says many things in defence of justice, it only sidesteps the real difficulties, which are moral. For, as every ordinary person knows, one cannot be 'just' to oneself any more than one can do favors for oneself. Moreover, no one needs reasons or values to learn to become kind to herself, because she is inclined to act that way anyway, so there is no pressing philosophical problem in this area. The real difficulty about justice is why one would play fair with others, and even if one could get away with cheating (cf. *Republic* 358E–360D)."

A first reply is that clearly Plato does not even *attempt* to model justice on ordinary conventions. But sidestepping the conventions of men in the street is *typical* for him, because he also sees democracy as unfree, the psyche as a teeming city, human life like a cave, etc. It is clearly not a priority for him to abide by common sense. He is prepared to shock.

But on what can he base instead? Scientists routinely by-pass everyday views of things, and they are entitled to do so because of the empirical evidence they consider. But what evidence does Plato have? He cannot use a telescope or a microscope to investigate justice, because justice can not be encounterd empirically (at least according to his own philosophy). The answer is that he reasons. But this can lead to results as well. For it turns out, by means of reasoning, that justice stands for even scales. If a weight n is placed on one side of the scale, the same number n belongs on the other side. The two sides must be equal. *That* is fair, no matter what any humans may happen to believe. Formally this is *nRn,* as in $\mathbb{R}$.

But if that is so then certain consequences follow. For it so happens that this view of justice is not essentially *inter*-subjective, contrary to ii. For we can also have *intra*-subjective versions of it (and 3.7 distinguished "ethics" and "morals" on this basis; cf. 3.13). But this refutes ii. Justice is a matter of reasoning, just as logic and mathematics are matters of reasoning (though the reasoning is not always exactly the same), and this reasoning shows that justice is not what it is ordinarily said to be.

iii. "Is there then no foundation for morals in Plato?"

3.13 already answered this, arguing that Plato's speakers become fair to each other in learning from each other. Hence, it is not their justice that makes them kind to each other, but their curiosity, their honesty, etc. (Gadamer p. 75 says instead that friendship with oneself is a *precondition* to friendships with others, but in my view this would make morals utopian indeed because Platonic self-friendship is so rare and difficult to attain, see 5.5. Thus it is the educational process that is moral, not its utopian result. Jaeger vol. 2 p. 201 compares Plato's educational utopia to other ancient Greek utopias, noting on p. 199 that for Plato the decisive thing is not, say, to uphold a rigid, Spartan tradition, to enforce Hippodamus' geometric order in urban planning, or to develop the economy. Plato is indeed all about *education,* also in the *Laws,* see 6. On ancient Greek utopias also in fiction literature compare Ferguson.)

iv. "Does *evil* require the same code, as Hammurabi says? Should criminals be made to feel the pains they inflict on others? The question arises because, after all, we are not all angels; so if we all act on our talents and inclinations then the results will not always be merry. For among us there are also sleeping tyrants and brooding sadists (the twentieth century witnessed extremes in this area: Mengele, etc.). We are not all merely waiting to play the flute and to speculate about the heavens. Again, if utopia is defined as a place where each individual pays for her deeds then we need to call that place a 'utopia', perversely, in which very negative things happen: shooters are shot and torturers are tortured (and who can torture them without deserving to be tortured in turn?). But surely utopia should be a happy place!"

The myth of Er envisions punishments in the here-after, not only rewards, so it promises hell for some and heaven only for others (see 5.4). However the issue of punishment is not treated seriously until the *Laws* (see 6.9). To anticipate what 6.9 will say, iv overlooks Plato's utopianism. For unlike e.g. Hammurabi Plato does not use his standard of justice to judge *present day* humans. Rather, it is the citizens of utopia who *would* reap what they sow. Why so? Because responsibility is a precondition of justice. After all, if a criminal acts badly due to an external force, say due to a drug's influence or because her parents beat her, then she is not to blame. In the *Laws'* world, only God is perfectly responsible, because God is the self-mover. We humans can only learn to be more or less divine, and to the extent that we learn that we begin to reap what we sow; but we are not like that automatically. To this background, it is fitting for Plato to say that criminals are not brought simply to *suffer* in Magnesia (the *Laws'* utopia). Rather, what they require more than anything is a sturdy theological education. For this will liberate their psyches! Hence the matter is altogether more complex than iv says.

v. "Let us examine this supposedly just *ethos* a little further. Is it to be interpreted literally as *the* just code? If yes, each individual psyche should reap *only* what it sows, and *all* of what it sows. But then we should each of us reinvent the wheel, and we would constantly be paying for our mistakes. Yet, if Plato's utopia is a place in which things are in general thus, then it is a terrible place, a dystopia! For it mut be extremely backward and painful. What really is the wiser attitude is actually to often forgive people's sins and to favor social co-operation (and Jesus says these things too)."

This is again to overlook that justice is a perfectionistic ideal for Plato. It is extremely difficult or impossible for humans to live by it. (See 5.5 below on God's justice and Chapter 6 on the *Laws*.)

5.4 ER (614B–621D)

The *Republic* closes with the myth of Er which repeats the same definition of justice as above but in more hyperbolical and colorful terms:

A. 615A–B: After death, persons are paid back manifold for what they did while alive. The unjust face tenfold penalties for their crimes (615A–B), suffering ten times the same pain that they previously inflicted on others (615B). On the positive side, the just and the pious are also paid back in kind (615B), reaping ample rewards. The number ten probably does no real work here and the point is only that all perpetrators will eventually be caught. But also, and quite abstractly, the ultimate fate of each person accords with the person's own deeds, so that e.g. shoemakers get shoes (or especially large or many shoes), quite as in 5.1–5.3 above.

But before long Plato is bound once again to complicate his picture somewhat:

B. 617D–618B: Persons choose how to live, but their choice is *not* perfectly informed. For in Plato's heaven the object of the choice is not a fully laid out biography but a mysterious *lottery ticket.* One may end up famous or a beggar, an animal or a tyrant, etc. Thus, the individual chooses, yes, but the outcome of the choice is never clear at the moment when the choice is made.

A little later Plato adjusts the setting further:

C. 618B–620D: The chooser always makes a choice *based on* the particular personality or character that she has or is, so the choice does not occur in vacuum. It is not a clean beginning from zero. Choosers must consider what will suit them and choose accordingly (618B–619B). A chooser can choose to become a tyrant and regret the decision because of the terrible things she will do to her children (619B). Some will choose to be animals, like swans, nightingales (620A), lions, eagles (620B), or monkeys (620C).

Now let us draw three lessons from these points (A–C).

The first is that in A Plato very clearly confirms the view of justice articulated in his name in 5.1–5.3. For the just reap what they sow, and so Hammurabi is at least roughly right by his lights.

Second, and additionally to the first point, in A–C Plato obviously thinks along the lines of the ethic of reincarnation articulated in Chapter 3 (see 3.7 on *Phaedo* 79E–84B). Thus the issue which the choosing individual faces is not as in e.g. the Golden Rule or the Categorical Imperative, because it is not about what *everyone* should do. Rather, the choice extends in personal time—not in social space. It is about what one can favor also in one's future lifetimes. (This gives us more confidence about Plato's *ethos*. It is not essentially moral at all. In certain ways it is existentialistic!)

However there are also some more problematic implications, which we can note briefly.

First, A–B (and especially 618C) presents us human individuals with one, decisive choosing situation for our *entire* lives, that is as if there were only *one* opportunity to make the fundamental choice (whenever that is). This can seem to accord well with the reincarnationist ethic, because now we would make some one grand decision and our entire biographies and future lifetimes would be determined as a result. (We would be a little like totalitarian dictators, repressing all our future selves at once.) Conversely, we would not get to shift directions later (like Plato's democractic personality at *Republic* 561C–E), so we would not have the opportunity to learn from our mistakes. But is this entailed by the reincarnationist ethic? In fact it is not, because it is imaginable that we form our biographies gradually, not suddenly, even if the doctrine of reincarnation is assumed. Thus, the myth of Er seems to slip a little to the wild side, saying things which do not belong properly in Plato's own program.

Second, Er includes the lottery of B above, and this element of contingency is not easy to factor into Plato's *ethos*. For the consistent picture that we would get *without* the contingency is that individuals should strive to plan their lives with a very extensive view of the consequences of their decisions (very extensive, because the effects extend beyond death), but this picture is ruined if (too much) contingency is added into it, because this would entail that the extensive effects cannot be *determined*. For no one could do long term planning if enough depended on chance or the unknown. But consequently the contingency, or too great an extent of it, would tell us that an *ethos* of reincarnation is actually impossible. Thus again Plato the poet seems to overstep his bounds.

Third, the opportunism of A robs us of the pure motives advertized in 5.2. For in 5.2 Plato said that justice is to be its own reward, but A says that it will be externally rewarded, and manifold. (What is perhaps even more alarming is that even *before* the myth of Er begins Plato's Socrates says that virtue is rewarded in heaven: 613E–614A. For due to this we cannot excuse Plato's blunder as merely poetic. Even some of his normal prose is contaminated!)

It is not easy to say how one should integrate these three points into Plato's overall position. Here that question must simply be set aside because there is more important ground to cover.

5.5 GOD (377E–392C)

The educational program of the *Republic* begins from physical exercise and narratives (376E), which is traditional enough. But the contents of the narratives that children need to hear should not be traditional, Plato says. Why not?

A. 377E–391E: The Gods of the traditional myths are too often shifting and deceptive, like magicians (380D). They change shape according to circumstance, misleading us humans. They are free to cheat, much like the poet Archilochus (365C), Gyges with his secret ring (359C–360D), or, apparently, the trickster deities of many traditional religions. But this will no longer do, Plato preaches. Why? Apparently the traditional Gods can not even be recognized properly *as* Gods in many cases (see B below). For Gods are *respectable,* not tricksters. They are role models. Hence, if Gods are portrayed in traditional ways, as in e.g. Homer and Hesiod, then Gods lose their authority.

B. 380E–382E: The Gods really worth learning about do not *change* as in A above. How is this known about them? Because the truly instructive role models would be perfect, and if x is perfect then x cannot change voluntarily or involuntarily (380E–381C). x cannot change voluntarily because a perfect being could not possibly wish to change into a less perfect being. But x cannot change involuntarily because, being perfect, *x* cannot be at the mercy of external forces (ibid.). (But an imperfect *x* is not a completely worthwhile role model.)

C. 380E–382E, 387B–E: In accordance with B above, the Gods (being perfect) are entirely self-sufficient or autonomous (380E–381A, 382E, 387D–E). If, then, the purpose of the educational narratives is to make their auditors want to be like the narratives' heroes (see A–B above and previous endnote), then the lessons learned from the proper type of education consist of lessons exactly in self-sufficiency or autonomy (387B, 387D–E). (In other words, Plato's educational program is about self-reliance! His is not a suppressive, totalitarian regime, contra Popper.) But why should the students learn to become self-sufficient? What do such values have to do with the earlier discussion of the *Republic,* which we analyzed already in 5.1–5.3? Plato's answer seems to be that the self-sufficient are *just* (381B–C). In other words, the Gods more than anyone reap what they sow. (This is entirely fitting because, after all, the self-sufficient get on by means of what they themselves do. This is the specific sense in which they are perfect. They are extreme in their *freedom*.)

D. 379B–C, 380D: Plato's Gods are not rulers of the world as it is (down here on Earth), because being what they are they could not possibly cause negative things to exist or occur. In this way Platonic theology, at least in the *Republic* (cf. 6 on the *Laws* and 12 on the *Timaeus:* their teachings are not exactly the same), is very different from e.g. Jewish or Christian positions. For Plato's Gods cannot make sure that everything will be alright in human life. They are too powerless in places where people (e.g. criminals, or else cancers, volcanoes etc.) do not learn or reason. Their force is felt only among those who strive to resemble them. Such idealists owe their physical or animal lives to their parents and e.g. plants and not to the Gods, but their awareness of the higher values may be of a divine origin (cf. 6.13–6.14; cf. Natorp on the Kantian possibility that the Gods are only values, not realities). At all events the *Republic*'s Gods are practically useless (contra Reeve, see 5.9).

E. 392C–398B: The *style* of a narrative may or may not imitate its object, so that for example a poet can pretend to be old when narrating about someone old (393A–B) or not. Plato's utopia would spell the end to this pretending. Moreover it is precisely the virtuous that are to be imitated (396B–E; the imitators must be specialists in their craft just like everyone else, 397D–398B, 395E–396D). It would seem to follow that in utopia we would hear only true stories about the just, and if plays were enacted on stage then all the actors would play themselves.

Selfishly, I will now first document what all this has to do with ℝ. A God is perfect in being exactly just or self-sufficient, as in *aRa.* We can learn to be more or less like *a,* so we can be placed as *b, c,* or *d* in *aRaRbRcRd...* Presumably, if we pay close attention as children in a utopian school then we rise from *d* to *c,* so we can begin our ascent while still quite young. (We cannot *complete* the ascent as children, by the *Republic*'s lights. Why not? A psyche's self-sufficiency will depend also on reasoning, especially in dialectics, see 5.7. Listening to stories does not teach one to reason!)

I mentioned earlier that the topic of God seems to build a bridge between the *Republic*'s two main topics, justice and the Good. How is this? The Gods' justice is *beyond our reach,* and so we are forced to rank the Gods *above* ourselves (see B and C above). But this is the situation also with the Forms: they rank above us. In contrast, nothing said about justice per se, in 5.1–5.4, implied this. For we talked about reaping what one sows, and there was never any mention of insuperable obstacles to this. If utopia is a place where each individual reaps what she sows, then why would one say that utopia is unreachable? Now we know: we are not Gods. We cannot be that free. (But how do we know this? Well, we depend on plants for food, and on (clean) air to breathe. In a different vein we do not decide where and when we are born, or with which innate characteristics. The Gods and Forms are not indebted to their environments in these ways. They are pure and sure. Chapter 6 will elaborate on this theme with the aid of the *Laws*.)

A few lighter clarifications may be in order to ensure that the overall message is interpreted in the right way.

Firstly, it is easy to see that Plato's concern is not at all to say, in the manner of a reductivist or a materialist, that there *are no* Gods, or that perfectionistic ideals which transcend ordinary human habits or traits do not exist (more on this in Chapter 6 on the *Laws,* where Plato's anti-materialism and anti-atheism are especially direct). Perhaps a Democritus would say that, or in modern times e.g. a Hume or a Marx. But Plato's interest is very different, because instead of ridding us of the Gods, he merely polishes them. He replaces mythical ones with rational ones. (This is "elevative," not reductive.) Accordingly, Plato is not a humanist in the sense of someone who says that nothing ranks above humans. He is not a "secular" humanist. However this should not be thought to make him a sadist, for the Gods and Forms are still the best things *we* can imagine. For the dialectical method which identifies them is made up of *our* reflections (if we philosophize properly). They are not *Hitler's* intuitions which we are made only to obey. Hence, though Plato is not a secular humanist this does not mean that he is inhumane (cf. Grant versus Popper). For he tells us to think freely and to trust our thoughts. (No naturalist can tell us that, because she will have to encourage trust in science, not in speculation. In this sense it is Plato who is more humane.)

A second clarification concerns Plato's relationship to traditional myths. We can see that he does not say, with e.g. Philo of Alexandria, that myths only use the wrong *idioms* but for the right things. (In ancient Alexandria Philo, presumably following the Stoics' lead, wants to show that the teachings of Jerusalem and Athens are one and the same: what the Hebrew Bible teaches in myths is only described differently in the reasoning of Plato and Aristotle. Many later Western theologians repeat this.) For we saw in A–B that Plato's rebellion is also substantial. Thus, Plato would not quite look to traditional stories for inspiration and merely rephrase their message. For he would *not* say that Homer and Hesiod need only to be translated into other symbols for them to qualify as something rational. But we must be careful. For this could tempt some readers to overgeneralize the point, as if myths *never* had rational imports according to Plato, and that is not quite correct either. I have two separate reasons for saying this, α and β.

α. Plato sometimes trusts the contents of myths at least roughly, we know, because if he did not then his own allegories of the Sun, Line, and Cave (and Er) would have to be pointless, which clearly goes against his need to express them (and against 506D–E). Therefore, myths must at least sometimes qualify as childish, helpless surrogates for properly authoritative accounts. They are not all simply silly.

β. It seems that the Gods of Homer and Hesiod do instance *some* autonomy, and *more* autonomy than humans. After all, they are immortal, and they move more freely than humans. Hence, Plato's rebellion may be only that their Gods are *still too* human. (God is no longer a bearded patriarch, or someone who can hide in a bush as at *Exodus* 3:4.) If so, then his mission is to separate the human and superhuman realms more clearly and deeply than his predecessors. (Jaeger vol. 2 p. 213 notes that Plato inherits this line of criticism from Xenophanes and Heraclitus, so his new beginning is not entirely new, or: his anti-traditionalism is also a tradition of its own! Per Jaeger (ibid.) some advances in rational criticism are taken even by Homer himself, for his later *Odyssey* corrects his earlier *Iliad* about the Gods. However this general direction seems not to be followed after the *Republic,* so it appears as the extreme.[4])

β will make a difference in 5.8 when we interpret the Sun, Line, and Cave.

5.6 RELATIVITY (472B–E, 475E–D, 476A–480A, 510B–511E, 522C–526A, 583B–588A)

It is often noted that Plato writes about some things being relative and others not, and that a Form or a Form of the Good belongs to this second set of

126   Chapter Five

things. However Plato has many different ways of saying this, and we need to explain them all. Hence we need to use a quite general explanatory pattern to capture his meaning. For this is how we can reconstruct a serious position from the ancient text.

A. 472B–E: The speakers seek a perfect model of justice based on which they mean to evaluate other things even if the other things cannot fully live up to the perfect standard. The issue is one of degrees. This is natual to interpret as a relational series *aRbRc...* because now there is something perfect (*a*) which stands in guiding relation (*R*) to its more or less perfect instances (like *b* and *c*), and the instances are more or less close or remote to the perfect *a*.
B. 475E–D: Beauty and ugliness, the just and the unjust, good and bad are opposites and their presence is mixed together in in many places, but the pure versions of each are at the extremes of the spectrum. Philosophers are awake in looking to the extremes and others are asleep in seeing only the mixed cases. This tells us more than A above in that the relational series *aRbRc.... yRz* now contains not only a perfect standard at its extreme (i.e. as *a*) but also, seemingly, a perfect or superlative instance of that standard. This needs to be read as *RRaRbRc...*, because now the extreme case is the same as the general standard. For we will omit either of the two functions unless we write *R* at the left hand extreme *and* repeat it throughout the string. The advantage of ℝ lies precisely in this, as noted already in 1.1: it makes the double function *explicit.* (Observe that the other, negative extreme of the same spectrum—i.e. the ugly, the unjust, badness—need not operate as a guiding standard as in A. At least, A does not convey such a role. Hence, the series *RRaRbRc...*, seems to end flatly with *...xRyRz,* i.e. only with an extremely negative instance. If so, then *RR* is unique to the positive end of the series, so the series is not symmetric. It is not shaped like a banana: it is not *RRaRbRcRR*. Cf. opposites in the *Phaedo* and the *Symposium:* 3.9, 4.5.)
C. 478E–480A: The beautiful itself is always beautiful and it always also seems beautiful, but different sights and sounds are, if at all beautiful, also ugly. Thus we again have extreme instances in a series, and a Form of Beauty is identified as one of the extremes. This is evidence that the Form could not possibly be identified merely as a universal or a standard. It must also be an extreme case. To illustrate, it cannot be merely like length in the abstract and it must (also) be like the longest thing. This may not be as obvious based on A or B above. (I here omit Plato's characteristic conflation of predication with existence, because it matters comparatively little to my argument. It is well known that Plato slips easily from *a is just*

to *a exists,* and from *a is just and unjust* to *a exists and a does not exist;* so, for any *a, a* does not properly exist unless *a* is a superlative instance (e.g. perfecly just). See 1.2 and e.g. Fine's "Knowledge and Belief in *Republic* V.")

D. 523A–525A: Some predicates raise questions and others do not, because only some predicates' instances are typically mixed or ambiguous. For example, ... *is a finger* is unproblematic, because your normal finger is entirely a finger. It is in no sense a non-finger or anti-finger. In contrast, ... *is long* is problematic, stimulating reflection, because most things that are long are long only in some comparison or other (as in *b* IS LONGER THAN *a*), and not in every comparison (like *c* IS LONGER THAN *b*, for now *b* is comparatively short and not comparatively long as in *b* IS LONGER THAN *a*; so *b* is changed from a long to a short thing simply by changing its point of comparison: *a* is replaced by *c*). But there are Forms exatcly for the problematic predicates, so there is a Form of Length but no Form of the Finger. This passage indicates that Plato connects Forms with *relations,* because comparative predicates are precisely the relational ones! (This overall message is again familiar from previous chapters of this book. But the following two are not: E, F.)

E. 522C–526A: On the same pages one finds something else said as well, and this needs to be considered separately. For when Plato's Socrates considers quantitative measures, such as thickness and length, he is led in these pages to philosophize about numbers. For he seems to hold, firstly, that if things are counted, using numbers, then this begs the prior question how to individuate units (524D–525A). In this spirit, before we have seven instances of something, or nine hundred, or indeed even one, we need to know what to *count* as one. (Where does one animal, one plant, one historical period, or indeed one thought end and the next one begin? Along somewhat different lines, how many *things* are in a room is impossible to say but how many *blue towels* are in it is easy to discover. See Chapter 9 on ordinary nouns as possible standards of individuation. Despite *Republic* 596A I do not hold that they are authoritative in Plato. His thought is a great deal deeper than his light-minded Wittgensteinian critics like to assume.) Hence we need a unit first. However also a second and more abstract question is raised in Plato's mind, and this is more purely a question for the philosophy of mathematics: What is one, or two, or any number, merely as such (524E, 525E)? Plato requires pure numbers of some kind (525D, 526B). How these pure numbers should be understood or defined raises complex questions specifically in the *Republic.* (These have been tackled in Platonic spirit at least in Krämer's Pythagoreanism and in Frege's and Russell's logicism. Dedekind's alternative is closer to

ℝ because Dedekind produces arithmetic and geometry from hierarchical series. For him, the number series (i.e., 1, 2, 3, ..., and the fractions in between) are only a special case of the generic hierarchical series. Thus, there is some vague hope that mathematics might be founded as in ℝ, i.e. that even Plato's interest in pure numbers would not force us outside the world of relations.[5])

F. 510B–511E: The Form of the Good is now said to depend only on the other Forms and not at all on empirical objects (510B, 511B–C). This is what happens when a philosopher reasons purely as a dialectician (511B–C). This clarity and purity is never attained or even sought in mathematics or the sciences because there mere hypotheses and empirical images are viewed as foundations even though they are not (510B–511D). The implication here seems to be that Forms other than the Form of the Good are not quite absolute after all, unlike in several of Plato's other works, so they are relativized. For now Forms other than Good seem to depend on Good in much the same way as empirical, material objects depend on the Forms (other than Good). If the dependence relation is the same in both cases then we attain a three-place relation, *non-Form: Form (minus Good): Good*. This would make Good the Form of the Forms, which is a result that several scholars have suggested (e.g. Natorp pp. 195 and 201 and Ross pp. 40–41; see Santas' "The Form of the Good in Plato's *Republic*" (2000) on Ross' many followers) even though it has no direct textual basis. But now, *if* we can add also that the Forms are relations, as this book urges, then we would have Forms other than Good, call them relations R-U, relating empirical givens a-h to each other, and Good, now as the relation X (not V because V looks like an "or" operator), relating R-U to each other. Thus we would get aRb, cSd, eTf, gUh, and on a higher level $R\,X\,S$, $T\,X\,U$. In less formal symbols, the thought in this is that if the role of normal Forms (i.e. R-U) is to order things in experience, though the Forms themselves are not objects of experience, then the role of X is to order those orderings. It is as if the Good were the commander of commanders, the authority of authorities—a kind of dictator in the world of thought. This view arises naturally if it is true that whatever the lower-level relations do is exactly what the *über*-relation must do also. (The only difference is that the *über*-relation's relata are the lower-level relations.) Thus X is the meta-cause, the cause of causes. If X conforms to ℝ exactly then we also need it to instance XX, and this would complete the formal structure.

G. 583B–588A: Experiences, pleasures, and evaluations often lead us to lose our way because of their relativity. For a person who is unfamiliar with the color white will be satisfied upon reaching gray after black (585A), mistaking gray for white. Similarly, a person moving to a central location after having been in a low place will think that she is then high (584D). Again, health will have value in the eyes of persons who have been ill (583C–D), and an end to pains will seem like a pleasure (583D). But only the reasoned person will know what is truly high or valuable (584E–585B), obviously because the reasoning being uses a *scale* of some kind. She does not simply let her experiences speak for themselves, drifting away to wherever they may lead her. Rather, she has her constant standard. It is like a map on which she can locate each of her then-current states. (In G we are back in familiar Plato-land, cf. 2–4.)

The easiest way to summarize this view is as a pyramid. At the tip is the Form of the Good (*XX*), and at the base are empirical, material individuals (*a-h*). In between there is the realm of the other Forms (*R-U*). Of course, the number of empirical particulars in this universe which we happen to inhabit is far above eight, so to be realistic we should list many more relata than *a-h*. (Similarly, there are many more relations to include than *R-U*.) Hence, the pyramid's base is much wider in the real world. The pyramid is not at all this narrow. But that is the only complication that we need to add to this simplistic idealization.

Is this pyramid a neutral representation of ℝ? Not quite, for something is added to the familiar picture. The complication is due to the introduction of the medial level in the pyramid. But this medial level must be added if the *Republic* requires it (see 510B–511E and F above). Without the medial level we could move from *a-z* to *X* directly (via *aXbXc...*) and then say that *XX*. But with the medial level we must use *{R, S, T, ...}* first on the pure relata *(a-z)*, and then we can use *X* only to *{R, S, T, ...}* and not directly to *a-z*. This has one glaringly obvious advantage: now relations like IS LONGER THAN (see D above) can be included into Plato's structure. They could not be before, because they do not conform to *aRa* or *aRR* (see 3.11). But they are not required to do that as *{R, S, T, ...}*. Thus Plato gets to cover the totality of all relations.

The *Phaedo* (in Chapter 3) omitted this medial level and the *Symposium* (in 4) did not, so we may compare the *Republic*'s pyramid to those other pictures briefly in order to avoid some logical errors.

First the *Phaedo*. A Form in the *Phaedo* is a relation to that same relation, but it is not a relation to any other relation. For in 3.3 we saw that the content EQUALS can be directed at itself, but if it is directed at other things (in however imperfect a manner) then those other things are *not* relations. They are for instance sticks and stones. (This is one difference with the *Republic*, because as I have just explained, *X does* have other relations as its relata: *R-U*.) A deeper logical difference is due to the *Phaedo*'s partless psyche (which cannot die because to die is to fall into pieces and a partless thing has

130   Chapter Five

no pieces to fall into). For its logic is *zRz,* not *RR:* the partless psyche is a relatum, not a relation. (It does relate to things, yes; but it is not the relation. It is a thing that is related *by* a relation. It is positioned like *a* in *aRb* and *aRa.*) A third reason why the *Phaedo*'s logic is different from the *Republic*'s (and the *Symposium*'s) is less exact. It is that the *Phaedo* often operates with pairs. Thus for instance a stick and a stone is a pair (*a:b*), and two sticks and two stones are a pair of pairs (*a:b::c:d*). These are not the longer series (*a:b:c:d:e*) of the *Republic* (and the *Symposium*). In accordance with this third logical difference, the *Phaedo* is more often dualistic (as in *psyche/body* or *Form/material-object*) and not as concerned with many degrees or levels like the *Republic* (and the *Symposium*). (In passing, none of this is to say that the *Phaedo* is *worse* than the *Republic*. Rather, it uses Platonic thinking on other topics. For example, as also the *Laws* will say in Chapter 6, the psyche is better viewed a la *aRa* than *RRa*. However relations like IS LONGER THAN are an authentic blunder in the *Phaedo,* as noted. Cf. 3.11 above and iii below.)

The *Symposium*'s logic is closer to the *Republic*'s. However this is not because they use the same *word* for their ideals (contra e.g. A.E. Taylor p. 287 and Voegelin p. 112 on "the Agathon"). Rather the kinship is logical. For the Form of Beauty was pictured as a harmony of harmonies, a la *RR* (see Chapter 5, endnote 3). There are harmonies in music which can be heard and also harmonies in poetry which can be read, but the harmony between these harmonies is inaudible and invisible. It is eternal and pure. Now, how does this differ from the *Republic*'s position? (I already noted the *causal* difference that the Good of the *Republic* is the first formal cause and the Beautiful of the *Symposium* is the first final cause, see 4 above and 5.7 below.) The *logical* difference is that the *Republic*'s relations are hierarchical and the *Symposium*'s are more balanced or organic ("democratic" would go too far). Visually this is to say that the *Republic*'s hierarchy is a pyramid with a sharp tip, but the *Symposium*'s hierarchy is not so sharp. The *Symposium*'s structure is more like a soft hill, with a rounder top. Why is this? Recall the *Republic*'s relations from above in this section (5.6): all of them rank things. *a* IS THICKER THAN *b,* or else IS MORE NUMEROUS THAN or IS JUSTIFIED BY, and so on. Relations like these lend themselves to straight-forward series like $a<b<c...$ In contrast, the beautiful relation in the *Symposium* is that of harmony, and this relation is not purely hierarchical. It is more like an analogy, as in $a \approx b \approx c...$ Why? Consider the notes that make up a melody or a chord: they require each other. They are not all merely *ranked* in an order. In a larger orchestra this becomes more obvious, because all the different instruments add to the whole. But this is likewise with paintings, in which all kinds of shades add to the total image. Similarly, a simile or an allegory makes at least two things seem alike to each other, but it does not thereby place one of

them *above* the other ("Juliet is the sun," says Shakespeare's Romeo, meaning that she is *as* warm, *as* bright, *as* central to life, etc., and not less or more). Its point is to make them *level*. *That* is why the metaphor is presented: it is to make two things seem the *same*. (However this does *not* imply that the purest harmony is not one of harmony with itself, see 4.6.)

Let us consider a number of objections in order to assess this.

i. "It is startling to hear the sweeping generalization that the Forms are relations, let alone that all of them are hierarchical ones. For where is the evidence for this grandiose generalization?"

In A–G above. The examples in A–C concerned the relative (or absolute) value that something could have, that is in being more or less just/unjust or beautiful/ugly. In D the stimulating predicates were exactly the relational ones, i.e. the ones which predicate of things only in certain conditions versus others. (The unstimulating ones like ... *is a finger* were not relational.) In E counting was seen to be relative to the prior issue how units are individuated (and after this the familiar numbers were supposed to have foundations in real or pure numbers of some kind). F was about the relations between Good and the other Forms. Finally, G contrasted relative experiences with measured realities. Hence relations popped up all the time. (To *not* see relations here would be strange.)

ii. "Perhaps the *Republic*'s Forms are relations but this does not make the Good into a relation R to that same R (as in *XX* above). For even if the Good is the Form of Forms and the Forms are relations it does not follow that *Plato* makes the connection that the Good is a relation R to R. For there is a difference between what an individual thinks and what the indivdual's thinking implies. If there were not then we would be logical machines, but instead we are humans, making errors all the time. (Moreover we are all busy wondering what to think. Who has a complete system?)"

A–C definitely instance the double function: it is both the firmest thing and that which gives firmness also to other things, so it has both roles, that of the superlative example (analogical to the longest thing) and that of the general measure (analogical to length). But this is charitable to read as RR. Conversely, if either of the functions is neglected in an expression describing the Form of the Good, then that expression does not cover all of A–C above. For, as already noted, the expression must assign the Good the role both of the extreme and the general standard, and how is this managed if not by presenting a graded series in which the Good is both (a) at one extreme (i.e. the first token of the relation "R," which is highlighted here: R$RaRbRc$...) and (b) the recurrently instanced organizer of the whole series (i.e. all the later tokens of the relation "R," which are highlighted here: RR$aRbRcRd$...)? ii would like to do without (a), but that contradicts Plato's text, as we have seen.

iii. "If the Good is a relation R to R and this R is a hierarchy then then it follows that the Good is a hierarchy of a hierarchy, which is nonsense. '<<' is nonsense just like IS LESS THAN IS LESS THAN."

First, as noted, in the *Republic* all Forms do not instance RR, and only the Good does (see F above in this section, 5.6). For example there is a Form of Length, yes, but it is not the longest thing.

Second, RR is not nonsense for all contents. We do not even need new examples to show this, if such relations as EQUALS or MEANS are hierarchical. (They are if a EQUALS b or a MEANS b implies that $a<b$, as it should, because then b is an advance on a: a more processed product, or more meaningful. In a DEFINES AS b b is more definite, etc. But then all we need is to refute iii is to use these relations on themselves, defining "defining" and giving the meaning of "meaning," as in 1.2, 2, 3.3, etc.)

However I am not suggesting that XX above has any of the preceding contents exactly. They make it especially easy to understand that iii is wrong in its sweeping condemnation. Hence they are as it were the minimally required premises for ridding us of iii. But a more honest or full-blooded view of XX is attained by taking R-U to be *scales*. Then one scale measures length, another justice, a third beauty, etc., quite as the text of the *Republic* would have it (see A–D and F above). To this textually firm background, X measures those scales and itself, so it is a scale of *all* scales. (It numbers among them.) The *mystery* which this scale of scales leaves one with is the content of this XX or Good. For what would really function as such an *über*-scale? How would one measure all these different measures? It is a breathtaking question, but it is not nonsense. (It is not nonsense because though the Good is especially good, Length is not especially long.)

iv. "But a hierarchy of hierarchies relatives itself. And in fact this happens to Plato himself because until the *Republic* the Forms are absolute enough for him, but inside the *Republic* he rises further to a Form of Forms, the Good. (Perhaps next he would introduce a Form of the Best which ranks still higher, that is if his creative powers continued to evolve.) Similarly with e.g. the allegories of the Sun and Cave (see 5.8 below). First, having recently fled the human cave, one may value light, but soon one will require more, until one can only stare at the sun itself. (And how long will that be enough? If the sun is studied, will a brighter center not be discovered from within it, and then a center from the center, etc.? Or will its dark spots at least be subtracted?) In other words, if each hierarchy is only an item in some further hierarchy, then each staircase will lead only to a further Escherian staircase, as in nightmare. Formally, on Monday you have $aRbRc$ (and $a<b<c$), but on Tuesday this changes into $cRdRe$, on Wednesday it becomes $eRfRg$, etc. Eveything flows and you never arrive. (This is much as in the paradox of ends in 4.4, but also

see 7 and 8. Plato forms a similar vicious circle at *Republic* 505C, where he objects to view the good is to know the good.)"

As in 4 one can stop at *RR* and refuse (for some reason) to go further to *RRR* or *RRRR*. For in 4 there was a harmony of harmonies, but no harmony of harmonies of harmonies. In the same spirit, the *Republic*'s text actually rises only so far. There is no call to extend the maneuvering to any hypothetical future. Thus, Plato relativizes Forms other than Good in the *Republic*, true, but he never rises further from there, and his Sun and Cave do not suggest any infinite ascent. Thus iv is a needless exaggeration. We say *XX*, not *XXX* or *XXXX*, etc.

v. "But the *Republic*'s central passages about the Good are really only poetic and elusive, and this is unsurprising because of course different persons have very different conceptions of the *summum bonum* of life. Plato *can* not say anything understandable about it to convince everyone: *that* is why he does not say it. Moreover, free thought would never generate believable results on a topic such as this. For even Hitler, Stalin, and Pol Pot have their utopian visions, so if uninhibited intuitions lead to something good in general then why not theirs as well? And who would be for their results? What fool would condone limitless free thought? It is better to think pragmatically and to finally forget about all this supposedly elevated nonsense."

These are misunderstandings because the Form of the Good in the *Republic* is actually a strictly rational ideal. It is not really a sentimenal life ideal even if Plato decorates it with so much rhetoric. Logically the Good is not relative to anything, but absolute or extreme like *a* or *d* in *aRbRcRd*. It is the first cause in a chain of reasons or arguments, as we will see next.

5.7 DIALECTIC (510B–511C, 532A–537C)

The *Republic's* assertions about dialecticians or philosophers arise to this background:

A. 473C–473E: Philosophers should become rulers or human suffering will be endless (473C–D). There is no other route to human happiness in public or private life (473E).

This begs the question who the "philosophers" are. What defines a philosopher (474B–C)? Plato has many answers:

B. 510B–511D: A dialectician seeks the first principle of things, whereas others are content with less (this is all we need from the Line at present).

C. 532A–B: A dialectician looks to the essence of each thing (532A) and in particular to the essence of the Good itself (532B). It is the limit of the intelligible (ibid.).
D. 533B–C: The dialectician studies the composition of each thing systematically (533B), giving an account of each of them (533C).
E. 533C: In dialectics one seeks the first principle of things, doing away with mere hypotheses. In other words, dialecticians seek the ultimate starting point on which other things depend.
F. 534B–C: Dialecticians give a precise account of the essence of each thing (534B), thereby explaining themselves (ibid.). But it is noted separately that they do this also for the Good (ibid.) and that a person who is unable to distinguish the Form of the Good from other things cannot possibly be a proper dialectician (534B–C).

Observe that now the dialectician's definitions *distinguish* things. They *abstract* or *separate* their objects. (Be forewarned that this is very different from the synoptic view of I below.)

G. 534D: Dialecticians ask and answer questions most carefully.

G accords well with B–F above if the questions which dialecticians characteristically answer always demand increasingly fundamental causes. But this would be the case with $\mathbb{R}$. (For then for each given a the dialectical questioner would ask what causes a, and if the answer given is b, the questioner asks next for the cause of b, etc. This operation is repeated with c, d, etc., until some ultimate point z is found.)

H. 534E: Dialectics ranks topmost in the hiearchy of cognitive authorities. Thus the first cause deciphered by the dialecticians seems to be the foundation for all other fields of inquiry.

By now this has a familiar ring. But this is something else:

I. 537C: If one can view things in interconnection then one is a dialectician. The dialectician presents a comprehensive survey of all the different things, noting their affinities. This is the chief test for determining who is by nature a dialectician and who is not.

By I, if someone's tendency is to separate objects then she is *no* dialectician, contrary to F. This marks an inconsistency which we will deal with presently. Before that let us note in passing how the *Republic* contains plenty of assertions about dialecticians (especially at 535A–536A) which take us still much further afield. For the philosophical rulers sought are most stable, most brave and enterprising (535A), virile and vigorous (535B), but also studious (ibid.). They are able to remember things well (535C). But they are also able at gymnastics (535B) and physical toil (535C–D). In fact they seem to love work (535D). However they also respect truth (535D) and their souls are lofty (536A) and they are in general virtuous in every respect (ibid.). (Elsewhere the *Republic* says the dialecticians learn quickly and remember vividly, and that they are brave as well as altogether magnificent (487A, 494B). They are indeed first at everything and natural leaders, their bodies being as excellent as their minds (494B).) What is one to make of all this? It has little to do with dialectics as in B–H or I above, because generally superhuman personal qualities do not connect necessarily with superior cognitive abilities. It seems to be fairer to say that dialecticians, being intellectual as in B–I, are useless star-gazers (488E–489A), because a certain impracticality goes with their territory. For a search for first principles is *bound* to be impractical. (After all, to put this in the *Theaetetus'* metaphors (174A; see Chapter 13), if one looks continually to the heavens then one cannot watch one's step. Looking up is not looking down.)

As noted, it is easy to sense that B–I are ambiguous between two alternatives. *Either* the dialectician separates her objects *or* her vision is synoptic. I will now argue that Plato is mistaken in his synoptic wish, for there are areas of life and inquiry which are not within the dialectician's reach (α). The issue this raises is what *is* (β). Thus we first assess what the dialectian cannot do and then what she can.

α. We may consider sciences first and then politics.

Sciences. It is not by means of a dialectic of question and answer that one discovers the properties of physical nature. Rather, science requires experiments (much more so than Plato knows, see Chapter 12 on the *Timaues* especially, but also 6.13 and 6.14 on science in the *Laws*). But also for instance historiography will differ markedly from speculative dialogue or debate, for it depends heavily on the extensive examination of historical sources. One does *not* attain a good overview of history by speculating dialectically. True, a person who happens to be a dialectician some of the time or even most of the time can use some of her time to learn about things other than dialectic and then speculate about them *also,* but if she does that then she does not know about the other things *as* a dialectician. For speculating is different from experimenting or examining sources in libraries: there is no way around that. (There are commonalities, but they go only so deep. There is trial an error in each type of inquiry, but the trials are not the same.)

But can a dialectician not form coherent wholes out of *others'* cognitive labors? Perhaps they need to do the dirty work and report to her and then she forms a single unified theory of everything based on their reports (cf. Reeve in 5.9 below). It seems that dialecticians are not really trusted in this way in point of fact. For example, if the Einsteinian physics of large wholes is difficult to fit together with the quantum physics of the smallest parts, as it has been in the physics of the past century, then it is not a dialectical philosopher who weaves these fabrics together. Rather, the task is left to physics itself. There is "string theory," for example, and its problems are problems in physics. Thus, philosophy does not seem to pull the different things together, contrary to the synoptic view. But consider that she is skilled in exploring extreme questions. E.g. if a current cosmologist has evidence for a Big Bang theory then it is easy for any philosopher to ask what there was before the Bang (and how it got there). The philosopher will have a collection of arguments about such matters because she has reflected on them before (and she knows her *Timaues* and *Laws* and her Kantian antinomies, etc.). By comparison the cosmologist will seem naive in not having thought all these avenues through. She will look like someone who merely collects data without a clear awareness of its potential status. So what if the known universe is expanding? What type of a conclusion can ever be established based on such data? That is a philosophical question, and it gives the dialectician the upper hand.

Politics. This is largely the same story. To begin with, dialogical speculation or debate is not *identical to* political life. Why not? Societies require roads, parks, health care, schools, institutions for criminal justice, and much else. (Why? We cannot simply speculate all the time. There is more to life than questions about first causes.) But one does not do all this by defining things or by seeking first principles. For the way that one comes to know about political realities is by living in society and observing behaviors, and that is often very different from doing dialectics (cf. 6). Despite this, one can philosophize dialectically about politics – of course. Plato himself benefits from several political parallels. Hence, the political life and political knowledge do not equate with dialectical speculation, yes, but for its part politics is speculative enough to consider its own ultimate grounds. What is a just order? What is moral, and what in the first place is a law? As with science, the philosopher has a role to play, but the role is that of a questioner, not that of the overall peacemaker.

The Hegelian Reply. Hegel may be said to reply to the preceding objections by projecting dialectical structures very widely: to history, to nature, art, religion, politics, etc. For in his view dialectical structures are *inside* all these things. History pulsates with the dialectic of progress, and nature is sleepy *Geist*. It is all *alike* to philosophy though it is not philosophy; it is a kind of mute debate.

The fault in this is easy to perceive: it is feigned. For if one insists on doing, say, mathematics by dialectical laws then the results are artificial. Soviet mathematicians were forced to pretend in this way, and they were thus held back from their real chores. But also consider the dialectical rhetoric of e.g. Mao. It is artificial and whimsical because it has no deeper connection to its subject matter. (What in a given phenomenon is inner and what outer? Which contradiction is the main one?, etc. Mao decides as he likes, because the subject matter does not do it for him. The subject matter does not intrinsically have anything to *do* with the theory. There is too much distance, or the data is of the wrong type.)

β. I have already stated many times now why dialectics is not silly even if it is not physics. For no one will seek first principles if the philosopher does not do it. But dialectic is just the right method for this. Why? The very *formulation* of first principles will require hierarchical idioms. For *to be* a first principle *is* to be the tip of a pyramid. It is to base on thing on another. Hence the formal philosopher cannot avoid the hierarchical syntax.

Here the holist may seem to have the opportunity for a counter-attack. For if several things, $a, b, c,$ etc., are founded in z, then must not the founded things—a-c etc.—be known as well? (Is a pyramid not so much more than its tip?) Hence, must not the dialectician be conversant in more than z? And must she not form a single, coherent whole out of *all* of a-z? The reply is that according to *Plato's Logic z* is a foundation *primarily* for z. a-c etc. figure only as so many springboards. They are not saved. (Thus Plato, unlike e.g. Spinoza. If Spinoza, the earth friend, does not know the facts of the earth, then that is embarrassing. For then what is he for? But Plato professes to be the expert of heaven, not of earth.)

A different question concerns Plato's *vocabularies*. As noted in 1.4, he uses many different ones (see i–v in 1.4). There are adjectives, verbs, negations, analogies, etc. (Also compare endnote 2 in Chapter 1, and 5.6 on mathematics.) Given this, must he not have some kind of a synoptic intuition about how all these different idioms work for the one main thing which he is so keen to communicate? Again the right reply seems to be hierarchical. For as in 5.6 above the situation in Plato is not only that there are different vocabularies for formulating hierarchies: the point is also that the vocabularies themselves form a hierarchy. Some hierarchies rank above others, and the Good is the scale of scales. True, Plato does not himself produce any precise definition of the Good, but that is a different matter. He would *like* to anyway, so by his own lights he is an imperfect being. We are discussing what he would like to be.

5.8 SUN, LINE, CAVE (507B–509C, 509D–511E, 514A–520A)

The *Republic* contains mythical descriptions of the Good because its author is unable to pronounce about the Good in a more definite way (506D–E). The three allegories leave us guessing what the Good may be because they are not more definite than they are. None the less the allegories tell us some crucial things. Here is a summary of each of them:

A. The Sun (507B–509C): The Good is to intelligence what the sun is to vision, so the Good makes things intelligible just as the sun makes things visible. We see trees, lakes, etc., and we grasp a range of things, and this is due to the sun and the Good.
B. The Cave (514A–520A): Human life is ordinarily like life in a cave in which objects are presented only artificially by other humans. For other humans prepare a show for us, and the show is a sham. If we manage to escape this underground city and to live life out in the open then we will be confronted with reality, but we will be able to face it only in a gradual way. For we cannot turn to look at the sun directly (515E–516B, 517B–C). We will begin with reflections on water and with shadows (516A). Only eventually will we be able to look directly at the sun (516B–C, 517B), and this is the endoint of the progression. Beyond that there is nothing higher to see anymore.

If the Sun Allegory in A is ambiguous whether the sun itself is the main object of sight then the Cave Allegory in B is unambiguous about the same point. For the Cave tells us that the sun is indeed the main object of vision (516B–C, 517B). This is made perfectly obvious also at 532B–D. By analogy, the Good is the prime object of thought (517B; cf. also 518C–D).

C. The Line (509D–511E): Human cognitive abilities or habits stand in a particular ratio to one another. For they are as in a line. The line is divided into two unequal sections and the same ratio is recurs in both of the sections. Per se this, like any, ratio is a relational pattern, so it sounds familiar from this book's structural point of view. (The Line is one geometric use of $a:b::c:d$, that is all.) Moreover it is obviously a hierarchical pattern. However the ratio in question seems insignificant, especially as it is merely geometric. (For what is in a *line* which is twice divided? I have yet to see a properly instructive interpretation of this.)

Here we must consider what to fasten on. The Sun and the Cave make the Good seem like an *experiential* object, and this suggests a mystical interpretation. The sun is seen, and the Good is somehow grasped, as e.g. by a mind's eye. There is perhaps a sudden flash, a euphoric "Heureka!," and then one understands the central thing. In contrast, *explaining* the Good to someone who has not "seen" it would then be like trying to argue inside the cave. It would be like talking of colors with persons who have always been blind: as pointless! But 506D–E entitles us to brush aside this mystical view (contra e.g. Wilamowitz p. IX, A.E. Taylor pp. 286–290, Voegelin p. 112, Grene p. 96, and Dahl p. 226; A. E. Taylor compares his mystical view to negative theology, seeing the *Republic*'s Good and the *Symposium*'s Beauty as the Christian God; G. E. Moore presents a simple view of good, but he does not relate this explicitly to Plato, though intuitionists like him are often viewed as Platonists, see e.g. Dahl). For as noted Plato tells us that he would wish to define it (506D–E), and of course he would not consciously wish for something he holds to be impossible. I want to suggest that it is the *structural* properties of the allegories that we need to fasten on, not the *experiential* ones. The mystics follow the wrong lead.

Perhaps the example of water is again most instructive. We know that water=H_2O, so we can define it. We know it is not simple, because it has an atomic structure. It is not even wet. It consists of two highly inflammable gases! But to the ancients this seemed otherwise. Water is water, they said—it is as simple as that. It *has* no underlying nature, they would say, because it *is* one of the underlying natures, along with e.g. air, earth, and fire (Aristotle, *De Caelo*)! Certainly, it is at times mixed with other things, as in *dirt: mud: water* or *ice: snow: water*. But that is the only way you can communicate about it, that is in external comparisons. You cannot give an internal definition, but you can compare externally. This is much as in Heraclitus' *child: man: god,* because this pattern does not state directly what god *is*. God is here presented only something which a man shares in more than an ape does. Then we are left guessing what the riddle may mean. For what is it that distinguishes the man from the ape? (IS MORE RESPONSIBLE THAN, IS MORE REFLECTIVE THAN, yes, but also, IS TALLER THAN, HAS LESS HAIR THAN, etc.) But this is the kind of description instanced in the Sun, Line, and Cave, above. To this background we can see how the mystical "Platonists" mentioned above could combine their view with the inevitablity of mythical communication.

Things change entirely if intrinsic definitions *are* possible. For think of water. We *can* penetrate into this topic. We can speak directly and positively. Intrinsic definitions are of course attained in many places: mathematical formulae, semantic theories, etc., as we have seen. Obviously, if we insist dogmatically that there is no deeper answer then we are like the ancients with water. Water is water and that is all there is to it. In the same spirit we would say that equality just is what it is, as everyone already knows (thus e.g. Wittgenstein in 9). But that is obviously *not* Plato's way with things: with him democracy turns out to be unfree, the psyche is shown to be like a busy city, mathematics depends on empirical illustrations, etc., so philosophy is full of groundbreaking innovations. Water is not water! (This is normal for *dialecticians* to say, e.g. Hegel, Marx, and Engels.)

The question this can seem to beg is how Plato can view the Good as something ultimate, as a *first* cause (see e.g. the Line), if it is not simple. Does its definability make it something less than absolute? But this is to confuse material and formal causes. The Good is the first formal cause, and that does not imply its simplicity. It is not a *part* in things but a type of *order* in which different parts can be arranged. For example, *a:b::c:d* is a structure. You can insert many different items for *a-d* and have a coherent result. (In Aristotelian terms, the same *form* is instanced in different *materials*.) Other structures abound: we find them in geometry as well as syntax, in music and architecture, etc. (You can make verbs out of smoke signals as well as Morse code, and you can build a dome of stone or glass. Many different materials can be used for the same format.)

Now we can turn around and explain Plato's actions. First off, what defines the Form of the Good? In 5.6 it was already identified as a hierarchical structure. Why then can Plato not define it? What forces him to myth? It is not credible that he cannot formulate a hierarchical structure, after all, because he does that so many times! (For recall the different ways he manages that, e.g. i–v in 1.4: adjectives and so on.)

Plato's own thinking seems to be *inadequately polarized* for his own needs. For this causes it to be the case that the Form of the Good does not stand out enough. It is too much like Homer's and Hesiod's Gods (in 5.5 above): it is too close to mundane affairs, too human. (Picture an accordion: if it is pulled open, then its parts are more differentiated, and this is what Plato wants as a formal philosopher per 5.5–5.7. But if the accordion is left closed, then its portions are jumbled together, as in a myth. Then Gods show up in surprising places and shapes and play tricks that are not really divine. As in a dream one thing becomes another and everything is fluid. See e.g. Snell p. 198 for the view that ancient Greek thought evolves from a clumsy materialism to something increasingly differentiated. A favorite illustration for this is the psyche, which originally stands for breathing not only in Greek or Latin but also e.g. Hindi and Finnish, but which comes to symbolize something utterly immaterial especially in Plato's *Phaedo*. Similarly also with Plato's Forms or Ideas, because they are separate, or above this world, though their etymology is visual. Again, there is a "heaven" of pure numbers, an unreachable archetype for a utopia at *Republic* 592A–B, and so on.)

But what evidence is there for this? What shows that Plato does not polarize his formal spectrum as much as he would wish in his allegories? I have two considerations.

First, Plato senses his chaos because he is too *imprecise* in this myths. The Line is more than a little off target logically, because it does not even sketch any kind of a center. (It gives a vague direction, but the numerical proportions are completely uninstructive.) But also the Sun and the Cave are off, because though the sun illuminates itself most in them, it is not identified as light itself. (Its structure is *aRa* not *RRa: the sun* ILLUMINATING *the sun* ILLUMINATING *a lake* ILLUMINATING *reflections on the water,* etc.) Thus, if Plato wants something that is at once the brightest thing and identical to light itself, then he misfires with the myths. He needs *RR* but he does not produce it. (No wonder he is discontented.)

A second answer is related to the first but its result is more spectacular. Plato is not aware that his Good is a yardstick because he thinks of it as a *totem*. (For in *aRa a* is not a yardstick, and *aRa* was just said to to be the logic of the Sun and Cave in the first answer. In *aRa a* is a relatum, not a relation (*R*), and only a relation (*R*) orders things in *aRaRbRcRd... a* does not do the work of measuring in *aRaRbRcRd...: R* does.) In other words, Plato is not, and he should be, fully aware that he needs a *standard* on top of his own pyramid. What can he be thinking, then? As a historical matter of fact, he may in the end think along the lines of a mythical primitive, that the Good is a like Brer rabbit, who in folklore is *the* rabbit of rabbits. (Similarly even today one American flag that is seen by a believing patriot is *the* American flag, Laguna p. 453; cf. Snell Chapter 10 on the Greek context.) Plato knows that he can not define his Brer, but on the other hand he very much feels the need to. Thus he is not quite aware how his philosophy should be properly formulated, and so he writes myths and feels unhappy with the result.

5.9 VERSUS REEVE (GOOD)

The best introduction to Reeve's version of Plato's Kallipolis in his *Philosopher-Kings* is negative. For Reeve juxtaposes the *Republic*'s Platonism with the supposedly very different Platonism of the *Meno,* the *Phaedo,* and the *Symposium,* denying that the earlier doctrines still survive in the *Republic.* Reeve says that in these three other works the Forms are at least occasionally "self-instantiating, nonidentical with sensibles, directly cognizable, cognitively reliable," and simple (Reeve p. 105), but in Reeve's eyes the *Republic*'s Forms are none of these things. Rather they lack the intrinsic perfection or autonomy of the earlier theory of Forms. They connect more flexibly to the mundane, material, and perceptual order of things, and in this way they are closer to Aristotle (Reeve pp. 105–107).

But then how do the Forms remain special? And how does the Form of the Good? Reeve says the Good is the substance of substances (p. 95), meaning that the Good has very many other things as its constituents (p. 84). This would seem to make the Good vastly complex (ibid.). Indeed, Reeve holds that the *Republic*'s philosophers who know the Good possess a generalized theory of everything (pp. 92, 71–79). He adds to this that the Good is as much a practical as a theoretic object (p. 84), so the philosophers who know it do not only interpret the world: they change it (p. 89). They know how to fashion the perfect cow, for example (p. 94). Reeve seems also to take the example of the Form of the Bed at *Republic* 596A literally, believing that philosophers are experts about beds (p. 86–90).

Could Reeve be right about these things? I do not want simply to repeat what was said in 5.7: that dialectic consists of debate and definitions, and that it is well used to track down first causes, but that it hardly combines well with political experience or scientific experiment. For we can actually find some additional errors in Reeve's position (here I list only the main ones).

The first fault to note is that Reeve sees other things as relating to the Good as its *constituents*. This would, it is true, make the Good vastly complex. But as in 5.8 constituents figure as material causes, not as formal ones. Conversely, if we have a formal structure for some object, let us say a cow, then a cow is surely not a *part* of that structure. (A cow is part of—say—a herd of cows, or of a farm, not of an abstract definition.) Formal patterns require something very different. In this spirit, take it that the utopian cow is orderly, and a Form of the Cow says what it is for a cow to be orderly. Then the Good (that substance of substances, as above) gets to be the order of orders. But then the optimal order that is imposed on things so that utopia is realized on earth is surely not *already everywhere* before the utopian reform is undertaken. For one thinks of it rather as an independent foothold which gives one an advantage over the current world. In fact, it seems that we cannot come along and correct the world unless we have something better than it to build on. (I now ignore the possibility of reforming one portion of the world to match another, so that e.g. China learns to build IT companies just as in Silicon Valley, because that prospect does not represent either Reeve's theory or mine.)

A second problem with Reeve's view is his neglect of all of those passages in the *Republic* in which philosophizing is clearly portrayed as an autonomous end in itself: philosophers live on the blessed isles (519C), breathing a purer air than the rest (520D), and their supreme object, the Good, is more certainly known (e.g. 510B–511D) and much more rewarding than other objects (see Cave). To top it all off, the Good is something above reasoning (508E–509A), so it is superhuman. These utterances would not make good sense if Reeve said that the *Republic*'s philosophers are *primarily* persons with very extensive political experience (p. 83), for how could the political philosopher be so happy merely in philosophizing? (Is philosophizing itself a political process? Habermas might say so, but not Reeve.) But Reeve's view seems rather to be that philosophizing is one thing and politics is another, and that philosophers must be brought to have political experience so that they can rule the Kallipolis. (This is like forcing two naturally independent circles to overlap.) He is not even *interested* in explaining how the philosophizing itself might be so rewarding, because his agenda is political. The philosophers' own, intrinsic agenda is not Reeve's problem—but it is Plato's, as the passages just listed attest.

A third and final main issue I have with Reeve's book is its recurrent insistence that the *Republic*'s Good is something *human,* that is as if it guided philosophers to design the optimal conditions for human beings to flourish happily (see especially Reeve pp. 82–85). The response this deserves is easiest to formulate theologically as in 5.5. For the Form of the Good is like God in 5.5 in *not* being on our side. Just as we can learn to be on *God's* side, if our level of thinking and feeling rises far enough above our vain, mundane concerns, similarly we can learn to follow the Good. The point is that we would need to become Godlike, changing ourselves to suit God, but that God would not reach downwards to us and show a human face. There is no divine forgiveness for our foolishness. Reeve wants to take this back, which sounds not only anti-Platonic (cf. 5.5–5.8 plus the *Laws,* the *Timaues,* and the *Theaetetus,* and see Chapters 6, 12, and 13), but also self-serving. For it is difficult or impossible to much respect anything that is merely useful.

5.10 SUMMARY

This chapter (5) began with four sections on justice (5.1–5.4), and then it turned briefly to God (5.5). After that came three sections on the Good (5.6–5.8) and finally there was a single section to refute a major current scholar (5.9). Justice and God instanced aRa and the Form of the Good instanced RR. These are the main reasons why they evidenced $\mathbb{R}$, though also the analysis of relativity and dialectical concflicts by means of $aRbRc...$ had some significance (in 5.6 and 5.7).

NOTES

1. If justice and goodness were of the same causal type then their relationship would be entirely logical: zRz to RR. The just (positioned as a) would instance a relation (R) which the Good would represent on a higher level (RR), as it were philosophizing about it and not only using it in practice. But what would this R be? E.g. EQUALS or REVEALING would seem to be too abstract for the needs of justice, which would demand e.g. DESERVES or PRODUCES. I.e., the just have to *do*

things in a way that the Good need not. They require a "moving" cause, not merely a structure. Cf. 6.

2. Utilitarians are of course free to make an *addition* to their view for example to the effect persons that who produce more happiness in a society need to be rewarded with more happiness than other persons in that society because this happens to cause there to be more happiness to distribute; but that is a separate matter, because it does not derive directly from the main utilitarian principle.

3. Why? At least because Plato's individuation of the rational part is simplistic in making all cognitive fields seem too much like philosophy. For seeking one kind of knowledge can be very different from seeking another kind, see 5.7.

4. We do not find the *Timaerus* or the *Laws,* let alone Aristotle, taking things further in the *Republic*'s direction, because those two later works and Aristotle *counteract* separation. For with them the divine is merged again with nature (even if not completely in some respects), see Chapters 12 and 6, cf. Feibleman and Solmsen.

5. Krämer notes (in 1959 at p. 260) that Plato's effort seems to be to provide the units in question on a purely *logical* basis and that this would easily involve the challenge of deriving quantities from qualities. Logicists might agree with this description of the problem. With Dedekind this is not so obvious. (Per Frege the reason for this is that Dedekind does not actually theorize sets or notice all their properies, see Gillies for discussion.)

My own impression is that Dedekind's hierarchies are like Plato's in depending on recursive series and not so much on sets (which Dedekind calls "systems"). For instance, Dedekind p. 64 presents a proof for a Theorem 66 which resembles the Third Man of Plato's *Parmenides.* (On that page Dedekind credits Bolzano, seeming to not know about Plato.) That proof says roughly that Dedekind's system of (possible) thoughts is an infinite system (call it S) because if s is one of thoughts in system S then so is s', where s' says that s is in S. This leads S to become infinite because then s'' can relate similarly to s', and s''' to s'', *ad infinitum.* (Thoughts about members of the system will *themselves be* additional members of the system, but then so will thoughts about those thoughts, and thoughts about those thoughts about thoughts, etc.) This proof is structurally analogical to the "third man" in Plato's *Parmenides* if we think of s' as linking $\{S,s\}$, and then of s'' as linking $\{S,s'\}$ (or $\{s,s'\}$), etc. For then we first build a bridge between two islands, and then a new bridge between between the old bridge and the (or either) island, etc. Dedekind says this in the language of sets, that is true, but he could as well use for instance relations and relata. For if aRb calls for bridge-building between $\{a,R\}$, then a' can be introduced as the bridge, and next a'' as the next bridge (i.e. from a' to a and/or R), etc. (Nothing in this requires Dedekind's talk of thoughts and egos in my view. Hence it is not pertinent, though it is correct, of Frege to object to Dedekind's psychologism, i.e. as if patterns such as that of Orion in outer space were merely thoughts of some *homo sapiens.*)

Chapter Six

The Laws

The *Laws*' argument is founded on a cosmological argument. According to it *a* MOVES *a* MOVES *b* MOVES *c*, etc., where *a=God* and *b*, *c*, etc., are the later events of history (the *Laws* shifts at times to Gods in the plural, but for simplicity I will mostly use the singular). The *Laws*' libertarian argument is that humans can become more or less Godlike and hence more or less free. But God's self-motion is psychic or spiritual, and this is why Godlikeness or freedom is attained philosophically (or theologically, cf. Laks p. 260). Hence freedom consists, once more, of thinking in a particular way, and the liberating process has the structure ℝ.

This chapter begins from the *Laws*' beginning. The work's first few pages already suggest its priorities (6.1). For the *Laws*' utopia, named Magnesia, is fashioned on a divine model. This model is used in many different areas of life, and in each of them it has its implications. The implication for the virtues is that wisdom must rank highest, because it is the most Godlike (6.2). For pleasures the divine implication is different, because there are no divine pleasures. Instead, pleasures have an instrumental role. Humans need to be led in a divine direction by means of patterns which please them (6.3). More specifically, such educating pleasures are instanced in gymnastics (6.4), music (6.5), and theater (6.6). The pleasures do not reach all the way to the divine conclusions, however, because the concluding portions of the educational process are intrinsically valid. They require reasoning, not pleasure. Similarly, the Magnesian educational philosophy begins from bodily exercises but it culminates in the study of mathematics and astronomy (6.7). Pleasures are associated with the body and valid relations with thought. Despite this, and somewhat surprisingly for Plato, the educational program of the *Laws* does not teach philosophical or theological speculation as such. Rather, the main point of entrance to God's realm is through science. However, speculation comes into the utopia through the back door, as a kind of safety net. For skeptical discourses are foreseen because there will be unanswered questions in some minds even when the utopian system of education is in place. The most significant discourses seem to consist of debating whether God exists (6.8).

The Magnesian system of criminal justice is founded on the same divine model in being therapeutic (6.9). The thought is that if only God is perfectly free then crime is involuntary, and so the criminal does not deserve punishment inherently. Rather, she is to be taught better. Her own interest lies in a religious direction. The divine implication for the Magnesian economy, again, is that individuals need to be materially self-sufficient and have ample spare time to live examined lives (6.10). Commercial activity and specialized professions would get in their way and make them too servile.

The *Laws* represents its divine norm as something conservative, because the utopia reverts to the most ancient of ways (6.11). Its myth of the deluge speculates about how human civilization can have had a beginning (6.12).

In 6.13 and 6.14 we finally reach the discussion on the first mover, God. In 6.13 my main concern will be to show how God is not a deterministic force in the universe. In 6.14 we assess what reason Plato has to say that God is a soul. Why is it that self-motion is possible only in thought?

As before, I will conclude the chapter by comparing my account of Plato with another scholar's (6.15), though also earlier sections will engage in some confrontations with competing views. The issue between us is much as in 2–5 in that once again the other scholars I discuss are more skeptical about Plato's perfectionistic philosophizing than I am. In particular, in 6.15 Bobonich holds that individuals do not need to become philosophers to qualify as virtuous or happy citizens in Magnesia, and I deny this. Philosophizing is Plato's central purpose, as always.

6.1 SELF-SUPERIORITY (625E–628E)

The first few pages of the first book of the *Laws* take us directly to a generalized and foundational question. Why should a state be ordered in one way rather than in another? What is the basis supposed to be (624A)?

At first this foundational question is political, concerning states, but soon its scope is expanded to concern villages, families, and individual persons as well (626C–D). The bridge from the specifically political version of the question to the generalized ethical dilemma is built by evaluating a particular hypothesis. On this hypothesis, expressed by Cleinias, the laws of a state should be formed with an aim to winning wars against other states (625D–626D).

The Athenian, who is (among other things) the Socrates-like questioner in the *Laws*, generalizes this principle by considering whether the same principle, if valid, should not be applied also to villages (626C), families (626C), and individual humans (626D). The other speakers of this dialogue concede that analogy rather easily. But this leads them to picture war everywhere. For not only would states then fight states. Also villages would fight villages, families families, and individuals individuals. Moreover each of them would also fight itself (626C–E), so everything would be at war, both within itself and without.

This result is so obviously displeasing (626E) that it seems naturally to lead the Athenian to consider a more positive alternative. The change appears to take place based on the reflection that universal war could be reversed (628A). For if an individual is divided against herself then she needs to have at least two separable parts. Moreover, if one of the parts wins against the other (assuming there to be only two parts for simplicity) then the winning part is superior and the loser is inferior. But on this basis the Athenian is able to speak of things being superior or inferior to themselves (626E–627C), and not only as something divided or conflicted as in war. Apparently the thought is that individuals, families, villages, and states may all be driven by what is best in them and therefore avoid war.

We will see later that the *Laws* uses this hierarchical thinking very widely, namely so as to cover individuals' thoughts and social stuctures as well as God and the cosmos as a whole. Everything is to be brought into peaceful harmony with itself and with everything else. In this way, the very first pages of the *Laws* already contain a sketch of what will turn out to be the ultimate cosmic utopia.

But what if anything does this have to do with $\mathbb{R}$? Quite a lot, because all of the above combinations are easy to map in relations and difficult to map otherwise. The negative scenario of universal strife generalizes a relation like CONFLICTS WITH or WARS AGAINST across the board, that is, from term to term. Thus, because a fights b, but also b fights c and c in turn fights d, and so on, we can form a single coherent series like a FIGHTS b FIGHTS c FIGHTS d FIGHTS.... In this scenario each fighter fights her neighbor. But this is not yet the whole story because each party has been said also to fight itself, as in z FIGHTS z, or zRz, and this takes us to a full-blown version of $\mathbb{R}$.

To this background it is not difficult to imagine how we might interpret the positive setting of universal peace or hierarchy. We need a different relation but the organizational principle is the same. Our relation needs to spell something like IS INFERIOR TO, HAS A SUPERIOR IN, or IS OVERCOME BY. The positive hypothesis says a HAS A SUPERIOR IN b HAS A SUPERIOR IN c HAS A SUPERIOR IN... z HAS A SUPERIOR IN z, which pattern instances ℝ (for less formal ways to organize much the same material to a similar effect see Stalley and Irwin 2010; Zuckert is misled by the Athenian's mild manner to dissociate him from Socrates' radicalism).

But what is questionable about the claims that I have made about the *Laws'* first pages? How can they be challenged?

i. "How is any a to be its own superior, as in $a<a$? This is no more possible for an individual than for a village. Everyone is as she is, and everything is at it happens to be—no different. No one is taller than she is, and no one is one iota smarter, stronger, or what have you. Hence, if the above is the true story about the *Laws*, then the *Laws* is really exposed as nonsense (cf. 5.3 for the same issue in the *Republic*)."

There is an easy reply to this and then also a not very easy one which we need also to decipher eventually in this chapter (in 6.14). The easy answer is to say that things have parts and the things are their own superiors when some of the parts, specifically the superior ones, rule over the others. Along these lines the Athenian's idea seems to be that if some a wins against a then a consists of something inferior (b) which loses and something superior (c) which wins (626E–627A). Here $a=b+c$, and $b<c$. This view involves no paradox of the type which i describes. But this answer will turn out to be too easy eventually because the *Laws* will take us to the God's self-motion (introduced in 6.13 below), and that will not be explained simply by a hierarchy of internal parts. For the time being we will take the easy way out but the reader has now been forewarned that things will be trickier later.

ii. "But Plato himself suggests no relational interpretation of the passages in question, and we are free to account for his message in so many different ways. Hence, there is no unique value to ℝ in this context. We might as well study the mores of Athens, Sparta, and Crete in historical detail, or else we could compare Zeno and Apollo as mythical Gods (624A). Also, we could use dialogical models or universals and particulars, and so on. The possibilities are endless. Plato can be read on so many different levels. None of them is *the* level."

This is incorrect because Plato does aspire to exhibit relational patterns: conflict, coherence, and hierachy. For his message is that one kind of relationship between individuals, families, villages, and states is sensible and another is not. The first is militant and the latter is peaceful. Moreover, Plato manages at the same time to consider internal relationships as well, so his topic is also about the relationships that individuals, families, villages, and states are to have to themselves. But all of these are relational patterns, and they are not accounted for by means of universals and particulars or dialogue per se (let alone by myths or historical details, which would not even pertain to reasoning). Put differently, if we use those vocabularies then we need to adjust them to cover the relational structures, because it is those structures that are the message in Plato's text. But then we need to introduce relational idioms in any case, in which case the universals and particulars or dialogical elements become dispensable and optional because the ground that needs covering is relational. We cannot account for the war and peace and hierarchy within and without except by relations because they *are* relations. Plato's *message* is relational.

iii. "But Plato nowhere says that these things are to be viewed as relations. This priority derives from one reader of Plato, not from Plato himself (compare the positivists of 1.4 again)."

As noted, without using relations it is not easy to map the two scenarios above, namely universal war and universal peace, but with relations it is achieved easily. Why that is so is no mystery, because conflict and concord are relations between things (or else within things, as was already made clear). But if that is so then Plato does not need additionally to come along to say use a word like "relation" to make plain that his topics are relational, for we can see that for ourselves. (Similarly, every statement does not need to be announced as a statement to be recognized as one, or as a word to be read as one, and so on.)

iv. "Is the law of the *Laws* now supposed to be that each thing, whether a person, a village, or a state, is an able judge of itself? If yes then this sounds oddly similar to the individualism and relativism of liberal thought in modern times, which again raises the suspicion that what is being described in this book is not inherently Platonic at all but an interpreter's wishful projection."

This demands two responses. The first is that the notion that things judge themselves is ancient, so it is not a modern projection (compare 5.1–5.5 and 3.7). It seems to be implicit in the Hindu norm that each living thing is to be reborn in accordance with its habits in the present life, which Chapter 3 also already mentioned when discussing reincarnation in the *Phaedo*. In ancient Babylon Hammurabi's law was that an eye should be taken for an eye, and Jesus in the New Testament says we reap what we sow (*Galatians* 6:7). Pythagoras had a mathematical version of this norm of justice according to some sources, so that for x the just standard to be applied is x itself, as in x times x, or x^2 (Sieroka p. 22). Hence it is not incredible to say that already in ancient times Plato could have maintained that we are best judged internally. But second, in the *Laws* Plato does not actually maintain that everyone is best judged internally: only the educated are, as we will see below. One must become at least somewhat divine before the norm begins literally to apply (644B, 726A–727A, 731D–732E, 904C–E), and I will interpret this requirement as saying that one must have a coherent internal principle in the first place: mixed and contradictory things cohere with everything and nothing.

6.2 VIRTUE (631B–D, 689D–E)

Cleinias values military valor, and so it is understandable that the main virtue for him is courage. But the pacifistic Athenian prioritizes wisdom instead (631B–D). He describes a hierarchy in which wisdom is topmost and other virtues such as temperance, justice, and courage rank lower. Below these other virtues we find such lesser values as health, wealth, and material comforts (on virtues in the *Laws* see Annas and Kraut).

That material values rank so low in Plato should surprise no one, but why is it supposed to be as clear as Plato seems to think it is that wisdom ranks so high? What is wisdom anyway? What do the wise do? Most coherently, they would seem not only to instance harmony 689D–E but also to know about it and to produce it in their surroundings (see 6.13 for the larger associations). This would make them the natural ambassadors of the kind of external and internal peace which was discussed in 6.1.

Now let us consider this in the light of $\mathbb{R}$. Is it wise of the Athenian to rank the virtues as above? If it is then wisdom seems to be the ordering relation in a series of the form $\mathbb{R}$ such that $RRaRaRbRcRdRe...$ and $a=wisdom$, $b=temperance$, and so on. Here R would be the characteristically HARMONIZING activity of the wise.

But does the *Laws* actually say that this order is established by the wise? There seems to be no such passage. As things will turn out later on, this is as it should be because the wise are not autonomous beings in Magnesia. Rather they are servants of the divine law. The divine model is above every human subject, so the only exact use of $\mathbb{R}$ that we can expect from the *Laws* will be divine and not human. Despite this the work is rife with human approximations of things divine, and these merit our attention.

6.3 PLEASURE (653A–654D, 659D–660A)

Pleasure has a role to play in Magnesia but it also has its strict limits. Bluntly, pleasures and pains rule over the actions of small children and animals but they do not determine the thoughts of the free or divine. Thus the *Laws'* hedonism is confined to a low order of things. It is there, but it is not central (cf. Dorothea Frede).

Here is how hedonism enters the utopian picture at all. Pleasure is initially the foundation of human motivation, 653A says, because children will tend to do what pleases them, moving around and making sounds (653D–E). Accordingly, if one wishes to teach them things then one should make the right things pleasing to them (659D–660A). Conversely, what there is no hope of is that the children understand, or perhaps even care, why it is that they are guided in a particular direction as opposed to another. For Plato holds that they will be focused more on the pleasures than on the reasons or reasonings (653B; this is an association of Plato's which I will question below). One aspect of this is that children should be taught by playing games, because it is unrealistic to expect them to stay silent and still for long or to follow an organized procedure (819BA–D). It is not good to scold youths, Plato says (729A–C). In general, authorities should be like loving parents and not like commanding and threatening tyrants (895A). The basis for these "soft" norms seems to be in their sheer realism, because Plato attempts to fashion Magnesia on a realistic conception of human nature. If this is correct then the "hardness" of a military drill is not as likely to really educate anyone.

But in what direction should the children be steered? What is it that they should learn to take pleasure in? This is the topic that will quickly take us outside the realm of pleasures and pains. For it is pleasure that children will learn to take in regularity and harmony through gymnastics and music (653D–E, 659D–660A); but they cannot appreciate music properly without being born anew as non-hedonic beings. They rank above (many) animals in being able to value rhythms and harmonic chords and melodies at all (653E–654A), to be sure, but it is still a further step to value music as such. For music like argument requires a characteristically Platonic focus on what is inherently valid in the object (667E–671A). Certain patterns are there in the rhythms and chords and melodies or else they are not, and accordingly the music is valuable or not (ibid.). The presence of this value-giving element is not indicated by any sensation of pleasure as such, Plato says (667E–671A). He appears to hold that pleasures (and pains) are like wishes or fears which may or may not accord with the important (and ultimately divine) realities, so the relationship seems contingent. One may or may not take pleasure in the valid things, and the things will be valid even if no one happens to find her way to value them (ibid.). Put differently, Plato seems to mean that pleasures can train us to pay heed to the right level of things but that we should begin at some point to value the level for its own sake and not because it has (artificially) been made into something fun by someone. (Here I omit a discussion regarding the relational character of pleasures in the *Laws*. On that topic in the *Phaedo* see 3.1; on it in the *Republic* see 5.6; also see 8 on the *Gorgias*. Dorothea Frede raises similar questions about relational pleasures in the *Laws*.)

6.4 GYMNASTICS (653A–654A, BOOK VII)

That pleasure is taken in the right kinds of order by human bodies is ensured first by exercises in gymnastics (795D; meanwhile music tends to the soul, ibid.). However gymnastics is a point of entry to the divine patterns of utopia not only for young children, as above, but for Magnesians of all ages (665C). All bodies need to be learn repeatedly about the right sorts of pleasures.

Now I will note only in passing that this thinking conforms well with this book's relational and structural orientation, because it is for regularity and order. We may imagine Magnesian gymnasts instancing the same pattern through many separate exercises, in which case they are much like the strings of a lyre in the *Phaedo* (see Chapter 3). In contrast it would once again be clumsy to speak of Plato's meaning only in terms of something like a property or a universal. The relevant wavelength is rather that of a ratio or pattern.

Here we should also begin to raise the issue of totalitarianism with regard to the *Laws*. For imagining collective gymnastics can easily awaken very negative associations from recent history. After all, we are accustomed to seeing pictures of masses of soldiers marching in straight lines and supposedly happy and colorfully clad Soviet children following carefully planned movements. In North Korea such ceremonies of public happiness seem still to be in fashion. However Plato seems to lack the notion of a large and anonymous mass, so these associations do not seem to accord exactly with his utopia. By our standards Magnesia is more like a village (with only 5040 free households). Moreover, we know that the totalitarians' ideologies are shams and fakes, but we should not assume too quickly that Magnesia is as hollow. Perhaps the more beneficial images will be of, say, collective exercises at Daoist cloisters. More questions about totalitarianism will arise later in this chapter (6; see C.C.W. Taylor for discussion).

6.5 MUSIC (653E–656C, 667E–671A, 700A–701C)

Music has a surprisingly important role in Magnesia: it educates the soul (795D). How can Plato expect this much from it? As mentioned, music introduces regularity to the soul (665A). But this is only the beginning, for Plato advances a sketch of a mimetic theory of music at 667E–671A. On this theory music has an external object just as a sculpture has one. A sculpture can portray a person's physical appearance more or less fairly, Plato seems to say, and accordingly it may or may not be a good sculpture (though this is not his only consideration). Just so, music can represent its object correctly or else fail to do so, and it needs to be evaluated in accordance with that. Plato admits that the represented object of a piece of music is more difficult to trace than the represented object of some words (669D–E). But he insists none the less that music is representative: it is to accord with something ulterior. What is that? Where is the object for music? Plato's most ambitious association would probably by like Pythagoras', for whom there is a music of the heavens, which is divine. Music of this kind would teach us to appreciate the utopian order of the cosmos (cf. Bourgault, who argues convincingly against Saunders' and Stalley's more conservative interpretations). However we are not told anything more specific about such divine music in the *Laws*. The music does not sound as one reads Plato, and the *Laws* contains no musical notes, chords, and so on. Hence, and like so often in Plato, we are given only rough directions, and much is left to our own imaginations.

Why ℝ accords with this was already noted in 3.8. Music is relational in consisting of ratios, and the ratios can be instanced by different material bodies. This is to say that for the relation R in $aRbRc$ we can shift the terms to $dReRf$ and retain the same rhythm, chord, or melody R. For only the ratio needs to be the same. One can play the same song on a tuba as on a piano, and on low keys as well as high. This is somewhat as with arithmetic, so that *1+1=2* applies to apples as well as oranges, so that *apple + apple = two apples*, of course. This would be entirely trivial to say were it not a fact that relational or structural interpretations of Plato are unusual in the current literature. It is *not* normal to consider the way or ways in which Plato's philosophizing has patterns similar to music.

We need to consider this fact from angle of an alternative. Imagine, for instance, that we think the vocabulary of universals and particulars or predicates and subjects to be central to the interpretation of Plato. With such tools we would not be adjusting to Plato's particular wavelength well at all, because both of those vocabularies are totally uninformative in the theory of music. In contrast, ℝ is at least in the right ball park. Plato's philosophy homes in on particular ratios, relations, or structures. Our interpretive tools need to accord with that highly general fact.

6.6 THEATER (657E–663D, 700A–701C)

At 657E–661A Plato imagines a festival with all kinds of performances from puppet theater, comic and tragic plays, readings of poetry, and even horse races. He considers how a competition between such different acts would lead to different winners depending who acts as the judge. If the children had the say then the puppet theater would win (658C), but the youths would elect a comedy (658D). The majority would nominate a tragedy (ibid.); but the old would side with the readings of Homer and Hesiod (ibid.).

Now which judge, if any, would be right? Who can judge the judges and qualify as the *über*-judge? Plato raises this issue at least in order to have an opportunity for rejecting the populistic theatrocracy (701A) in which there is a democratic raise of hands, for again it is not the maximization of pleasure which should have the say in his book (659B–C, 660D–661D). Rather, the judge of judges is the most educated party (658D–E). Such a party is to fashion the festivals in such a way that there is a clear moral lesson to be learned every time. The festivities are to teach the population that only the virtuous or the reasoning will be rewarded with pleasures (660D–E; this rule binds the poets at 801B–D). However even Plato himself seems to have some doubts as to whether this is true about human life (662A–663E), so it may need to be taught merely as a useful lie (663D). Also, he seems to be somewhat uncertain whether people will in general accept the morals that are taught (663E). If they do then clearly it is a comparatively pleasant option for all to have the instruction take place through entertaining festivities. Probably comparatively few people would delight as much in attending lectures and taking graded tests.

It is perhaps a little monotonous to hear once again that $\mathbb{R}$ can be used to explain Plato's thought. But against this there is the possibility of maintaining that it is Plato himself who is the monotonous one, because he keeps returning to his pedagogical program and picturing optimal human affairs in terms of hierarchical relations. In this section (6.6) the version of $\mathbb{R}$ that we get places the educated theatre critics at the top of the hierarchy. They value their own evaluations (as in *RR*), and moreover they set the standards for the other segments of the utopian population (as in *aRbRc*).

6.7 EDUCATION (643A–645C, 653A–673D, 788A–822D)

In approaching the Magnesian philosophy of education we should note at the outset that Plato is an early adherent to public education. Already small children are to be shaped by the utopian state. The tradition this contrasts with is one in which education, and especially early childhood education, is left to the private discretion of the family or household. In Plato the public sphere of state planning intrudes into the traditionally private realm and takes rational control of what is there, for the traditional intuitions about education and ethics are simply not trusted (despite Plato's frequent adherence to many things ancient, see 6.11 below). For it is reason that must rule in human life, across the board. In Magnesia even sleeping patterns are regulated, and foods. Humans are to study the implications of reason and to implement their findings throughout. Consequently it is no surprise that Magnesia is run by teachers (718C–D, 720D, 723A, 857D–E, 885D–E, 888A–D). It resembles a giant school. (See Clearey for an overview. In keeping with Plato, the Renaissance utopias of Europe, as for instance Campanella's, Bacon's, and Comenius', are often places precisely of education, though perhaps Bacon's is more aptly assimilated to a research institute.)

What does the educational process consist of? We receive an initial impression of this by first considering its earliest stage. At 790C–791B infants are to be rocked as at sea to comfort them, for such a regular movement gives them a sense of harmony as silence and stillness do not. Thus, right from the beginning Plato's educational philosophy in the *Laws* instances regular movement, just as the pinnacle of the *Laws'* hierarchy, God, is a regular *mover*. The coherence of this contrasts with a different coherence that Plato instanced earlier, for the Plato of the *Laws* is no longer the adherent of the *eternal stillness* of the Forms as in the *Phaedo* and the *Symposium*. The emphasis is on motion, and more specifically on regular motion. In this same spirit, as the children age they participate in musical and gymnastic education, the point of which is to learn to value regular movements, as already mentioned. But something very similar seems to be planned also for higher education, which consists of arithmetic, geometry, and astronomy (817E–822D). For these fields of knowledge take Magnesians to the most direct grasp of God's thoughts in the regular motions of the heavens (644D–645C, 659D, 716C–E, 726A–734E), which are regular in the extreme (and which we will come to in 6.14 below).

Now let us turn again to $\mathbb{R}$. Magnesia appears as a giant school, we said, and it is hierarchical. To this background it comes as no surprise that, at 728C, each Magnesian individual is to improve her inferiors and follow her superiors. This we may interpret as a generalization about the Magnesian social order. Then a IS IMPROVED BY b IS IMPROVED BY c... or, because the more specific character of the improvements is educational, a IS TAUGHT BY b IS TAUGHT BY c... On these premises we are close to having an instance of $\mathbb{R}$ because the series has the structure $aRbRc$, where R=IS TAUGHT BY. What is still missing is the hierarchy's tip, however. Is either pattern, zRz or zRR, in the text? More specifically, who exactly is to teach the teachers (as in zRR), or who is self-taught (as in zRz)? We will learn this in 6.13–6.14.

Now let us have objections again.

i. "This talk of invading the traditionally private sphere of the home with the most homogenous of patterns invites associations of totalitarianism in a different way than before. For is the privacy of homes and persons not being abolished in Plato's utopia by a single generic rule for all?"

There is also a sense in which Magnesian education is not totalitarian, namely because it is "soft," as noted. It is not about strict discipline, for youths are best taught by example and not admonished (729A–C). Teachers benefit from trying to learn as they teach, and should be like loving parents and not like threatening tyrants (895A). Also, as in Egypt, mathematical games are valued for children, so learning should be made into something pleasing (819BA–D). In these terms, progress does not need to be painful. Beyond this, it is also worth nothing in passing that the *Laws* shows no great animosity to human nature even when it is not utopian, holding that humans are normally tame animals as they stand. But education serves to raise their level to something divine (766A). Hence, for Plato humans are not innately evil, as they have been for many Christians who believe in original sin, for example. For this reason the utopian educator can afford to be comparatively kind to her students.

ii. "But rationalist thought, too, can be a straitjacket. For we saw that the educational authorities of the *Laws* are to follow Magnesia's laws to the letter, and this goes against their free thought. For then there is to be no leeway left over for them to think through on their own. How can such a setting possible be called free? Is the *Laws* not rather about compelling thought and education to abide by certain eternal and supposedly holy rules which should never be changed in any way? The reply to ii does not contradict this prospect because there is also a totalitarianism of the mind."

The *best* rules would not need changing: that seems to be what Plato is after. If the laws are not optimal they leave room for improvement, but there will clearly be less reason to improve anything if the result is perfect already. In the utopian scenario the warranted option seems to be to abide by the rules, that is by living by them and teaching them to others. But this is freedom-friendly thinking if the perfect pattern in question leads one to instance self-motion. Plato's argument is that there is no alternative route to self-motion. Self-motion requires a particular, divine structure. It is not a matter of taste or dispute. Everyday agents do not instance it for instance in choosing between coffee and tea in normal life. It is something perfect, not something that is already familiar from common experience.

iii. "But how are the best rules to be found if they are not to be questioned?"

But they *are*. Even materialists and atheists will be confronted with civilized arguments if they deny the foundational value of the divine sanction (see 6.8 below). Plato's Academy is not a military academy. It is a highly intellectual place, with philosophers and theologians at the helm. Magnesia is generally not a city of arbitrary traditions or fashions and its laws can always be questioned, as we will now see.

6.8 DISCOURSE (720A–724A, 880D–E, 885B–899D)

We saw in 6.7 that Magnesia's educational program does not involve philosophical speculation in speech or writing, because the training is focused on gymnastics, music, and science. The program seems to be geared to deliver definite results which conform to stable patterns, not to raising questions. However, despite this, there seems to be an expectation that among humans questions still will arise, for philosophical discourse is far from being absent from this utopia. Let us now first examine two passages in which this matter is discussed and then consider the extent to which the *Laws* is self-consistent in its discursive idealizations.

The first passage to look at is 720A–724A, where the Athenian compares medication among the free with medication among slaves (this is crucial to both Zuckert above and Bobonich below). Among slaves doctors simply prescribe treatments but among the free they also explain why they prescribe them, so among the free patients are treated not only as patients but also as co-doctors. Similar thinking is applied to legislation at 721B–D, so the legislator of the free gives her reasons to the legislated. This appears to be a general point about how free citizens need to be treated. They are not to be made to undergo any changes as uninformed patients and rather they are educated so that they can participate actively in the deliberate procedures. Magnesia comes thus to seem even more like a school society, because even medication is viewed pedagogically. (It is notable also that Plato expects the free citizens to care about the facts pertaining to their medication and legislation. This expectation seems rather exotic compared to the realities of today's liberal societies. For instance my own sister, a practicing gynecologist, tells me that patients tend to be rather uninterested in hearing about the science on which their treatments are based. Plato's view of human nature seems to be more flattering than the modern reality.)

A second passage, 880D–E, shows how even atheists will be confronted fairly and openly in Plato's theocracy. For a materialistic atheist is not simply imprisoned or silenced in Magnesia, but reasoned with (885B–899D). This is the highpoint of all of the utopian discourses, it is said (887B–C; thus I cannot agree with Laks p. 290 that discourse is not a Magnesian ideal). The atheist or materialist is an especially radical critic of Magnesia because she has a reversed view of reality and values. She holds that body is prior to soul (892A–C) and that the heavenly bodies are made up of earth and stone (886D). According to her the material things have originated earlier in history, and reason and God have arisen only later as human creations (889B–E). Materially all there is to justice is force (890A), she says. It is notable that Plato's response to persons with brutish views of this type is not brutish but civilized and that the civilized discourse that he foresees between the utopian rulers and the materialistic rebels is in a way already in utopian terms. For it does not involve the use of violence. It is to strive to overpower the body not with the body but with the soul or thought, which is exactly the main message which the utopians wish to teach the rebels anyway! Hence, if the rebels agree to this practice then their conversion into utopians has already begun. In general, there seems to be a deep coherence to the Magnesian adherence to reason. A similar coherence does not appear to attach to materialistic arguments.

Beyond the above two main points the text of the *Laws* repeatedly describes the norms it sets for itself as a self-conscious piece of discourse (the performative awareness is registered for instance at 722C–D). Some of them are followed quite well in the text, such as those which were referred to in 3.6 and 3.13 as "cognitive communism" (in the *Laws* cf. 629A, 633A, 667A–B). On the other hand certain passages idealize hierarchical priorities and the actual text of the *Laws* seems often to be rather too unstable or unfocused to meet such ideals. The overall view seems to be that some topics have priority and demand most attention but that there are also lighter topics which demand their share of time (816D–E, 803C). At 631B–632D the Athenian outlines his preferred manner of presentation, which consists at least of a hierarchy of different values and the relations these have to political authorities and institutions. On an even more abstract level he says at 630E–631A and 632E to prioritze the whole and not particular contexts, and at 638C–D that things are not to be evaluated in isolation but in their diverse inter-relations. However the *Laws* itself does not seem to be systematic or orderly in this way, and if that is so then it does not practice what it preaches. It does not qualify as an ideal piece of discourse (or thought) by its own lights because it frequently drifts from detail to detail (which claim I do not think I need to prove).

6.9 CRIME (859D–864B)

The utopian model of education is expected to leave gaps also in a further sense. It is not only, as above, that philosophical explanations will be necessary to make to atheistic materialists or that medical and legislative facts need to be taught to Magnesia's citizens despite the education they receive. For there will not be gaps only in knowledge. Also moral gaps will remain, and so crime is expected to survive inside the bounds of Magnesia (853B–D).

What is the Magnesian response to crime? Is the response based on desert or reform? The latter (857C–858A, 854A–E; cf. Jaeger vol. 3 p. 216 for the view that Plato is inspired to this view by an analogy with the practice of medicine). For 860C–D says that bad deeds are involuntary (cf. especially the *Gorgias'* "intellectualism"). This truth has general implications because all legislation regarding crime, in every state, is premised on the distinction between voluntary and involuntary acts (861B–C). Why is that? Because, says 861E, individuals hurt other individuals often —this is what gives us a stock of data to consider as potential issues for criminal cases at all—but such deeds will not always be voluntary. Perpetrators may be too ignorant or too weak in character (863A–864B). Accordingly, crime really requires a pedagogical or a medical response. At 862C–D crimes are dealt with medically by curing souls' diseases, and at 862D–E crimes are dealt with pedagogically by educating criminals about what to do in life. The generalization is that criminals need to be helped, not tortured. This is not to imply that they *can* always be helped, however. If a criminal is incapable enough of improving her ways then she is put to death as a hopeless case (862E–863A, 854E–855A).

Plato has an interesting view regarding the severity of the measures which need taking in response to criminal behavior. For the severity does not vary by the size of the crime but by the curability of the criminal (941C–D). Thus, even a petty thief may require extensive treatment if her soul is very corrupt. For if her soul is corrupt enough then that means that she would in fact commit greater thefts if she only could (ibid.). Thus, the state of her soul cannot be assessed based on what she actually *manages* to steal. Comparatively, another thief may take vast sums from another person and simply happen to have such an opportunity as a one-time affair (ibid.; also see 944B–C). She may require almost no measures from the authorities to steer her back to a life of virtue and innocence. This is to say that the punishment (or rather the therapeutic measure) is not made to fit the crime: it is made to fit the criminal, and specifically the criminal's soul (also see 944A–D).

But why is Plato so confident that the free can not commit crimes? Could someone not do evil voluntarily? What is supposed to rule out such a possibility? The Magnesian answer to this seems to be based on its divine ideal. For freedom pure and simple is instanced by God alone, which we will identify God's self-motions with certain manners of thought below. Lesser motions are not exactly free because they are not exactly self-moved. This is to say that they are at least partly moved by other things, not only by themselves. But an entirely voluntary action would be entirely self-moved, and every action that is not voluntary is involuntary. The final premise that we need is that a criminal is not self-sufficient because she harms another. In other words, crimes cannot be free because crimes consist of external relations, and the relations of the free are internal. On these premises, which appear to underlie Plato's therapeutic view on crime, free criminals are erased from the utopian picture entirely as an impossibility, and the utopians can only "re-educate" evil-doers but they can not punish them.

Notice that on this view crime becomes an object of rational treatment. By contrast, criminal actions would be much less understandable and explainable if they originated in uncaused acts of free wills. For the evils that would be willed freely would be mysterious, because their causes could not be located. Meanwhile, Plato's therapeutic view makes crime something less than exotic, because then criminals are in principle only like so many other humans. Like everyone else they are not yet free, and like everyone else they need instruction about how to manage liberation eventually. This is because, in ℝ's symbols, something can be free only in divine isolation from other things (as in ...*zRz* or ...*zRR*) and because this freedom can be sought in grades (as in *aRbRc*...). A criminal is at most only further away from the shared goal than the many others who are more innocent. Accordingly, crime is an educational issue on a par with so many others.

However, we need to note in fairness that the text of the *Laws* complicates the above picture in two wide-ranging ways which we cannot study at length in the context of this book. First, the *Laws* adopts the idioms of other philosophies of criminal justice and, second, its particular laws regarding crime can often seem arbitrary in their extensive details. The first type of complication arises because Plato does not strive in all, or in many enough, passages to make a completely clear break with the view that is his main traditional competitor on issues bearing on crime, namely the tradition according to which punishments must match crimes due to desert (as in Hammurabi's "Eye for an eye" once more, see 5.3–5.4 and 6.1). That tradition arguably has more to do with (irrational) revenge than with (rational) solutions, and it is clearly and deeply at odds with Plato's own position. To this background the terms of Plato's attack against it are surprisingly mild. There are few sharp edges. (The younger Plato would probably have differentiated the competing positions more clearly.) The second kind of complication arises because Plato seems to have more than timeless philosophical principles in mind when he authors the *Laws*. His effort appears to be to legislate for a concrete utopia with the name Magnesia in actual historical fact. For his laws regarding crime become quite detailed (cf. 865A–885B, 907E–945B). To illustrate this one example, at 916A anyone selling products worth more than fifty drachmas is made to remain in the city for ten days. Now of course this is not something which we can explain philosophically (any more than we could derive the optimal size for windows from God in 6.7). The relation between fifty drachmas and ten days is purely arbitrary from a philosophical point of view. However, one needs to keep in mind that it may not be arbitrary in practical affairs, for perhaps it will have effects which happen to conform the high-minded, theocratic principles in the specific locality of central Crete over two millenia ago.

6.10 LABOR (704D–705B, 806D–E, 918C–919E)

The Magnesian economy consists of 5040 land-owning households located in central Crete. The farms are safely removed from the coastline and its commercial affairs. But though the utopia's households are farms, its citizens themselves are not farmers, and there are slaves to perform the actual physical labor (806D–E). The same holds for the specialized crafts, which are too mechanical to take any of the free utopians' precious time (846D, 741E). Farming and the crafts are the lot of the slaves and not of the free because the free need to devote all their time to cultivating virtue, most of all through leaning (807C–808D, 846D, 847E; this differs strikingly from More's utopia, in which honest toil is good for one's moral character).

We may respond to the topic of slavery in passing. On the one hand it is of course disturbing that Plato seems not to say a word about giving the slaves a fair chance to flourish as well. This may remind one of Thomas Jefferson who is said to have advocated the lifestyle of small farmers as a model of freedom for all while at the same time owning slaves who operated his farm. However, on the other hand, we should not associate slavery too closely with Plato's utopianism, because his main concern is to enable humans to live examined lives and not to enslave others. He may be correct that examined lives demand a lot of time. Moreover, we should not rush to the conclusion that ample free time is an unrealistic ideal economically. For as utopians of a more Marxist stripe would say, modern technology can provide modern humans with the tools to extend their leisurely hours without slavery (cf. Marcuse). There may be nothing wrong with the utopian aim of extending free time as such. It need not necessarily base on slavery, because there is an alternative foundation for it in technology.

On a different level, the Magnesians are free not only of manual labor but also of commerce. Trade is forbidden for two main reasons. First, it is liable to distort one's priorities, because humans are too frequently drawn by greed to seek much more wealth than they need (704D–705B, 918C–D). In reality both poverty and wealth need to be avoided so as to maintain the appropriate focus in life. Second, commerce is servile, and performing services to other humans is below the dignity of the free (919D–E; also see 831E–832A). The free serve God, not other humans (919D). Here we see why it is important for the free to have their own self-sufficient households. Indeed, their material independence appears in a way to resemble God's perfect freedom.

All of this is clearly to consider the economy as something external to freedom as such. For Plato does not predicate freedom of any economic activity, be it production or exchange. (Hence by his lights there is also no such thing as "free trade" unlike in Adam Smith, for example.) But then does his economic thought not fall outside his libertarianism? And does that not count as evidence against his supposedly constant libertarianism, which thesis this book has defended? The reply to this is unexciting: $\mathbb{R}$ is not meant to cover everything that Plato says, for $\mathbb{R}$ is a hypothesis for explaining his philosophizing. It only so happens that he does not always only philosophize. Things would be otherwise if he founded his economic system on philosophical principles, but that he appears never to do. If he did that, and if the philosophical principles in question did not conform to ℝ, then we would have evidence against ℝ, but now it is not so.

6.11 ANCESTOR WORSHIP (656D–657C, 715D–718D)

We look back to Plato, but he looks backwards too. He looks to the Egyptians with admiration (656D–657C, 690A, 799A). In a more extended sense he looks backward also all the way to God, the first and original mover of the universe (see 6.13 below). Beyond this the *Laws* contains backward thinking in family traditions, so that persons need to respect their elders (716C–718D). It also states repeatedly that older persons tend to have cognitive advantages which youths lack (715D–E, 888A–B, 634E). Even children's games are not mere fun and games, because it is important for their education that the games retain their ancient ways (797A–799D). To top it all off we seem to know that Plato is himself an old man when he writes the *Laws* (see Nails and Thesleff on the origins of the *Laws*). In general we seem here to have someone old praising things old. The more ancient and the more original things are, the better.

There is a coherence to these associations mainly because the main authority of the *Laws* is a self-moving God, that is an efficient cause, and efficient causes appear to precede their effects in time. It would follow that efficient causes are always more ancient than their effects, and so as students of efficient causes we would naturally focus on the things that happen first in time. What is more, if there is also a cause *of* causes, that is some one original root from which all the other things are able to grow later as offshoots, then that first cause will be the most ancient of things and it will be of the most interest of all. On these premises the focus of students of efficient causes will naturally fall on the ultimate origin of everything. Religious persons can seek this mythically, relying for instance on the Book of Genesis, and scientists can aspire to the same cosmologically, for instance by theorizing about a Big Bang, but the principle guiding both seems to be the same, as Plato appears to realize.

ℝ provides us with a way to organize the *Laws*' backward-looking associations, for in series of the form form $aRbRc...zRz$ R can be assigned the content IS MOVED BY and $z=God$. Then somewhere along the same line we should place the Egyptians (say at r), Plato (for instance at m), our parents (d), ourselves (c), and so on.

Now we can address a few complications concerning the *Laws*' position. 717B–C supplies us with the somewhat different content IS INDEBTED TO, because it says that individuals have debts to their parents. Now of course everyone owes their existence to their parents, but as in the *Symposium* one may stress how debts like offspring come in many shapes and sizes, and the *Laws* is disappointingly insensitive to such differences. For example, Ficino is indebted to Plato though Plato is not Ficino's biological father, of course. Also, Ficino is indebted to the Medici family who finance his research, but his debt to Plato is still something different. But the *Laws* seems to say nothing to make room for distinctions of this kind. On a different level, there happen also to be parents who harm their children, and here is another blind spot for the *Laws*' paternal way of thinking. More generally, where exactly the positive debts are in each individual's case seems to be a highly complex affair, and very little of this complexity seems to be recognized by the author of the *Laws* (unlike the author of the *Symposium*, who is of course the same man but at a different time).

A second complication with the *Laws*' conservatism arises due to 690A, where Plato appears to advocate a form of progenitor's justice: whoever begins a thing is to rule over it. Parents are to rule over their offspring and the old should rule over the young, it says. Along similar lines God is of course right to rule over us all. But this connection between origins and authority seems quite artificial, for no sense of ownership seems to derive directly from the moving cause. The *Laws*' insistence to the contrary seems to be one more case of monomania in Plato, for again a single consideration is to answer all kinds of questions in human life in a sweeping way. The more realistic approach seems to be to say that issues about efficient causes have their legitimate and consistent place, but that those issues are not automatically similar to ones about ownership or ethical authority. More generally, one cause type should never be thought to rule over all.

6.12 THE DELUGE (677A–682E)

In passing, and only in a few pages, but in a quite vivid and memorable way, the *Laws* takes note of a foundational question regarding human civilization. On these pages it is imagined, or else stated as a historical fact, that a long time ago there was a deluge which destroyed all human creations and forced humans to make a fresh start (677A–D). The foundational question is how any new beginning could possible be made, given that everything old had been swept away (677D, 678A–B). By contrast, if a beginning is given then the continuity or evolution of things is not as difficult to explain, for people teach their children, and the children have further children, and so on (691A–B), as in a relational chain (*aRbRc...: R*=HAS A CHILD gives us *a* HAS A CHILD *b* HAS A CHILD *c*, etc.; we must use the singular if we are to avoid complicating the pattern into a network). But what can or could have been the first cause in the series? This is roughly similar to asking how something could come out of nothing.

The striking thing about this issue is that it seems to be so well suited to function as an excuse for the kind of question to which the *Laws*' theology (which is surveyed in the next section, 6.13) is a fitting answer. For the theology identifies a first mover in God, and so God begins something out of nothing in one sense, namely in initiating motion where there is no motion. In other words, if we picture a series of questions concerning the origins of human inventions and discoveries, such that the series penetrates continually further and further into the past (that is to more and more ancient causes), then the last question in the series would portray a scenario like that of the deluge above. (How did *a* originate? In *b*. How about *b*, in what way did *b* emerge? Through *c*. But *c* – and so on, as always in $\mathbb{R}$.)

Of course, Plato is not alone in envisioning origins for human civilization after a flood, for we have similar stories also for instance in the Old Testament, the Akkadian *Gilgamesh*, and the Finnish *Kalevala*. However, these other ancient sources differ deeply from Plato in that Plato's answer to the mythically motivated question about origins is itself far from being mythical. It is an argument. Let us turn to it now.

6.13 GOD (893B–899E)

The *Laws* finally arrives at its foundational argument in Book X, at 893B–895C. It defends the existence of God as a self-moving soul on the grounds that the beginning of motion in reality must have come about due to an intelligent self-mover. There are nine other types of movers besides the self-moving God but since they depend for their motion on prior movers which affect them they cannot be first in line. Only a self-mover can begin the chain. (The assumption is that there is a beginning.) The later links in the same chain seem to instance circular motions, for spinning around an internal center is comparatively close to God whereas revolving around an external center is further away. In this way the suggestion is made that the shape of a circle is somehow connected with the divine self-relation, but this connection is left unexplained.

We may interpret a portion of this position with $\mathbb{R}$ if *R*=MOVES, *a*=God, and *aRaRbRcRdReRfRgRhRiRj*, for now *God* MOVES *God* MOVES *b*..., so God is a self-mover and God begins the causal chain (for less formally oriented interpretations of the *Laws'* theology see Mayhew and Schofield 2003). Moreover, the chain consists of a hierarchy of ten links, and the thought is that the closer one is to God the more one is an agent and the less one is a patient.

Several of the other things the *Laws* says about God accord well with the above picture. Because God, as the first cause, is ultimately responsible for the whole show it is fitting for Plato to say that God is placed not only at the beginning but also at the middle and the end of the temporal series (715E–716A; see Mohr for the argument that the *Laws'* world is a theodicy). For God's force is felt throughout. It is also fitting to say, on these premises, that theology makes up the most serious topic of all, or the only topic that is of utmost importance (803C). Beyond this, it may be coherent to say as well that God abides by, and that God does not dictate, necessity, at least if we can conceive of God's self-motion as something necessitated by the relation which makes for God's own motion (741A, 818B). The most straightforward interpretation of this would be to identify "God" with the relation directly, in which case God would be the relation and not anything outside or above it.

However, there are also some less easily domesticated passages, and these raise deep questions. We will address two, and the first one only briefly. Odd as it is, Plato also introduces an evil deity (897B); but if a self-moving soul is capable also of perpetrating evil then the perfectionism of the *Laws* seems to be undermined. For in that case Gods, souls, or self-movers are not always or entirely self-sufficient or perfect after all. Moreover, then the perfect God does not rule over the cosmos any more than the evil god does, for rather the universe is made bipolar. This would complicate the *Laws'* total image to such a great extent that at least within the bounds of this book we need to categorize Plato's introduction of the evil deity as an isolated blunder, though I admit that this way to react to a passage is far from being optimal.

The second of the deep questions will preoccupy us throughout the remainder of this section (6.13), and it is once again in the general neighborhood of totalitarianism. For how is human liberation supposed to be possible in a cosmos which is entirely dominated by God? The universe should not be a deterministic or fatalistic clockwork if human thoughts are to be able to become divine in their powers (this seems to contradict Mohr's theodicy thesis). But if human thinking cannot evolve into something divine then the educational program of Magnesia will be flawed, for then it will attempt to teach us things which we are not able to learn (like flying). In that event the divine ideal would be as unreachable as in Woodruff's account of the *Hippias Major* (see Chapter 2 above), and so the name of God would be invoked without any humanly understandable meaning or function. We would then need only to bow down before God; we could not seek to rise. Clearly, then, there should be a way for God to act as God in a way that allows other free agents to form as well. But does Plato perceive this need? Yes. Here are the main ways in which he seeks to provide the needed leeway (A–E):

A. 631C–D: Certain higher goods, which have to do with the virtues and especially with the thoughtful virtue of wisdom, are called divine, and God and wise human souls are said to reflect one another, apparently corresponding to each other in some way. Thus, all human patterns are not as divine, or as similar to God, and so everything in human reality is not simply a reflection of God. (To misuse Orwell's "Some are more equal than others.") The irony in this is that those who are more closely connected to God seem also to be represented as freer. Hence, as we move right in a series $aRaRbRcRd...$ and $a=God$, b is *less* determined than c. For b has more of God's freedom than c has it. This is ironic because the expectation can have been that the effects that are closer to the most powerful cause are *more* determined by the main cause than the remoter effects. This is an important clue as to what type of a relation Plato might actually use to explain the content of MOVES, and we will come to this topic in this section below.
B. 644D–645C: God is a puppeteer and humans are puppets, so God pulls a particular chord and a human being moves. The Athenian seems to identify this principle of divine rule with the rule of reason and of law, thereby suggesting that God operates as soon as reason or law operates, which again appears to be a way of saying that as appropriately reasoning beings we are Godlike, and hence also that some type of reasoning is our ticket to becoming puppeteers instead of puppets. Conversely, if we do not live by reason and law then we are patients and not agents: puppets instead of puppeteers. The moral here seems to be much like in (A) above.
C. 709A–C: The Athenian presents the competing possibilities that chance governs everything, that chance conspires with God, and that God governs everything; but against all such generalizations the Athenian states also that human skills play a part in the overall drama as well. This is not much more than a denial of fatalism or determinism, but it is a sure signal that the religion of the *Laws* is not opposed to human effort.
D. 713C–716E: Oxen ought not to rule over oxen, the Athenian says. In general, every kind of entity needs to be ruled by a kind that is superior to it, just as parents ought to rule over their children (presumably Plato means good parents specifically, cf. 895A). By the same token, humans should be ruled not by humans, contrary to the relativist Protagoras (discussed in Chapter 10 below), but by God. But once more the real mean-

ing of this is that human affairs need to be active and ruled by reason, so the Athenian is not implying that humans should simply wait passively until God appears in person to save everyone. Rather, God seems to stand for the best kind of human action. (In accordance with this, perhaps children *should* after all rule over themselves *if* they can imagine what their parents, or their idealized parents, would most likely have them do in the circumstances.)

E. 903B–905D: God orders all of reality (903B), ascribing everything and everyone more or less active and passive roles in it (903B–C). All of these parts serve the whole (903C–D), but the specific roles of the parts keep shifting based on merit (903D–E). God sees to it that there is justice throughout the cosmos, so that the virtuous get treated well and the vicious badly (904D–E). There is no escaping this fate of judgment (905A–C). God does not determine everyone's performance compeletely, however, because each agent makes part of the decision regarding her own merits and consequently also regarding her own fate (904B–C). In general, like is done to like (904A). This passage appears to be coherent in much the same way as (A)–(D), for God would not seem to be able to judge humans by their merits unless they did things themselves. (Otherwise God would judge God and leave the humans out of the picture.)

(A)–(E) are ways in which the text of the *Laws* makes room for human freedom in a world that is also controlled by God, its creator. Now the following objections seem to arise.

i. "What is the exact relation for efficient causation if it is not a strictly mechanical MOVES? For if God does not determine everything down to human thoughts, values, and decisions then it is false to say that *God* MOVES *God* MOVES *a* MOVES *b* MOVES *c* MOVES... *us*. For in that event the connection is looser. MOVES is too rigid a relation if there is to be human liberty. There needs to be, instead of a hard, iron chain, something more like a mild influence or a tacit suggestion. But this is opposed to the content MOVES, and hence Plato's (deterministic) cosmology is inconsistent with his (freedom-friendly) *ethos*."

We already encountered a looser relation in TEACHES (or its converse, IS TAUGHT BY). For, first, Magnesia seems to be run by teachers and the teachers model themselves on God. This gives us a reason to identify R not exactly with MOVES, or with just any type of motion, but with TEACHES. Moreover, secondly, we already saw in 6.7 that Magnesian education is liberal and not tyrannical. Children are not admonished, for instance, and in general they are not forced or commanded. The instruction is "soft," not dictatorial, and this squares with the less than completely determining affect. In consequencce Magnesian teachers leave some or much of the work of learning to the children themselves. 6.14 will return to this theme.

ii. "This section's (6.13) ironies are avoided more easily and realistically by compatibilism, which never occurred to Plato (who lived so long before Hobbes and Hume). For causal determinism may be true and still we would be free to act in accordance with our wishes and plans. What needs to happen for us to be free is only that our actions accord with our wishes and plans. Hence, there is no need to go so far as to imitate God's self-motion, because our freedom does not require that."

But as in (B) Plato would say that the less than divine wishes or plans are determined, like the puppets and unlike the puppeteers, and that would not be free. If the puppets applaud something or sense that there is an injustice then it is only the puppeteer who makes them feel in those ways, but that means they are not free. Again, if the puppets manage to act on their feelings then that is no sign of their freedom because then they are only obeying the puppeteer. But this great puppeteer is God, and the only way out the hellish scenario of the puppet theater is to become more and more like God the self-mover (for a similar view in recent metaphysics, see van Inwagen).

iii. "The *Laws'* divine law is against itself in numerous ways. First, it was said in (D) above that oxen should not rule over oxen, but by the same rule God should not rule God. If oxen need to be ruled by their superiors then why not God? Why is the rule changed all of a sudden when God comes around? Second, God cannot be self-superior unless God has a superior and an inferior part as in 6.1, but then God is not somehow pure and free of inferior elements altogether, which is contrary to several purist passages in the *Laws*. Third, if God's self-motion consists of thought then it cannot be modeled on movements like rotation or spinning as above in this section (6.13) because rotating and spinning are bodily movements, not thoughts. Thoughts do not extend spatially, so they cannot revolve or spin."

The circular shapes may be only so many illustrations for zRz or zRR, so they need not literally be the shapes of God (cf. Sedley 2000, pp. 317–319, 324–328). Moreover we know that certain relations can be superior to themselves at least if we are allowed to distinguish between their intensions and their extensions. Otherwise there could not be non-tautological (meaningful) accounts of meaning, see 3, or evolutions in loves, see 4. 6.14 will come to this as well.

iv. "If one claims God to be on one's side then one claims a superhuman authority, and that is always dangerous because it entitles one to trample over things merely human."

But this is not so if doctors must explain their procedures to their patients, or if rulers must be teachers, as in Magnesia (see 6.7 and 6.8). For then social relations will consist either of research or instruction, and not for instance of violence or compulsion, and there will be public reasoning.

But we can also turn this around and speak of the dangers that are involved if humans rank nothing above their own subjective preferences. For then each human being can say "Me, me, me" and bow before nothing. This can lead one to disrespect the wider world, education, and one's very own better abilities.

6.14 GOD'S THOUGHTS (895E–897B)

This is not to have said *how* God is a soul. What links self-motion to thought?

First we may determine, in passing, that there is no doubt about this connection in *Plato's* mind. This is a certainty, for he says at 895E–896B that self-movers are souls (on the general connections between soul and God in Plato see Sedley 2000; more widely on Gods in ancient Greece see Snell Chapter 7; on ancient creationism see Sedley 2007). Moreover, what a soul is is not left entirely open because at 896D he lists as things of the soul moods, wishes, calculations and memories, and as things of the body, length, breadth, depth, and strength. Also, at 897A he adds that souls have forethought, counsel, joy, grief, confidence, fear, hate, and love; and, in contrast, the body now has heat and coldness, heaviness and lightness, softness and hardness, colors, and tastes (897A–B).

But *why* is Plato so convinced that the self-mover is thoughtful and immaterial? We need to distinguish between (A) a way to understand him and (B) a way to to accept that he is right.

A. Plato appears to conflate two kinds of law which moderns tend to draw apart (apparently since Galileo, see Losee chapter 7 part 1 for discussion). One kind of law is as in a legal code and the other as in an explanatory theory; and Plato means both. Hence, to illustrate, God is viewed like a dictator or a monarch who makes the laws which all beings should obey *and* which the beings more or less do in fact obey as well (903B–905D; also see Chapter 12 on the *Timaeus*). On these premises it is rational to explain things by invoking God's plan because God's activity realizes God's plan in the cosmos.

But how does a thinking soul come into the picture? Due to the first of the two roles; for it is highly plausible to view planning, designing, evaluating as impossibilities without thinking or intending, and moreover it appears that material things do not do such things. The material, thoughtless beings can follow the laws but they not make them. (There is, of course, a rich contemporary literature about what material things can do, see Rey.)

B. Why would one follow Plato in conflating the two said functions, that is the legislative and the explanatory? Recall that the *Laws* is focused on the efficient cause, so what we should now accept as a mover is a thinker. This is of course what is most usually discussed as "causality" in our time, and mental or intentional causation is a major topic in the modern philosophy of mind. Now, Plato's view both is and is not an exotic candidate for the current philosophical landscape. It is exotic because it predicates so much causal power of God's thought. God's plans rule the cosmos. But Plato is somewhat less exotic in predicating causal force primarily of mental acts *Laws* (897A). If we interpret the *Laws'* distinction between primary and secondary causes in terms of movement from within and movement from without then we imply, plausibly, that material things instance only secondary causes, because they are moved by other things. This is something that physicalistic determinists in our day would seem to accept, for they do not seem to maintain that material things move themselves. Our other, and main, implication would be that mental self-motion is primary in originating causal chains. Since this seems to have the form zRz (as in *God* MOVES *God*), the issue we are left with is the mental or intentional content of this R. A rather loose but plausible answer is INTERPRETS, so that *God* INTERPRETS *God* in some way, because we are all familiar with the activity of self-interpretation and can well conceive of its originating force. We engage in self-interpretation when we say what is on our minds or when we clarify the symbols or actions which we have produced. But such activities seem to quality as intentional causes in a self-moving sense by many figures in the contemporary philosophy of mind. Thus the *Laws'* views on mental causation appear valid based on contemporary standards.

Now let us look at the two last objections of this book.

i. "Modern science does not undermine cosmic idealism alone, for it also disproves mental self-motion altogether."

This we need to deny or Plato's philosophy becomes quite unserious, for he depends heavily on the power of the mind or soul. Luckily for him, the issue of intentional causation is actually wide open to this day, so it would be false to portray Plato as the underdog on this score (see Rey; also see Sedley 2000, pp. 317–319).

ii. "But we have no conception of God's thoughts, so the *Laws* really provides us with nothing definite to model on."

This is to be denied and affirmed. It is false because we do know that God's thoughts are self-moved, so we have some rather clear-cut knowledge about them. After all, it is due to their self-motion that they are so deeply original. For as Plato insists, a series of causes cannot begin from what is caused from without; the first mover must be self-moved. But this is not redundant. What is more, it is also not mystical in the way that some religious perspectives are, because it is not metaphorical (cf. "God is love," "God is light," "God is something utterly unfathomable"). It is literal and relational and it is formally or structurally precise.

None the less, it is true to say that Plato does not give God's thinking any specific *content*. As in the earlier chapters of this book, he is focused primarily on the structure of things. He tends to leave us with many questions.

But notice, crucially, that in this way his philosophizing has of course generated further philosophizing by others in great abundance. Hence, ironic as it may sound, this fact of his great influence leads us to e a promising way to compensate for his failure as a cosmologist, as follows.

It is difficult for philosophers to deny the vast influence of the field's classics, and especially of Plato (and Aristotle), and this implies intentional causation in the history of ideas! Moreover, as 6.11 noted, the causes do not go back only as far as Plato: he also looks back to the Egyptions and to God. Hence it is true to say that we relate to him in the way that he relates to them, so $aRbRc$, and R=IS INDEBTED TO or IS MOTIVATED BY, a=*Tommi*, b=*Plato*, and c=*God*. This is a realistic pattern if it is indeed difficult for contemporary philosophers *not* to place themselves at a in this series and if Plato is right that he has a further past to look back to. But if this pattern holds then Plato's failure as an idealistic cosmologist (as in i above) is made up for by his enormous influence on the history of philosophy, for though we do not attain a realistic history of efficient causation in one way through his work, we do in another. To this background the contents of the self-moving thoughts of God should be sought in the intellectual tradition which precedes Plato and not in the disenchanted cosmos. To advance along these lines we might seek to interpret, from times before Plato, for instance Heraclitus, Pythagoras, and diverse sources from further in the East.[1]

6.15 VERSUS BOBONICH (NON-PHILOSOPHERS)

Bobonich makes the surprising claim that in the *Laws* also non-philosophers live fully worthwhile lives. He says this is a change from what Plato held when he was younger, especially in the *Phaedo* and the *Republic*. The enthusiasm for philosophizing is supposed to have waned as Plato aged.

Bobonich's *Plato's Utopia Recast* (2002) is a thick book, and the best way for us to analyze it is by identifying some representative portions in it.

The first of these is Bobonich's section 3.6. This interprets the scene in the *Laws* (644D–645B) in which God is the puppeteer and humans are puppets (cf. 6.13). The decisive thing for Bobonich's view of the *Laws* seems to be that there is not simply a black and white dichotomy between the puppeteer and the puppets. Rather there are gradations in gray, because a human being can be more or less in control. A human being is, then, not always utterly divine or else totally passive. Rather, she can be more or less divine. In Plato's metaphors, the picture is not only that God pulls chords or sinews in the puppets and the puppets move. Rather, the puppets can pull along. They can be agents of divine reason in the human world, and to a greater or lesser extent.

Bobonich is that the *Laws* recognizes different gradations between the agents and patients. But does the main point of the work not remain that the more one manages to be an agent, and the less one is a patient, the better? Is not the central moral of the *Laws* that humans should become as alike to God as possible and hence think in self-motion? No matter how many shades of gray we recognize, is there still not a hierarchy with white and black at the extremes?

Bobonich never quite faces this question. Rather, he keeps returning to the foundations of morals. The virtuous should prove to be happy. On the first page of his book (page 1) Bobonich quotes Plutarch saying that for Xenocrates only philosophers do voluntarily what the rest of humanity must be forced to do. On the pages 2–3 Bobonich asserts that for more modern humans everyone has this ability to reason internally. This seems to be the view which he wishes to find also in the *Laws*. Divine or utopian constructions must be downplayed because democracy is good (cf. the Anubis Analogy in 1).

Bobonich finds further support for his view from the *Laws'* discussion of the preludes (Bobonich 2002, pp. 97–119), for it is here that the non-philosophical citizens of Magnesia are most obviously treated as persons to be reasoned with. The model is as in 6.8 above, that is with doctors explaining diseases and treatments to their free patients and merely medicating their slave patients. Based on this it is certain that the free citizens of Magnesia are dealt with as reasoning beings by its rulers. The relevant contrast seems to be especially with the *Republic*, where the philosophical elite lies to the population, because the population cannot deal with the truth. This appears to be the decisive break for Bobonich, for here we have something we can fasten on as a non-philosophers' crucial ability in the setting of the *Laws*.

Now is Bobonich not right about this? It is true that the free Magnesians are reasoned with even if they are not philosophers. But it is none the less false to suggest that the *Laws* values the non-philosophers equally with the philosophers. For the *Laws'* main program is indisputably for humans to become Godlike. Put differently, the *Laws* is not as pessimistic about non-philosophers as the *Republic*, so that is true as Bobonich says. But despite this the Magnesian non-philosophers rank comparatively low in its hierarchy. The human optimum remains philosophical throughout Plato, and Bobonich is biased in making this seem otherwise.

6.16 SUMMARY

In this Chapter (6) we first encountered the familiar relational pattern $\mathbb{R}$ in the *Laws'* early ethical generalization (6.1). Then it seemed to be approximated also in this work's views of virtue (6.2), pleasure (6.3), gymnastics (6.4), music (6.5), theater (6.6), education (6.7), norms of discourse (6.8), ancestor worship (6.9), criminal justice (6.10), and the economy (6.11). The deluge was a more speculative philosophical topic in 6.12. Next we studied the *Laws'* core, that is its theology (6.13), which discussion we supplemented with some insights about God's actual thoughts (6.14). Finally there was a confrontation with Bobonich (6.15).

NOTE

1. The inspiration for this speculative paragraph is Nietzsche's *Genealogy of Morals*, Book 2, § 19, where it seems to be suggested that the later members of declining traditions rank themselves below, and consider themselves indebted to, their ancestors, and that a radically declining tradition would go so far along the same lines as to view its origin as divine. In such traditions the debt to the original divinity would be immense. Apparently God would here be conceived on the model of an especially powerful human being in the remote past.

A viewpoint of this kind is at odds most of all with the Plotinian or Neoplatonic tradition of Platonic scholarship, which is cosmic and not humanistic, cf. Dillon, Feibleman.

Chapter Seven

The Lysis?

The *Lysis* contains

a. an especially transparent series of final causes in questions and answers, and
b. an apparent termination for the series in happiness,

and in these ways it provides evidence for ℝ. However we need also to confess openly that

c. the happiness in question may not be self-relational,

and so the *Lysis* provides us with only partial support for ℝ. It does not give us the whole story.

    a. Young Lysis' parents wish him to be happy (207D), and happiness consists, it seems, of doing what one wants (207E); but Lysis' parents do not allow him to do as he pleases (207E–208E). Is this not a paradox? It is not because Lysis' parents may believe, even truly, that Lysis does not know what makes him happy (209C–210C). If they thought him more competent then they would trust him more, and then he would be allowed to act more independently. At present, however, as Lysis is still lacking by this standard, his parents trust in the services of certain authorities, for those services are instrumental to Lysis' happiness. The authorities still know more about Lysis' happiness than he does himself, but if Lysis can change that then he will be self-sufficient and free (cf. 215A–B).

    To this background Socrates proceeds to consider how it is generally so that unfree things, that is beings which are not sufficient to themselves, have the need to depend on other things (215B–C). But he also adds to this picture the possibility of *series* of dependencies, so that if a depends on b, b can in turn depend on c. For instance, at 219C $a=medicine$, $b=health$, and $c=?$, where c is something Socrates inquires about. Similarly at 219E, where $a=a$ *vessel*, $b=wine$, $c=health$.

Clearly this is evidence for $aRbRc...$ and hence for a portion of $\mathbb{R}$. But how about the rest of it? Do we get $...zRz$ or $...zRR$ or not?

b. In a above I already spoke of freedom and self-sufficiency in connection with $aRbRc$, so the general way in which the rest of the libertarian pattern could emerge from the *Lysis* is not altogether mysterious. We know what to seek. Something should be self-sufficient to terminate the series. But is anything like that in the *Lysis?*

At 219D and 220B Socrates provides us with a promising lead in not considering causes other than first causes real or proper causes at all. For he seems to say that everything in the chain $aRbRc...$ except for the extreme and final point is illusory. We may imagine what this means in the light of the example from 219C: a sick person may consider that health is all she needs, that is as if b were the end of the series—though it is not. In this spirit we have all heard also of dreams of wealth from the poor, or of fame by the unpopular, or of justice from the oppressed, and so on. All of these would seem like illusions on Socrates' way of thinking if the fulfilled wishes would not prove to be as conclusively rewarding as they seemed when they were not yet fulfilled. If this is so then it makes sense to say, with Socrates, that there are illusions about final causes, because, in short, there is a tendency to take the next step forward to be the last step that needs taking. Many series of actions or events that are viewed as something progressive would merely lead to the dark unknown.

What is also promising, though perhaps in a less obvious way, is that Socrates presents a familiar paradox at 215A–B and 220B–221A. This is much as in 4.4 above and 7 below: further aims make sense only in the light of lacks in the present, but without further aims there is nothing more to want, and therefore there could not be happiness, or contentment purely in the present. If this is correct then a series of final causes can have no end, and in that case illusions are not found only before the end, as in he preceding paragraph, but everywhere, and final causation is in a state of crisis altogether.

To the background of these points we may expect Socrates to present the real or absolutely final cause, for instance as a Form or a God, much as in Plato's several other works.

c. But this does not occur. Instead, at 223B Socrates summarizes the *Lysis'* result as a skeptical one, and clearly this goes against the hypothesis that it proves that happiness or self-sufficiency resides in anything of the form zRz or zRR (contrary to the appearance raised at a above). Hence we must conclude that the *Lysis* endorses this book's thesis only in part. It is an important part, but it is not the whole.

Chapter Eight

The Gorgias?

The *Gorgias* contains

a. an interesting paradox, which we may compare with the *Lysis*' and the *Symposium*'s and
b. its solution.

However this involves the uncomfortable assumption that

c. some things Socrates clearly says in the *Gorgias* are actually mistaken,

which is never a comfortable prospect given that Plato tends to idealize Socrates so often in most places. Due to this the *Gorgias*' endorsement of ℝ is not necessarily wholesale. For the ingredients are there but the manner in which they are presented leaves one slightly uneasy.

    a. At 493A–494B Socrates states a paradox according to which the search for satisfaction is like an unwinnable rat race in that it always involves a prior dissatisfaction. Before drink gives pleasure there must be thirst, for instance. Scratching is nothing if there is no itching, as it were. But then the quest for happiness, pleasure, or satisfaction seems like a merry-go-round, for on these premises one needs always to go down in order to get to rise again. One cannot remain up.

    Callicles' response to this is to embrace the restless manner of living (494A–C). He will take the pains as well as the pleasures. However this is to overlook what appears to be a deeper challenge in Socrates' argument, namely that as a deliberate agent Callicles needs now to create dissatisfaction on purpose. He must make himself unbelieving and forgetful (cf. 493C). If he were lucky enough merely to suffer such a fate as to have a disease then he would have direction in his life because he could wish for health. Similarly, as a poor person he could dream consistently of wealth. But he is not sick or poor, and so he knows that his only route forward on these premises is masochistic. He must indulge in strange behaviors so as to complicate his life on his own initiative.

This paradox is largely as in the *Phaedo*, the *Symposium,* and the *Lysis*, see 3.1, 4.4, and 7 above. It arises for a series of final causes which aims at satisfaction, so the content for $\mathbb{R}$ is IS A MEANS TO and the endpoint should be some z which is an end in itself.

b. At 482E–484C and 488B–C Callicles' position is exposed as the view that might is right. The strong should receive greater rewards than the weak. Socrates' challenge is first to question the nature of this might or strength. For what is it that one should have strength in? However his most challenging sanction seems to be to inquire about strengths which *cohere* with the rewards they are to receive. For instance, is a shoemaker to receive especially large shoes, or especially many shoes (490D–491A)? Again, is a maker of coats not to fairly obtain coats in particlar? The assumption in these questions is that it is natural for agents to reap what they sow, which is a value we have already frequently encountered in this book (see e.g. 3.7, 4.2, 5.3–5.4, and 6.1) and which we have repeatedly interpreted in terms of $\mathbb{R}$. Stated comparatively, the present view is that if one makes shoes then one should not receive coats as a reward for this, for that is not what one produces. Coats are not what one gets for making shoes unless the world is somehow mixed up artificially. In fishing we get fish (if anything), not french fries. The issue is somewhat as with the philosophy of reincarnation: one is to be reborn according to one's own way of life. If one lives like a dog then one should be reborn as a dog (see 3.7 above). Alternatives to this seem artificial.

Now notice how this solves the paradox in a above. The basic idea is the familiar one of self-sufficiency. There needs to be an activity which questions and answers in a continually progressive way, thereby generating needs to work on without merely revolving in a circle.

The *Gorgias*' way of presenting this message is by contrasting philosophy and rhetoric as follows. The sophist teaches rhetoric for the sake of an external reward (money) and her skill is to be used for all possible social ends. In contrast, the reward of philosophizing is intrinsic, so there is no ulterior merit or prize. On Callicles' view, this is a fault in philosophy, because one's thinking ought to lead to greater, ulterior things (484C–D). It is not good to merely think and talk like Socrates. Studies and discussions like Socrates' are childish and small (484E–485C). Philosophy is useful for education (485A) but education is only a means among the young, in Callicles' world. Socrates' way of life leads him to whisper in corners, whereas the real life of grown-ups is in politics and commerce (485D). Socrates should ceaze refuting and playing with toys and trifles (486C–D).

But Callicles' *ethos* leads to the above paradox, and Socrates' *ethos* leads out of it. Bluntly stated the crucial difference is that Socrates' alternative is self-sufficient—free. External dependencies enslave Callicles just like they enslave the sophists. Callicles and the sophists serve others for the sake of extrinsic rewards and forget about themselves, but this leads them to a curious regress.

c. The uncomfortable aspect of the *Gorgias* is that in it Socrates' actual position is not always like the above (in b). For he tries rather to minimize needs or wishes, as if asceticism solved the paradox (490B–C). Callicles remarks correctly that if it did then stones and the dead would be the most fortunate of beings (492E), which Socrates appears to concede. The oddity in this is that Socrates' mistake is so outrageous, which is a rather unusual outcome in the Platonic corpus. Much more usually Socrates figures as the hero, of course. To be sure, we have encountered his failure with a similar problem also in the *Symposium*, see 4.4. Moreover there is always the *Parmenides,* where Socrates is an even more helpless figure. Thus we know that Socrates is not always a perfect human model of a free thinker. The possibility is that Plato attributes faults to Socrates to communicate that he, too, is only human. But this is only a speculative possibility, and it is not the best way to conclude an interpretive account.

Hence, the *Gorgias* does support $\mathbb{R}$, but not in as unambiguous a way as some other Platonic works.

Chapter Nine

The Meno?

The *Meno* raises a number of interesting philosophical issues, such as

a. whether Socrates believes that for every word there must be a single object, which belief Ryle refers to as the "Fido-Fido" theory and which coheres with the so-called "Socratic Fallacy" (Geach 1966), and
b. how the so-called "paradox of inquiry" is to be solved.

I am about to argue that both topics, (a) and (b), are well understood by means of $\mathbb{R}$. However, as always in Chapters 7–13, we need also to note a shortcoming. This time it is

c. the absence of the transparent self-relations in the *Meno*,

for which reason this dialogue provides only imperfect evidence for the generalization $\mathbb{R}$. We find some evidence, but not all the evidence we need.

 a. The Socrates of the *Meno* asks Meno for a single definition of all virtue. What is he after? He compares virtue with bees (72A–D), saying that bees have a single, constant nature even though they differ in for instance beauty and size. Another comparison is with health at 72D–E. By analogy also virtue should have a center or essence of some kind.

 But why should this analogy hold? What reason is there to think that virtue is just like bees or health? Most of all, why trust that also virtue can be defined? It may be claimed that Socrates' reason for thinking thus is merely verbal. If so, he is misled by the existence of a single word to trust that it conceals a single, unified essence. On this way of thinking an informative, realistic definition can be produced for "virtue" as well as for "bees" and "health." Things are not named the same for nothing, after all. They stand for unities.

If this is Socrates' basis then he is wrong. The mistake would be as in the Fido-Fido theory, as Ryle calls it (see Ryle), which states that for every single word there is a separable and unified object. In this spirit, the word "bees" stands specifically for bees and "health" stands uniquely for health. There would then be such a separable and coherent species as *bees* out there in the world which can be studied scientifically and which may be definable in some way. Similarly health would have its stable and distinct features no matter where it happens to be found.

What would be wrong with this? What is wrong with the Fido-Fido theory? It generalizes too widely. This is apparent as soon as we think of a word like "game" in the later writings of Wittgenstein (see Wittgenstein). "Game" is, of course, a single word, but games do not have any strict commonality across the board, Wittgenstein teaches. Some games share one feature and others another: only some have a ball, and only some have points, and only some involve several players, and so on. The games do not have a single common core that one could capture in a definition. Hence the recurrence of the word "game" is not a sure sign of a constant essence lurking anywhere, and more widely words are not always such as to conceal essences that one could expose with definitions. Is there then no reason why a single word stands for all the different games? Wittgenstein answers that they are held together by a relation of "family resemblance," like the members of a family. Some of a family's members share the same type of nose and others have a hair color in common, and so on. There are numerous overlapping circles but there is no point at which they all overlap, so there is no center. If this is true about games and many other things, as Wittgenstein thinks, then there is not even usually a single essence to define behind every word.

The same thinking would be even more obvious if we take a word such as "thing." Things will often be very different from each other, indeed so different that there will not be even a family resemblance between them. One might as well try to define all x's of the world. But others would use as their example not "game" or "thing" but "good" (cf. Mackie), and this already takes us to the general territory of virtue, that is to the territory of ethical topics. Perhaps virtue is as heterogenous as things, games, families, and goods. (A still further way to make this point would be on the basis of thought or freedom, both of which are of course central to this book. There are different kinds of thinking, as for instance memories, computations, guessing riddles, and so on; cf. Wittgenstein § 23. There are also different types of freedom, say, in Grotius' freedom of the seas, Smith's free trade, many liberals' free speech, Marxian free labor, and so on. Everyone is for "freedom" from the fascists to the communists and the Christians, but each party means a different thing by the word.)

Does Socrates not see this? As a first response to this one should note that he does discuss the possibility that there may be many virtues, like virtues *for* women or men (71E–72A, 72D) or else virtues *of* justice or of temperance (e.g. 73B). Hence, it is not that the prospect is unimaginable to him. This raises the issue why he expects a uniform answer concerning virtue. It is not because altenatives to it are unimaginable, we now know. *Is* it because there is a single word for virtue? Or is there another reason? Or is there none?

Before we answer that let us note briefly how the so-called "Socratic Fallacy" would arise *if* Socrates depended on the mere word (Geach). Then it would be consistent of him to assume that anyone who understands the word is able to provide a definition for the word's meaning. On this view of Socrates' semantic position, every word has a definition and to understand the word implies an ability to define that word. But this, we saw, would not be a tenable position, due to examples such as "game," "thing," and so on, as above. For those words are understood and used well enough without any definitons.

Now we have seen how Socrates could be guilty of the errors described by Ryle and Geach. But is he in fact guilty as alleged? Is he a "definitionalist" in semantics, as one might say?

We may note now how it would not be consistent of him to be a definitionalist. For his desire is to *correct* everyday intuitions about virtue. After all, he wants to argue for instance that virtue is one and that virtue is knowledge (cf. e.g. *Meno* 77B–78B, *Protagoras* 358C, *Gorgias* 468C; *Gorgias* 460B–D and 509E, *Protagoras* 345E and 360D), and he clearly wishes to *change* the thinking of people who do not yet think or act in accordance with this. This suggests that he does not want only to explain everyday concepts or words. He seems rather to want to improve them.

But if so then how does Socrates propose to make the improvements? What are better words or concepts like? As Irwin says, Socrates models on the crafts—that is a part of the answer. For Socrates wants words or concepts to be more like geometry, for example (74B–76A). But this gives a different color to his demand of definitions. For we do in fact have definitions in geometry, and people can know certain unified things about geometrical topics. (Moreover, the persons who know about bees or health and produce orderly definitions about such topics may also be experts of some kind in Socrates' mind, so perhaps the craft analogy was really the intended analogy already at 72A–E above.) But this is not everyday language. This is to turn to technicalities. Now, this is the background to which Socrates' quest for definitions makes sense, for now he does get to correct everyday opinions and habits. Moreover, on this view Socrates does not have a definitionalist theory of meaning, so he does not make the mistakes that Geach and Ryle find so silly. Rather he has an idealized standard based on expert knowledge, and he wants virtue ethics to be shaped into a technical art of its own.

So far so good. Now let us add some further complications.

b. At 80D–81D Socrates asks Meno how Meno knows what to look for in his search for virtue. For, on the one hand, if he does not know what he is looking for then how will be recognize it if he finds it? On the other hand, if he already knows what he is looking for then what need does he still have to look for it? This is the well known "paradox of inquiry" (also see *Euthydemus* 275D–278C).

The first thing I want to highlight is that now Socrates' sanction is different from a. For this is not geometrical thinking. The paradox is also not derived from any other familiar craft such as arithmetic, medicine, pottery, or others. Rather, this is a paradox which reminds us of the acrobatics of Socrates himself (and of his cousins, the sophists). It is a normal part of his elenchtic or dialectical philosophizing. For he quite usually comes to speakers with paradoxes (as about the equal (3.3), the ends of life (see 4.4, 7, 8), self-consistency (5.3, 5.6, 6.1), and so on). Moreover, higher-level self-relational topics are exactly his cup of tea. What are such higher-level topics? Now he inquires into inquiry: that is one example. But elsewhere he seeks knowledge about knowledge (*Theaetetus*, see Chapter 13), equals the equal (*Phaedo*, see Chapter 3), and so on, as in zRz or zRR throughout this book. But notice that like the paradoxes, the higher orders are Socrates' own affair, not the craftsmen's. He is the self-conscious speaker who reflects on human practices with a critical eye. He seems quite like a philosopher as in $\mathbb{R}$, not like a scientist or a craftsman.

c. But now, *is* the *Meno's* Socrates a philosopher as above (i.e. as in $\mathbb{R}$)? He is not because he (still) confuses his characteristic activity with the crafts. The type or slot for "the philosopher" is not yet born—that is one part of it. However the more significant part is that the *Meno*'s Socrates does not see how exotic his sought-after objects are.

Chapter Ten

The Protagoras?

The *Protagoras* provides important explanations

a. why episodes of speech or thought need to be interrupted;
b. how deliberate efforts have an opposite in a kind of state of nature in which humans are at the mercy of fate;
c. in what way at least some things may be individuated in relation to their opposites; and
d. how an individual may be superior or inferior to herself.

However we need also to note

e. how the *Protagoras* fails to specify any ideal outcome for its project.

Hence, despite all the helpful evidence, the *Protagoras* cannot be seen as one of the main sources for ℝ in Plato.

a. Close to the beginning of the dialogue Socrates asks why Hippocrates desires to be taught by a sophist (311B). For what does he hope to become? What indeed can a sophist make out of one? A sophist, the answer goes (312A). Next it turns out that a sophist delivers eloquent speeches about things. But about which things (312C–E)? What does she know about? What is the range of her particular expertise? A little later Protagoras, a sophist, answers that a sophist provides one with skills in the art of politics in particular. But this, too, he should explain in responsive (328E–329A), brief (334E–335A), and sincere terms (331C–D), Socrates dictates. He should not simply ramble on like a book that is closed to its reader's responses, even if that is something that a sophist might characteristically do professionally.

Here we may already interrupt the flow of the dialogue and pause to raise some philosophical issues.

Socrates' questioning has a constant topic throughout the *Protagoras*, and this is identified as virtue or art. His questioning is consistently concerned to discover the character and product of this particular relation to things, that is the virtuous or skilled relation. But as above he keeps calling "cut," thereby holding the other speakers back. Why? The rather obvious answer is that he wants to keep track of what is going on. If relations do not have external sanctions to answer to then they get out of control, turning into something that is neither policed nor understood. They escape to their own worlds. This is precisely the danger that sophists seem to face in Socrates' view above.

A different way to explain the same danger is by reference to a premature circularity. If for instance a sophist makes one a sophist as above then there is an "answer" to the question about what a sophist does or can do but not a responsible answer or an answer which would explain anything to a party who is *not* already familiar with and accepting of the answer. The sophist's circular "answer" would contain no authentic news. To explain things authentically we need to break out of circles of this kind, and this is to say that we need to bring our relations (as for example our sophistry, our virtue, or our skill) to bear on what is independent and ulterior. We do not want sophistry to produce sophisms about sophistry.

This is much as with Heraclitus in 2.1: talk of God is to begin in mundane terms. If we talked of God directly in a divine vocabulary then we would not understand what we are saying. In relational terminology, we should not proceed first with relations to relations as in *RR* or *RRR*. Rather, we need to chop up the series, as in *aRbRc*, where *a*, *b*, and *c* are something different from *R* and also something more familiar and less elevated or problematic than *R*. A different way of saying this is that even the most exalted theologies need to use earth-bound examples for us to grasp what is going on in them. Otherwise they become symbols of symbols of symbols without any bearing on anything.

b. Once Protagoras has said that he trains his students specifically in the art of politics (319A) he narrates a long myth about the general historical and perhaps also about the metaphysical significance of this art. In the myth it is documented how different animals initially received particular gifts from nature and human beings received none (320C–321C). We did not have the fortune to attain the speed of some animals or the strength of others as a birthright. Instead nature left us naked out in the woods. However in Protagoras' narrative the introduction of Promethean skills or arts changes this entirely (321C–D), and in this way our species attains its particular advantage over fate (and its comparative advantage over other animals). This situation resembles the one sketched later in the *Laws:* the deluge (see 5.12).

c. "Self-predicated" expressions (cf. 1.2 and 3.3) occur twice in the *Protagoras*, once about justice (330C) and once about holiness (330D–E). In the light of 329D–330B Socrates seems to use them in order to ponder whether each of the virtues, such as for instance justice or holiness, is what it is independently of the others. For there he asks whether they are like parts of a face which together form a single face (nose, eyes, etc.) or, instead, like gold so that every part is the same as every other. Headway is not made directly by phrasing the issue in these self-predicated terms, because in view of them it is too easy to agree that each virtue is self-sufficient. Of course justice is just and holiness is holy, the speakers agree, apparently because these sound to them like mere tautologies (330C–E).

A somewhat more decisive question is phrased differently, namely by considering whether just things are at least a little holy (331B). This is to consider whether the scope of each virtue overlaps with the others. If there is no overlap then just things are not at all holy, for instance, in which case the different virtues seem like parts of a face and not like gold. But Protagoras is not overcome by this type of a consideration so no progress is made on its foundation.

Luckily, however, there is a third way of posing the issue that is more revealing, namely whether each of the virtues has the same opposite or not (332A–333C). The idea here is to say that if x and y have the same opposite z then $x=y$. But this is how things turn out to be with the virtues, and so the virtues are said to be one and the same because each of them has an opposite in the same z.

In the light of this the *Protagoras* seems to be a comparatively advanced Platonic discussion on the topic which it covers. For instance the *Phaedo*, discussed in Chapter 3, was not clearer or more reflected than this about individuation by opposites. The main point for this book's purposes, however, is the presence once again of $aRbRb....yRz$, that is of at least a portion of $\mathbb{R}$. That portion has been discovered in the *Protagoras* above because of its talk of opposites. But do we find zRz or zRR?

d. The self-predicated passages in the *Protagoras* do not contain interesting self-relations, because they are only as in c above; but the dialogue's concern with moral psychological intellectualism is more interesting and more informative. For towards the dialogue's end we arrive at a discussion about how persons can act or fail to act on their knowledge, and this is explained in hedonic terms by comparing mild but easily attained pleasures with intense but laborious ones (356A–B, 358B–C). The point seems to be for instance that if one is lazy one settles for less but if one does all one can then one attains more. Moreover, to settle for less is to not really *know* about the more rewarding alternative, for Socrates seems to hold that the knowing think impartially in numbers and do not suffer from sloth or biases. (The idea appears to be that one may be at a distance of, say, 5 units from a pleasure of 6 units and at a distance of 10 units from a pleasure of 20 units, in which case the 6 units would have a "price" of 5 (so to speak) and the 20 unit would have a price of 10. Then one would face a decision between the two alternatives, and the latter would be the more knowing choice strictly because of the numbers: 20-10=10, 6-5=1.) In any case his interest is clearly to advocate the strongest type of agency imaginable (356B–C). Hence we know that he uses the dialogical series and polar oppositions really to guide humans once more towards the most perfect freedom, and this is in keeping with the overall message of *Plato's Logic*.

e. Finally for this chapter (10) we need to note briefly why the *Protagoras* has not been prioritized more in this book. Its tone and structures are often progressive, but the endpoints are not represented logically enough. For instance the calculations of utility in d above do not register anything as self-consistent as *zRz* or *zRR*. We would optimally need talk of a self-mover, a Form, or something similar.

Chapter Eleven

The Phaedrus?

The *Phaedrus* is a dialogue about rhetoric and its concern is to advertize a type of presentation which combines diverse philosophically interesting elements, such as

a. the psyche's self-motion,
b. the value of knowledge,
c. the structure of organic wholes,
d. a dialectic of collection and division, and
e. interactive speech as opposed to dead writing.

However

f. the *Phaedrus* does not combine these elements in any string like $\mathbb{R}$,

and this is why the dialogue does not count as unambiguous evidence for this book's thesis as a whole.

    a. At 245C–E Socrates states briefly that a psyche moves itself and that it is therefore immortal. Hence we know that the psyche has a relation to itself as in *aRa* and that *R*=MOVES. The cause type is efficient, of course.

    But how does the psyche manage this? How exactly does something move itself? The *Phaedrus* is explicit that only the philosopher's psyche can do this (248C–E, 249A–C) but its descriptions of philosophers' actions in those passages are mythical and metaphorical. Hence we need to ask what it is that a philosopher's psyche does elsewhere in the *Phaedrus* that makes the psyche free.

    b. One lead is provided at 262A–C, where Socrates says that to speak of things properly one needs to know about them. This is to steer away from the values and habits of the sophists, who appear as Socrates' opponents in the *Phaedrus* like in so many of the other Platonic works (*Hippias Major, Protagoras, Gorgias,* and so on).

But in what way does a philosophizing psyche have knowledge? And what kind of knowledge is at issue here? Also, how does having it lead one to initiate movements?

c. 264A–C requires speaking in organic wholes, so that different parts in a presentation must come together to form a single body. There are to be feet, a body, and a head; or else there should be a beginning, a middle, and an end. Hence it may be that the knowing compile their subjects properly. They know them *as* orderly wholes with fitting parts. Moreover:

d. 265D–266B requires individuating things according to real distinctions in definitions. One should not impose differences or continuities artificially. There is to be one whole and then there need to be the many things which make it up.

This seems to accord well with c above. Based on this view we may take it that the production of definitions is the philosophizing psyche's activity. She has access to wholes and their parts because she knows how to define things. The definition of a definition would then be roughly that it explains things as wholes and parts.

But what of questions? Are they not a part of the philosophizing psyche's movement as well? That is what Plato's Socrates would typically say.

e. At 274B–277A Plato writes that speech is superior to writing, the principal reason for the ranking seeming to be that speakers respond to misled interpretations of themselves whereas texts remain quiet and defenceless (275D–276B).

In this way questioning has come into the *Phaedrus'* picture. Apparently we should think that philosophers produce definitions in response to questions and that this makes them move themselves. If their dialectic is internal to their own minds then they are self-movers as individual psyches. What is more, if they define themselves or define defining then they instance zRz or zRR and the match with $\mathbb{R}$ is perfect.

f. However the *connections* that have been made in this chapter (11) are not actually said in the text of the *Phaedrus*, so we do not know for certain that this is Socrates' meaning. The flowery language in his mythical descriptions leaves too much leeway. Hence we do not here have a firm textual basis foundation for $\mathbb{R}$.

We can put this problem in a different way. There seems to be no non-arbitrary way of organizing the *Phaedrus'* overabundant colors, fascinating as they are. If the imagery were structured more coherently as a series like $aRbRc...$ then it could convey a philosophical message which would combine elements like a–e above in an intelligible way and thereby do something to explain each of a–e by reference to the other items of that series. But as things stand, so many typically Platonic associations, as in a–e, are only mentioned in passing in the *Phaedrus* without any coherent order. (There are also mentions of self-knowledge, recollection, Godlikeness, and so, but they seem only like mentions, so they appear as loose ends.)

In sum, the "freedom" of the *Phaedrus* is flighty and restless, and while it is a stimulating read it is not reasoned enough as an artefact to be trusted as a solid foundation for $\mathbb{R}$.

Chapter Twelve

The Timaeus?

The *Timaeus* teaches that

a. human individuals should strive to be like a self-moving God, and that
b. God's traces are perceptible in physical nature.

Hence humans are to read the "book" of nature to learn how to be free. However we need also to acknowledge that

c. God's self-motion is perceptible in nature only in a quite approximate way even according to the *Timaeus* itself, and more dramatically that
d. the facts of modern science show that the divine, free order is not in fact perceptible in physical nature at all.

The conclusion we need to draw from the *Timaueus* is that in it ℝ is supported only in an incomplete way. The connections with physical nature are simply too blurry and implausible to give us a broader foundation, though the intent to liberate by means of a perfect structure is there.

    a. That humans ought to emulate God is stated at 47B–E and 90A–C. God is optimally free, and specifically as an intelligent soul. Throughout the *Timaeus* the contrast is with thoughtless bodies, which lack the intelligence to organize things according to perfect patterns. Material, empirical bodies merely obey thinking souls (cf. e.g. 46C–E, 36E–37A). The soul takes the lead. But God's lead is only a larger version of what humans can learn to do, so where God rules over the entire cosmos, humans can aspire to do the same in miniature. Our influence is much smaller than God's, but the principle is the same (cf. Sedley 2000 pp. 316–328).

We have here come by a position in the *Timaeus* which resembles that of the *Laws*. For in both works human souls are freed by becoming Godlike and God is responsible for the order that is perceived in nature. (However, unlike Christian creationists Plato does not in general imagine God as the *creator* of the liberating order. Rather, Plato's God is the perfect exemplar and the universal overseer; cf. Sedley 2000 p. 314 and Sedley 2007.) The two dialogues agree also in their general interest in causal origins. Both look back to Egypt and narrate floods which purge human civilization, and so on.

b. To put this in a little more detail, the *Timaeus* actually describes two separate Gods. The first models on the Forms to shape the material universe in an orderly and optimal way (27E–30B). Material things would be in chaos without it. But from this act of creation by the first God a second God emerges, and the second God appears to be in charge of the world's sustenance (33E–35A). It is this second God who seems to be purely self-relational (33D–34B), and the *Timaeus'* message appears to be that humans need to mimic the second, conservative God and not the first, creative one.

The *Timaeus* portrays nature like a book that has been made for us to read, for God gave us eyesight so that we could learn about the divine order in the outer universe (46E–47C). In this way things have been set up optimally for us. We have been born with exactly the right abilities and reality contains just the things we need. All we have to do now is inquire and the great story of human liberation will begin to unfold. We will be divine.

But what exactly are we supposed to do? How are we to see God in nature?

c. We are not supposed to engage in thoughtless, passive observation because nothing more than approximate traces of God's thoughts are actually perceptible in physical nature (27E–29C). Hence, there will not be direct evidence of God. Rather, and in keeping with what he so often says elsewhere, Plato finds the empirical senses unreliable. Reasoning is a firmer pathway to knowledge and reality. None the less, the *Timaeus* wishes to rely on perception as well.

But how, exactly? In what way does empirical, material nature have God's imprint?

The *Timaeus* answers this question by means of proportions or ratios (31B–32C). These recur in nature, so there is a constant order. This is, of course, at least a vaguely relational suggestion, because now we would expect nature to have patterns like $a{:}b{:}c{:}d,$ or else $a{:}b{::}c{:}d,$ or something similar. We would then only seem to need to fill in contents for the variables and we would be well on our way to discovering the divine ratio or formula.

If this is correct then the next question is after the more exact ratio or relation which the *Timaues* ascribes to the cosmos. What recurrent ratio should be expect to find from physical nature? What reason is there to suppose that a single ratio to cover it all?

The text seems to be of many minds about this. The first answer would seem to take us to the shape of a circle. It is elected as the ideal form of movement for the universe (33A–34B), and so we may conjecture that this is the structure which we are to seek more widely in nature. The same form seemed to be of cardinal importance already in the *Laws*, as we saw in Chapter 5. We also saw then that circularity coheres well with autonomy or independence especially on such patterns as *zRz* and *zRR*.

But the *Timaeus* has other answers as well. It proceeds to theorize also in terms of the four elements of air, earth, water, and fire (31B–32C), to compare the cosmos to an animal (32E–34B), and to set proportions in terms of divisions into three (31C–32A, 35A–36D). All of these moves as well as several others make it plain that the *Timaeus* does not operate with any one overall ratio. Rather there are multiple considerations. There is not one rule but several. But this means that the prospects of finding one's way to God's model by reading the book of nature are not very great, for on these premises one cannot open the book at any given page and see the *same* imprint of God. For what is now being implied is that the order on every page will *not* be the same. God's presence will be more elusive.

d. Finally we should note briefly that the *Timaeus* is far from qualifying as a credible source on nature because it is so radically outdated in comparison to modern natural science (cf. Losee). The world which modern scientists have discovered is entirely devoid of intelligence and freedom, so it offers no basis for Plato's idealism.

Chapter Thirteen

The Theaetetus?

The *Theaetetus* is a remarkably relational piece of philosophy primarily due to its

a. aim of attaining knowledge about knowledge and
b. critique of relativism.

Moreover it coheres nicely with ℝ in its

c. method of question and answer and
d. ideal of a divine outcome.

However it has the drawback of

e. producing a merely skeptical result,

so we are not actually informed about any superior relation or higher order. For the knowledge about knowledge that is sought is simply not attained in the *Theaetetus*.

    a. The *Theaetetus* begins as a quest for knowledge about knowledge (146A). Socrates is after knowledge as such, so he does not care to hear about its uses in different contexts or specialized fields (146C–147C). The comparison is with clay (147A–C), which is moistened earth no matter who uses it and for what. Similarly, knowledge is the same everywhere. Like clay it has a general definition.

    This is a self-relational aim with the logic of $...zRR$, for knowledge is a relation and knowledge about knowledge relates the relation to itself. Apparently the cause type is formal.

The haunting issue throughout the *Theaetetus* is what relation this can be. How can it be substantiated? If it were discovered then the foundational issue of epistemology would be solved, but as noted the *Theaetetus* does not actually reach this goal.

b. The prospect of epistemic relativism is pondered repeatedly in the first half of this dialogue. Let us first assess how Plato's Socrates sees it and then compare it briefly with ℝ.

Protagoras the arch-relativist is introduced at 151E–152A by considering the hypothesis that knowledge is perception. 152B illustrates this doctrine with the wind, which is cold to some but not to others, though it is the same wind. 159B–D brings up taste, so that something tastes good when one is healthy but not when one is sick. More theoretically, 159A–B speaks of pairs of agents and patients, such that both agents and patients exist in infinite numbers and each pairing produces a unique result. This generates a great many possible combinations, of course, so there should be an infinite number of different perspectives, each with its relative or local "knowledge."

Stated more negatively the relativistic doctrine is that nothing exists independently (153E). Everything is related to other things, so nothing is pure, clean or free. Thus, we are all stuck together with so many others, as it were in a large and inescapably interconnected world, and our characteristics change with the company we happen to keep. Nothing simply is, and everything flows.

The Socrates of the *Theaetetus* presents a number of arguments against relativism of this general type, and several are in a light or polemical vein. For example, at 158A–C it is questioned whether the insane or dreamers think truly, and how we know that we are not asleep. In other words *every* perspective would not seem to be true, contrary to Protagorean relativism. At 161C–D it is asked whether a pig or an ape might as well be measures of truth as a human. At 161D–E it is questioned how Protagoras can go around teaching others and getting paid for it if his lesson is only that everyone already knows all they need to know.

However the most important point with regard to ℝ is made at 171A–B, where Protagoras is said to say that even those persons are right who *deny* that he, Protagoras, is right in his relativism. Hence the relativism swallows up its own opposition, as it were. But the implication of this is clearly contradictory, because then the relativist will say that relativism is true as well as false (false because also those who oppose it are right).

Now we can specify how ℝ compares to this. We may distinguish between three differences, which we can lable realism, selectivity, and Platonism. Realism about relations implies that the relations are real. If for instance *a* IS TALLER THAN *b* IS TALLER THAN *c* then there is a real pattern. Then the situation is not that anyone *seems* taller *according* to *a* as opposed to *b*, for example. Realists say "is," not "seems." In contrast, Protagoras is an anti-realist in saying the reverse of this, that is, in presenting relations only as subjective appearances or perceptions. Second, $\mathbb{R}$, or on this book's view Plato, is not concerned with all relations. For instance *a* IS TALLER THAN *b* IS TALLER THAN *c* cannot conform to $\mathbb{R}$ because it does not work in the structures *zRz* or *zRR* (though see 5.6 for a more inclusive possibility). Similarly, there are no Forms for mud, hair, or dirt (*Parmenides* 130B–C). Plato's idealistic viewpoint is not a sweeping generalization about *everything*. But Protagoras' is. This leads us to the third difference: $\mathbb{R}$ requires intrinsicness or absolutism as in *zRz* or *zRR*, because relations or relata are required to relate to themselves. Hence there are things that are perfectly separate and pure, and divine freedom is real. In contrast, Protagoras pictured infinite interdependencies. He said nothing is independent, but for Plato the Gods and Forms are independent.

c. Socrates describes his method of question and answer at 150B–151D, explaining at 167E–168A that this method is a way to make individuals dissatisfied with themselves and to turn them into philosophers who seek to change. For persons do not blame the questioner for the answers which they produce, Socrates explains. Apparently the questioning Socrates is a kind of mirror which is held up to one face after another. At 177B Socrates says also that people are revealed in arguments. In the same passage he seems to say that persons who do not philosophize hide from themselves in rhetoric. They do not seek self-knowledge: they avoid it.

d. A digression on philosophy runs from 172C to 177C (on this see Sedley 2000, pp. 311–314). It draws several illustrative contrasts. Professionals such as jurists are tied to specific obligations, whereas philosophers have the leisure to explore things freely (172C–173A). The jurist must always serve some client or other, for example, but not so the philosopher. If a fresh question pops up the philosopher can pursue it without limit, because her lifestyle is independent. She does not have external commitments to hold her back. She does not need payment from anyone. She does not need to maintain stubbornly and artificially that her client is right. She may change her mind if there is reason to do so.

This leads to humor as well, because in the words of Socrates philosophers are like Thales who admires the heavens so much that he does not watch his step and falls into a ditch (174A). Similarly, philosophers do not know their own neighbors (174B). Philosophers are not concerned with their family traditions because they look to more remote ancestors (174E–175A). They live in a larger world, at least in their thoughts. This makes them comic at times, and Socrates reports this honestly.

In passing we should note that these are clearly generalizations about philosophy which have to do more with its initial than its advanced stages. For all of the preceding paragraph's descriptions portray a remoteness between the philosopher and what she seeks. But of course the distance diminishes if one begins to find what one is looking for, so it seems false to present the philosopher always merely as an absent-minded dreamer. However that image fits well with the questioner in c. After all, the questioner is not the answerer. The questioner seeks perfection and does *not* have it. The answerer may have it.

What would the answer be like? Does the *Theaetetus* ignore that side of the philosopher's landscape? It is described briefly at 176A–177A. Mortal life is inevitably infested with evils, Socrates says there, but luckily there is the option of striving to live like God. Socrates clearly holds, as usual, that philosophers reach much nearer to this end than the city's busybodies with their narrow minds (175B–176E). But as noted the reality in the *Theaetetus* tends to be that philosophers do not in fact get very close to their divine end at all, and this is why 172C–177C is a mere digression and not the dialogue's highpoint. (On this view Hamlyn p. 300 is quite mistaken in thinking that the *Theaetetus*' goal is to "vindicate ordinary knowledge." Cornford is closer to being correct in saying that the dialogue aims to show knowledge proper to be impossible without the Forms. Cornford's error is only in ignoring that the *Theatetus*' idealistic standard is in God, not in the Forms; see Sedley 2000, p. 312.)

e. The *Theaetetus*' Socrates is convincing in his opposition to relativism, but his hypotheses about the kind of knowledge that is superior to the Protagorean are only a set of failures (as the second half of the *Theaetetus* reveals). The problem this raises for the interpreter is why he follows such unpromising tracks. Why did Plato not fashion a work with more encouraging results? There seems to be no determinate answer to this question, and this is the reason why the *Theaetetus* cannot be treated as a main source for the kind of positive and self-consistent philosophizing for which ℝ stands.

Bibliography

Ahbel-Rappe, Sara and Kamtekar, Rachana, eds. *A Companion to Socrates*. Oxford: Blackwell, 2006.
Allen, Reginald E. "Forms and Standards," *The Philosophical Quarterly*, Vol. 9, No. 35 (Arp. 1959), 164–167.
Annas, Julia. *An Introduction to Plato's* Republic. Oxford: Clarendon, 1981.
———. "Aristotle on Inefficient Causes," *Philosophical Quarterly* 32 (1982), 311–326.
———. "Plato," in Simon Hornblower and Antony Spawforth (eds.), pp. 1190–3.
———. "Plato and Common Morality," *The Classical Quarterly*, Vol. 28, No. 2 (1978), pp. 437–451.
———. "Virtue and Law in Plato," in Christopher Bobonich (ed.), pp. 71–91.
Anscombe, G. E. M. and Geach, P. T. *Three Philosophers*. Ithaca, N.Y.: Cornell University Press, 1961.
Aristotle. *The Works of Aristotle*, 2 Vols., transl. W.D. Ross. London: Britannica, 1952.
Armstrong, D. M. *Universals and Scientific Realism*, 2 vols. Cambridge: Cambridge University Press, 1978.
Ayer, Alfred Jules, ed. *Logical Positivism*. New York: Free Press, 1959.
Bailey, D. T. J. "Logic and Music in Plato's 'Phaedo,'" *Phronesis*, Vol. 50, No. 2 (2005), pp. 95–115.
Baldwin, Anna, and Hutton, Sarah, eds. *Platonism and the English Imagination*. Cambridge: Cambridge University Press, 1994.
Baldwin, Thomas. "Editor's Introduction," in G. E. Moore, pp. ix–xxxvii.
Baltzly, Dirk. "Socratic Anti-Empiricism in the *Phaedo*," *Apeiron: A Journal for Ancient Philosophy and Science*, Vol. 29, No. 4 (1996), 121–142.
Barnes, Jonathan. *The Pre-Socratic Philosophers*. London: Routledge, 1983.
Beets, M.G.B. *Socrates on Death and the Beyond:* A Companion to Plato's *Phaedo*. Amsterdam: Duna, 1997.

Benson, Hugh, ed. *A Companion to Plato*. Oxford: Wiley-Blackwell, 2008.
Beversluis, John. *Cross-Examining Socrates:* A Defense of the Interlocutors in Plato's Early Dialogues. Cambridge: Cambridge University Press, 2000.
Bhaskar, Roy. *Plato Etc.:* The Problems of Philosophy and their Resolution. London: Routledge, 2009.
Bobonich, Christopher. *Plato's Utopia Recast:* His Later Ethics and Politics. Oxford: Oxford University Press, 2002.
———. ed. *Plato's Laws: A Critical Guide.* Cambridge: Cambridge University Press, 2010.
Bostock, David. *Plato's Phaedo*. Oxford: Oxford University Press, 1986.
Bourgault, Sophie. "Music and Pedagogy in the Platonic City," *The Journal of Aesthetic Education*, Vol. 46, No. 1 (Spring 2012), 59–72.
Broadie, Sarah. *Nature and Divinity in Plato's Timaeus.* Cambridge: Cambridge University Press, 2011.
Burnyeat, M. F. *The Theaetetus of Plato*, transl. M. J. Levett. Indianapolis: Hackett, 1990.
Campbell, Keith. *Abstract Particulars.* Oxford: Blackwell, 1990.
Camus, Albert. *The Myth of Sisyphus and Other Essays*. London: Vintage, 1991.
Carnap, Rudolf. "The Old and the New Logic," reprinted in A. J. Ayer (ed.), pp. 133–146.
Castañeda, Hector-Neri. "Plato's *Phaedo* Theory of Relations," *Journal of Philosophical Logic*, 1 (1972): 467–480.
Charles, David. "Types of Definition in the *Meno*," in L. Judson and V. Karasmanis, eds., pp. 110–128.
Chen, Ludwig C.H. "Knowledge of Beauty in Plato's *Symposium*," *The Classical Quarterly*, Vol. 33, No. 1 (1983), 66–74.
Chomsky, Noam. "A Review of B. F. Skinner's *Verbal Behavior*," in Leon A. Jakobovits and Murray S. Miron (eds.), pp. 142–143.
———. *The Knowledge of Language:* Its Nature, Origins, and Use. New York: Praeger, 1986.
Clearey, John. "*Paideia* in Plato's *Laws*," in Samuel Scolnicov and Luc Brisson (eds.), pp. 165–173.
Cohen, S. Marc. "The Logic of the Third Man," *The Philosophical Review*, Volume 80, Issue 4 (Oct., 1971), 448–475.
Cooper, John M. "Stoic Autonomy," in Paul Miller Paul et al. (eds.) pp. 1–29.
Cornford, Francis M. *Plato's Theory of Knowledge: The* Theaetetus *and the* Sophist. London: Routledge & Kegan Paul, 1951.
Craig, William Lane. *The Cosmological Argument from Plato to Leibniz*. London: Macmillan, 1980.
Cross, R.C. and Woozley, A.D. *Plato's* Republic: *A Philosophical Commentary*. London: Palgrve Macmillan, 1964.
Dahl, Norman O. "Plato's Defence of Justice," reprinted in Gail Fine (ed.) vol. 2, pp. 207–234.
Dedekind, Richard. *Essays on the Theory of Numbers*, transl. Wooster Woodruff Beman. New York: Dover, 1963.

Dillon, John. *The Heirs of Plato:* A Study of the Old Academy. Oxford: Oxford University Press, 2003.
Dorter, Kenneth. "The Significance of the Speeches in Plato's *Symposium*," *Philosophy & Rhetoric*, Vol. 2, No. 4 (1969), 215–234.
Feibleman, James K. *Religious Platonism: The Influence of Religion on Plato and the Influence of Plato on Religion.* London: Routledge, 2013.
Ferguson, John. *Utopias of the Classical World.* Ithaca, N.Y.: Cornell University Press, 1975.
Fine, Gail. "Introduction," in Gail Fine (ed.) vol. 1, pp. 1–35.
———. "Knowledge and Belief in *Republic* V." *Archiv für Geschichte der Philosophie* 60 (1978), 121–139.
———. ed. *Plato*, 2 Vols. Oxford: Oxford University Press, 2000.
———. *On Ideas: Aristotle's Criticism of Plato's Theory of Forms.* Oxford: Clarendon Press, 1993.
———. *Plato on Knowledge and the Forms.* Oxford: Oxford University Press, 2003.
———. "Separation," reprinted in *Plato on Knowledge and the Forms.* Oxford: Oxford University Press, 2003.
———. *The Possibility of Inquiry: Meno's Paradox from Socrates to Sextus.* Oxford: Oxford University Press, 2014.
Frankfurt, Harry G. "Freedom of the Will and the Concept of a Person," reprinted in Gary Watson (ed.), pp. 322–336.
Fränkel, Hermann. "A Thought Pattern in Heraclitus," reprinted in Alexander Mourelatos, ed., pp. 214–228.
Frede, Dorothea. *Platons Phaidon: Der Traum von der Unsterblichkeit der Seele.* Darmstadt: Wissenschaftliche Buchgesellschaft, 2005.
———. "Puppets on Strings: Moral Psychology in *Laws* Books 1 and 2," in Christopher Bobonich (ed.), pp. 108–126.
Frede, Michael. *A Free Will: Origins of the Notion in Ancient Thought.* Berkeley: University of California Press, 2012.
Frege, Gottlob. "On Sense and Reference," in Peter Geach and Max Black (eds.), pp. 25–50.
Friedländer, Paul. *Platon*, 3 vols. Berlin: Gruyter, 1960.
Frye, Northrop. *Anatomy of Criticism: Four Essays.* Princeton: Princeton University Press, 2000.
Gadamer, Hans-Georg. *Dialogue and Dialectic: Eight Hermeneutical Studies on Plato*, transl. P. Christopher Smith. New Haven: Yale University Press, 1983.
Gaiser, Konrad, ed. *Das Platonbild: Zehn Beiträge zum Platonverständnis.* Hildesheim: Georg Olms, 1969.
Gallop, David. *Plato's Phaedo*, transl. David Gallop. Oxford: Clarendon, 1975.
———. "Relations in the *Phaedo*," in Roger A. Shiner and John King-Farlow, eds., *New Essays on Plato and the Pre-Socratics* (Canadian Journal of Philosophy, Supplementary Volume 2, 1976), 149–163.
Geach, Peter. "The Third Man Again," *Philosophical Review*, ixv (1956), 74.
———. "Plato's *Euthyphro:* An Analysis and Commentary," *Monist* 50 (1966), 369–382.

———. and Black, Max, eds. and transl. *Translations from the Philosophical Writings of Gottlob Frege*, 3rd ed. Oxford: Blackwell, 1980.
Gerhardt, Volker. *Pathos und Distanz: Studien zur Philosophie Friedrich Nietzsches*. Stuttgart: Reclam, 1988.
Gerson, Lloyd P. "A Platonic Reading of Plato's *Symposium*," in J. H. Lesher, Debra Nails, and Frisbee C. C. Sheffield (eds.), pp. 47–67.
Gill, Mary Louise. "Problems for Forms," in Hugh Benson (ed.), pp. 184–198.
Gillies, D. A. *Frege, Dedekind, and Peano on the Foundations of Arithmetic*. Assen, the Netherlands: Van Gorcum, 1982.
Gosling, J. B. C. "*Doxa* and *Dunamis* in Plato's *Republic*." *Phronesis* 13 (1968), 119–130.
———. *Plato.* London: Routledge & Kegan Paul, 1983.
———. "*Republic* V: *ta polla kala* etc." *Phronesis* 5 (1960), 116–128.
Grant, G. P. "Plato and Popper," *The Canadian Journal of Economics and Political Science*, Vol. 20, No. 2 (May, 1964), pp. 185–194.
Gregory, Andrew. *Plato's Philosophy of Science*. London: Bloomsbury, 2001.
Grene, David. *Greek Political Theory*. Chicago: University of Chicago Press, 1965.
Griswold, Charles L., ed. *Platonic Writings, Platonic Readings*. New York: Routledge, Chapman & Hall, 1988.
Grube, G. M. A. "The Logic and Language of the *Hippias Major*," *Classical Philology*, Vol. 24, No. 4 (Oct., 1929), 369–375.
Guthrie, W. C. K. *A History of Greek Philosophy*, Vol. 4. Cambridge: Cambridge University Press, 1975.
Habermas, Jürgen. *The Theory of Communicative Action*, 2 Vols. Boston: Beacon, 1985.
Halper, Edward C. "Soul, Soul's Motions, and Virtue," in Samuel Scolnicov and Luc Brisson (eds.), pp. 257–267.
Hamlyn, D. W. "The Communion of Forms and the Development of Plato's Logic," *The Philosophical Quarterly* Vol. 5 No. 2 (Oct. 1955), 289–302.
Hanhijärvi, Tommi Juhani. *Dialectical Thinking: Zeno, Socrates, Kant, Marx*. New York: Algora, 2015.
———. *Socrates' Criteria: A Libertarian Interpretation*. Lanham: University Press of America, 2012.
Hornblower, Simon, and Spawforth, Antony, eds. *Oxford Classical Dictionary*. Oxford: Oxford University Press, 1996.
Hylton, Peter. *Russell, Idealism, and the Emergence of Analytical Philosophy*. Oxford: Clarendon, 1990.
Irigaray, Luce and Kuykendall, Eleanor H. "Sorcerer Love: A Reading of Plato's *Symposium*, Diotima's Speech," *Hypatia*, Vol. 3, No. 3, French Feminist Philosophy (1989), 32–44.
Irwin, Terence. "Morality as Law and Morality in the *Laws*," in Christopher Bobonich (ed.), pp. 92–107.
———. *Plato's Ethics*. Oxford: Oxford University Press, 1995.
———. ed. *Plato's Metaphysics and Epistemology*. New York: Garland Publishing Inc., 1995.

———. *Plato's Moral Theory*. Oxford: Oxford University Press, 1977.
Jacquette, Dale, ed. *A Companion to Philosophical Logic*. Oxford: Blackwell, 2002.
Jaeger, Werner. *Paideia*, 3 Vols., transl. Gilbert Highet. Oxford: Oxford University Press, 1944.
Jakobovits, Leon A. and Miron, Murray S., eds., *Readings in the Psychology of Language*. Upper Saddle River, New Jersey: Prentice-Hall, 1967.
Janaway, Christopher. *Images of Excellence: Plato's Critique of the Arts*. Oxford: Clarendon, 1995.
Jeremiah, Edward. "The Development, Logic, and Legacy or Reflexive Concepts in Greek Philosophy," *Journal of the History of Ideas*, Vol. 74, No. 4 (October 2013), 508–529.
Jubien, Michael. *Contemporary Metaphysics: An Introduction*. Oxford: Blackwell, 1997.
Judson, L., and Karasmanis, V., eds. *Remembering Socrates*. Oxford: Clarendon Press, 2006.
Jung, Carl Gustav. *The Archetypes and the Collective Unconscious*, transl. R.F.C. Hull. Princeton: Princeton University Press, 1969.
Kahn, Charles. *Plato and the Socratic Dialogue: The Philosophical Use of a Literary Form*. Cambridge: Cambridge University Press, 1996.
Kant, Immanuel. *Critique of Pure Reason*, transl. John Miller Dow Meiklejohn. New York: Prometheus, 1991.
Kierkegaard, Søren. *Concluding Unscientific Postscript*, transl. Alastair Hannay. Cambridge: Cambridge University Press, 2009.
———. *Either/Or: A Fragment of Life*. London: Penguin, 1992.
———. *Philosophical Fragments*, transl. Edna H. Hong and Howard V. Hong. Princeton: Princeton University Press, 1985.
Kim, Alan. *Plato in Germany: Kant— Natorp—Heidegger*. Sankt Augustin: Academia, 2010.
Kirwan, C. "Plato and Relativity." *Phronesis* (1974), 112–129.
Kneale, William and Kneale, Martha. *The Development of Logic*. Oxford: Oxford University Press, 1962.
Krämer, Hans Joachim. *Arete bei Platon und Aristoteles*. Heidelberg: C. Winter, 1959.
———. "Die platonische Akademie und das Problem einer systematischen Interpretation der Philosophie Platons," in Konrad Gaiser (ed.), pp. 198–230.
Laguna, Theodore de. "Notes on the Theory of Ideas," *The Philosophical Review*, Vol. 43, No. 5 (Sep. 1934), pp. 443–470.
Laks, Andre. "The Laws," in Christopher Rowe and Malcolm Schofield (eds.), pp. 258–292.
Langford, C.H. "The Notion of Analysis in Moore's Philosophy," in P.A. Schilpp, ed., pp. 319–342.
Lear, Jonathan. "Socratic Method and Psychoanalysis," in Sara Ahbel-Rappe and Rachana Kamtekar (eds.), pp. 442–462.
Leibniz, Gottfried Wilhelm. *Discourse on Metaphysics and Other Essays*. Indianapolis: Hackett, 1991.

Lesher, J.H., Nails, Debra, and Sheffield, Frisbee C.C., eds. *Plato's* Symposium: Issues in Interpretation and Reception. Washington, D.C.: Center for Hellenic Studies, 2006.

Levy, Donald. "The Definition of Love in Plato's *Symposium*, *Journal of the History of Ideas*, Vol. 40, No. 2 (1979), 285–291.

Lipman, Matthew, and Bynam, Terrell Ward, eds. *Philosophy for Children.* Oxford: Basil Blackwell, 1976.

Losee, John. *A Historical Introduction to the Philosophy of Science.* Oxford: Oxford University Press, 1972.

Lutoslawski, Wincenty. *The Origin and Growth of Plato's Logic.* London: Longmans, Green, and Co., 1905.

Mackie, John L. *Ethics: Inventing Right and Wrong.* New York: Penguin, 1991.

Magnus, Bernd. *Nietzsche's Existential Imperative.* Indianapolis: University of Indiana Press, 1978.

Malcolm, John. *Plato on the Self-Predication of Forms.* Oxford: Clarendon: 1991.

Marcuse, Herbert. *One-Dimensional Man.* Boston: Beacon, 1964.

Maslow, Abraham H. *Motivation and Personality.* New York: Harper and Bros., 1954.

Matthen, Mohan. "Plato's Treatment of Relational Statements in the *Phaedo*," *Phronesis* Vol. 27, No. 1 (1982), 90–100.

———. "Relationality in Plato's Metaphysics: Reply to McPherran," *Phronesis* Vol. 29, No. 3 (1984), 304–312.

Matthews, Gareth B. and Cohen, S. Marc. "The One and the Many," *Review of Metaphysics*, 21 (1968), 630–655.

Mayhew, Robert. "The Theology of the *Laws*," in Christopher Bobonich (ed.), pp. 197–216.

Meyer, Sauve Susan. "The Moral Dangers of Labor and Commerce in the *Laws*," in Samuel Scolnicov and Luc Brisson (eds.), pp. 207–214.

Milhaud, G. *Les Philosophes-Géomètres de la Grèce: Platon et ses prédécesseurs.* Paris: Alcan, 1900.

Mohr, Richard. "Plato's Final Thoughts on Evil: Laws X," *Mind*, New Series, Vol. 87, No. 348 (Oct., 1978), 572–575.

Moore, G. E. *Principia Ethica,* Revised Edition. Cambridge: Cambridge University Press, 1993.

———. "A Reply to my Critics," in P.A. Schilpp (ed.), pp. 533–677.

Morgan, Michael. "The Continuity Theory of Reality in Plato's *Hippias Major*," *Journal of the History of Philosophy* 21 (1983), 135–58.

Mourelatos, Alexander, ed. *The Pre-Socratics: A Collection of Critical Essays.* Princeton: Princeton University Press, 1994.

Murdoch, Iris. *The Sovereignty of Good.* London: Routledge & Kegan Paul, 1970.

Nails, Debra, and Thesleff, Holger. "Early Academic Editing: Plato's Laws," in Samuel Scolnicov and Luc Brisson (eds.), pp. 14–29.

Natorp, Paul. *Platons Ideenlehre: Eine Einführung in den Idealismus.* Hamburg: Meiner, 1922.

Nehamas, Alexander. "Confusing Universals and Particulars in Plato's Early Dialogues," *Review of Metaphysics* XXIX (1975), 287–306.

———. "Plato on the Imperfection of the Sensible World," *American Philosophical Quarterly* XII (1975), 105–117.

———. "Predication and Forms of Opposites in the *Phaedo*," *Review of Metaphysics* XXVI (1973), 461–491.

———. "Self-Predication and Plato's Theory of Forms," *American Philosophical Quarterly* XVI (1979), 93–103.

Nietzsche, Friedrich. *The Birth of Tragedy: Out of the Spirit of Music*, transl. Shaun Whiteside. London: Penguin, 1994.

———. *Beyond Good and Evil: Prelude to a Philosophy of the Future*, transl. Helen Zimmern. Mineola: Dover, 1997.

———. *On the Genealogy of Morals*, transl. Douglas Smith. Oxford: Oxford University Press, 2009.

Nightingale, A. W. "Historiography and Cosmology in Plato's *Laws*," *Ancient Philosophy* 19 (1999), 299–326.

Nozick, Robert. *Anarchy, State, and Utopia*. New York: Basic Books, 2013.

Nussbaum, Martha C. *The Fragility of Goodness: Luck and Ethics in Greek Tragedy and Philosophy*. Cambridge: Cambridge University Press, 1986.

Ogden, Charles K. and Richards, I. A. *The Meaning of Meaning: A Study of the Influence of Language upon Thought and of the Science of Symbolism*. London: Routledge & Kegan Paul, 1923.

Owen, G. E. L. "A Proof in the *Peri Ideon*," *Journal of Hellenistic Studies* 77 (1957), 103–111.

———. *Logic, Science, and Dialectic: Collected Papers in Greek Philosophy*, ed. Martha Nussbaum. Ithaca: Cornell University Press, 1986.

———. "Notes on Ryle's Plato" in *Logic, Science, and Dialectic: Collected Papers in Greek Philosophy*, pp. 85–103.

Passmore, John. *A Hundred Years of Philosophy*. Harmondsworth: Penguin, 1957.

———. *The Perfectibility of Man*. New York: Charles Scribner's Sons, 1970.

Penner, Terry. *The Ascent from Nominalism: Some Existence Arguments in Plato's Middle Dialogues*. New York: Springer, 1987.

———. "The Unity of Virtue," reprinted in Gail Fine (ed.), vol. 2, pp. 67–88.

Plato. *The Collected Dialogues, including the Letters*. Hamilton, Edith, and Cairns, Huntington, eds. Princeton: Princeton University Press, 1961.

Putnam, Hilary. *Philosophical Papers*, Vol. 1. Cambridge: Cambridge University Press, 1975.

Quine, Willard van. "Existence and Quantification," reprinted in *Ontological Relativity & Other Essays*, pp. 91–113.

———. *Ontological Relativity & Other Essays*. New York: Columbia University Press, 1969.

———. *Word and Object*. Cambridge, M.A.: MIT Press, 1960.

Reeve, C. D. C. *Philosopher-Kings: The Argument of Plato's Republic*. Indianapolis: Hacket, 2006.

Rey, Georges. *Contemporary Philosophy of Mind: A Contentiously Classical Approach*. Oxford: Blackwell, 1997.

Robin, Léon. *La théorie platonicienne des idées et des nombres d'après Aristoteles*. Paris: Alcan, 1908.

Robinson, Richard. *Plato's Earlier Dialectic*. Ithaca, N.Y.: Cornell University Press, 1941.

———. "Up and Down in Plato's Logic," *The American Journal of Philology*, Vol. 84, No. 3 (Jul. 1963), 300–303.

Rogers, Carl. *On Becoming a Person: A Therapist's View of Psychotherapy*. London: Constable, 1961.

Roochnik, David. "Socrates' Use of the *Techne*-Analogy," *The Journal of the History of Philosophy* 24 (1986), 295–310.

Rosen, Stanley. *Plato's Symposium*. London: Yale University Press, 1968.

Ross, W. D. *Plato's Theory of Ideas*. Oxford: Oxford University Press, 1951.

Rothstein, Edward. *Emblems of Mind: The Inner Life of Music and Mathematics*. Chicago: University of Chicago Press, 2006.

Rowe, Christopher and Schofield, Malcolm, eds. *The Cambridge History of Greek and Roman Political Thought*. Cambridge: Cambridge University Press, 2000.

———. "Interpreting Plato," in in Hugh Benson (ed.), pp. 13–24.

Russell, Bertrand. *A History of Western Philosophy and Its Connection with Political and Social Circumstances from the Earliest Times to the Present Day*. New York: Simon and Schuster, 1945.

———. *The Principles of Mathematics*. Cambridge: Cambridge University Press, 1903.

Ryle, Gilbert. *The Concept of Mind*. New York: Barnes and Noble, 1949.

Sachs, David. "A Fallacy in Plato's Republic," reprinted in Vlastos (ed.) vol. 2, pp. 35–51.

Santas, Gerasimos Xenophon. "The Form of the Good in Plato's *Republic*," reprinted in Gail Fine (ed.) vol. 1, pp. 247–274.

———. *Platon and Freud: Two Theories of Love*. London: Blackwell, 1991.

———. "Plato's Criticism of the 'Democratic Man' in the *Republic*," *The Journal of Ethics*, Vol. 5, No. 1, Ancient Greek Ethics (2001), 57–71.

———. *Socrates*. London: Routledge, 1983.

Scheibe, Erhard. "Über Relativbegriffe in der Philosophie Platons," *Phronesis*, Vol. 12, No. 1 (1967), 28–49.

Schilpp, Paul A., ed. *The Philosophy of G.E. Moore*. Evanston: Northwestern University Press, 1942.

Schofield, Malcolm. "Religion and Philosophy in the Laws," in Samuel Scolnicov and Luc Brisson (eds.), pp. 1–13.

———. *Plato: Political Philosophy*. Oxford: Oxford University Press, 2006.

Schopenhauer, Arthur. *The World as Will and Idea*, vol. 1, transl. R. B. Haldane and J. Kemp. London: Kegan Paul, Trench, Trübner & Co., 1909.

Scolnicov, Samuel and Brisson, Luc, eds. *Plato's Laws: From Theory into Practice*. Sankt Augustin: Academia, 2003.

Scott, Dominic. "Platonic Recollection," in Gail Fine (ed.) vol. 1. pp. 93–124.

Sedley, David. *Creationism and Its Critics in Antiquity*. Berkeley: University of California Press, 2007.

———. "Form-Particular Resemblance in Plato's *Phaedo*," *Proceedings of the Aristotelian Society*, Vol. 106 (2006), 311–327.

———. "The Ideal of Godlikeness," in Gail Fine (ed.) vol. 2, pp. 309–328.
———. "Plato on Language," in Hugh Benson (ed.), pp. 214–227.
———. "Platonic Causes," *Phronesis* Vol. 43, No. 2 (1998), 114–132.
Sharma, Ravi. "From Definitions to Forms?," *Apeiron: A Journal for Ancient Philosophy and Science*, Vol. 40, No. 4 (2007), 375–395.
Sheffield, Frisbee. *Plato's Symposium: The Ethics of Desire*. New York and Oxford: Oxford University Press, 2009.
Sider, David. "Plato's Early Aesthetics: The *Hippias Major*," *The Journal of Aesthetics and Art Criticism*, Vol. 35, No. 4 (1977), 465–470.
Sieroka, Norman. *Philosophie der Physik: Eine Einführung*. Beck: Munich, 2014.
Silverman, Allan. *The Dialectic of Essence: A Study of Plato's Metaphysics*. Princeton: Princeton University Press, 2003.
Sluga, Hans. *Gottlob Frege*. London: Routledge & Kegan Paul, 1980.
Snell, Bruno. *The Discovery of the Mind: The Greek Origins of European Thought*, transl. T. G. Rosenmeyer. London: Blackwell, 1953.
Soble, Alan. "Love Is Not Beautiful: *Symposium* 200e–201c," *Apeiron: A Journal for Ancient Philosophy and Science*, Vol. 19, No. 1 (1985), 43–52.
Solmsen, Friedrich. *Plato's Theology*. Ithaca: Cornell University Press, 1942.
Stahl, Donald E. "Nehamas on Platonic Predication," *Apeiron: A Journal for Ancient Philosophy and Science*, Vol. 18, No. 1 (1984), 31–33.
Stalley, Richard Frank. "Justice in Plato's *Laws*," in Samuel Scolnicov and Luc Brisson (eds.), pp. 174–185.
Stenzel, Julius. *Kleine Schriften zur griechischen Philosophie*. Darmstadt: Wissenschaftliche Buchgesellschaft, 1956.
———. *Studien zur Entwicklung der platonischen Dialektik von Sokrates zu Aristoteles*, 2nd Ed. Stuttgart: B. G. Teubner, 1931.
Svavarsson, Svavar Hrafn. "Plato on Forms and Conflicting Appearances: The Argument of *Phaedo* 74A9–C6," *The Classical Quarterly, New Series*, Vol. 59, No. 1 (2009), 60–74.
Szlezak, Thomas Alexander. *Platon und die Schriftlichkeit der Philosophie*. Berlin: Walter de Gruyter, 1985.
Tarrant, Dorothy. "Plato, *Phaedo* 74 A–B," *Journal of Hellenic Studies*, Vol. 77, Part 1 (1957), 124–126.
Tarski, Alfred. "On the Calculus of Relations," *The Journal of Symbolic Logic*, Vol. 6, No. 3 (Sep., 1941), 73–89.
Taylor, A. E. *Plato: The Man and His Work*. London: Methuen, 1926.
Taylor, C. C. W. "Plato's Totalitarianism" in Gail Fine (ed.) vol. 2., pp. 280–296.
Taylor, H. M., ed. *Euclid's Elements of Geometry*. Cambridge: Cambridge University Press, 1893.
Teloh, Henry. *Socratic Education in Plato's Early Dialogues*. Notre Dame: University of Notre Dame Press, 1986.
Thorson, Thomas Landon, ed. *Plato: Totalitarian or Democrat?* Upper Saddle River, New Jersey: Prentice Hall, 1963.
Tuana, Nancy, ed. *Feminist Interpretations of Plato*. University Park, Pennsylvania: Penn State University Press, 1994.

van Inwagen, Peter. *An Essay on Free Will*. Oxford: Oxford University Press, 1983.
Verdenius, W.J. "Notes on Plato's *Phaedo*," *Mnemosyne*, Fourth Series, Vol. 11, Fasc. 3 (1958), 193–243.
Vlastos, Gregory. "Degrees of Reality in Plato" reprinted in Gregory Vlastos, *Platonic Studies*, pp. 58–75.
———. "Justice and Happiness in the *Republic*," reprinted in *Platonic Studies*, pp. 111–139.
———. ed. *Plato: A Collection of Critical Essays*, 2 Vols. Garden City, N.Y.: Doubleday, 1971.
———. *Platonic Studies*. Princeton: Princeton University Press, 1981.
———. "Reasons and Causes in the *Phaedo*," reprinted in Gregory Vlastos (ed.) vol. 1, 132–166.
———. "Socrates' Disavowal of Knowledge," reprinted in Gail Fine (ed.) vol. 1, pp. 64–92.
———. *Socrates: Ironist and Moral Philosopher*. Ithaca: Cornell University Press, 1991.
———. "The Socratic Elenchus," reprinted in Gail Fine (ed.) vol. 1, pp. 36–63.
———. "The Third Man Argument in the *Parmenides*," *Philosophical Review*, 63 (1954), 319–349.
Voegelin, Eric. *Plato*. Baton Rouge: Louisiana State University Press, 1966.
Watson, Gary. "Free Agency," reprinted in Gary Watson (ed.), pp. 337–351.
———. ed. *Free Will*. Oxford: Oxford University Press, 2003.
Wedgwood, Ralph. "Diotima's Eudaemonism: Intrinsic Value and Rational Motivation in Plato's *Symposium*," *Phronesis*, Vol. 54, No. 4/5 (2009), 297–325.
White, F. C. "Beauty of Soul and Speech in Plato's *Symposium*," *The Classical Quarterly, New Series*, Vol. 58, No. 1 (2008), 69–81.
———. "Socrates, Philosophers and Death: Two Contrasting Arguments in Plato's *Phaedo*," *The Classical Quarterly* New Series, Vol. 56, No. 2 (2006), pp. 445–458.
———. "Forms and Sensibles: *Phaedo* 74B–C," *Philosophical Topics*, Vol. 15, No. 2, *Ancient Greek Philosophy* (1987), 197–214.
Wilamowitz-Moellendorff, Ulrich von. *Platon: Leben und Werk*. Berlin: Weidmannsche Buchhandlung, 1920.
Wittgenstein, Ludwig. *Philosophical Investigations*, transl. G. E. M. Anscombe, 2nd Ed. London: Basil Blackwell, 1968.
Wolsdorf, David. "*Hippias Major* 301B2–C2: Plato's Critique of a Corporeal Conception of Forms and of the Form-Participant Relation," *Apeiron: A Journal for Ancient Philosophy and Science*, Vol. 39, No. 3 (2006), 221–256.
Woodruff, Paul. *Plato: Hippias Major*. Indianapolis: Hackett, 1982.
Wos, Larry and Fitelson, Branden. "The Automation of Sound Reasoning and Successful Proof Finding," in Dale Jacquette (ed.), pp. 709–723.
Wright, Georg Henrik von. *Logik, filosofi och språk*. Nora, Sweden: Nya Doxa, 1993.
Zeller, Eduard. *Outlines of the History of Greek Philosophy*, transl. Wilhelm Nestle. Mineola, N.Y.: Dover, 1980.
Zuckert, Catherine H. "Plato's *Laws:* Postlude or Prelude to Socratic Political Philosophy?" *The Journal of Politics*, Vol. 66, No. 2 (May, 2004), pp. 374–395.

www.ingramcontent.com/pod-product-compliance
Lightning Source LLC
Chambersburg PA
CBHW022012300426
44117CB00005B/143